Tales from Facebook

By the same author:

Comfort of Things

'The very best kind of micro-ethnography. Miller writes better – and with more insight and compassion – than most novelists.'

Kate Fox, author of *Watching the English*

'An outstanding piece of work: a fine example of modern anthropological fieldwork, a powerful corrective to the banal notion that materialism is synonymous with excessive individualism and, perhaps above all, an informed, sensitive, and wholly sympathetic guide to the human diversity to be found through the keyholes of our capital city.'

Laurie Taylor, *Independent*

'A wonderful and unusual antidote to the fear that humanity and individuality is losing its battle with modern consumerism. In his book, even the most trivial product of consumerism can be rendered almost magical by its owners.'

Financial Times

'Daniel Miller's moving account, *The Comfort of Things*, is a stout defence of that pejorative notion: "only sentimental value". He builds up a tapestry of the variety of ways in which people use things to express themselves and make meaning in their lives. The nondescript, the ordinary, can be invested with great value. In Miller's account, people knit rich associations with objects, caring for each, using them to express relationships.'

Guardian

Stuff

'[*Stuff*] really is a little gem. Timely, well-written and highly accessible, it is a concise and grounded resource in the struggle to analyse the complexities of contemporary cultural life . . . For undergraduates and general critical readers alike, it will be a welcome and thought-provoking reminder that the material world of things we have created, and which in turn helps to create us, needs to be understood dialectically – for better and for worse.'

Times Higher Education

'[T]here are fascinating things here: a seven-page description of how a woman who wears a sari navigates daily life through the garment; a portrait of council tenants as "artists" redecorating their flats in different ways; and analyses of fashion, furnishing and "mobile phone relationships" in Jamaica. When Miller is focused on the details, the writing hums with empathetic colour and detail.'

Guardian

Au Pair (with Zuzana Burikova)

'*Au Pair* is a ripping good read, full of salacious details of the indignities of trying to live and work as a foreigner in middle-class London households.'

Times Higher Education

With its fine-grained ethnographic detail, skilfully presented in vivid prose, this book illuminates every aspect of the hopes, fantasies and frustrations that constitute the frequently troubled ties and misunderstandings between au pairs and their employers. A huge pleasure to read, *Au Pair* provides a definitive, indispensable text for addressing this increasingly prevalent facet of family life, with its own suggestions for improving the lives of both au pairs and the families in which they reside.'

Lynne Segal, author of *Why Feminism?*

The Theory of Shopping

'Miller begins with an excellent and sensitive ethnography of shopping firmly rooted among his own native north Londoners. It is a fine example of what an anthropologist can achieve at home.'

Times Higher Education

'His demystification of what appears to be, on the surface, straightforward juggling of cost, quantity and quality is absorbing reading.'

Will Self, *New Statesman and Society*

Tales from Facebook

Daniel Miller

polity

Copyright © Daniel Miller 2011

The right of Daniel Miller to be identified as Author of this Work has been asserted in accordance with the UK Copyright, Designs and Patents Act 1988.

First published in 2011 by Polity Press
Reprinted 2011 (twice), 2012, 2013

Polity Press
65 Bridge Street
Cambridge CB2 1UR, UK

Polity Press
350 Main Street
Malden, MA 02148, USA

ISBN-13: 978-0-7456-5209-2
ISBN-13: 978-0-7456-5210-8(pb)

A catalogue record for this book is available from the British Library.

Typeset in 11 on 13 pt Sabon
by Servis Filmsetting Ltd, Stockport, Cheshire
Printed and bound in the USA by Edwards Brothers, Inc.

The publisher has used its best endeavours to ensure that the URLs for external websites referred to in this book are correct and active at the time of going to press. However, the publisher has no responsibility for the websites and can make no guarantee that a site will remain live or that the content is or will remain appropriate.

Every effort has been made to trace all copyright holders, but if any have been inadvertently overlooked the publisher will be pleased to include any necessary credits in any subsequent reprint or edition.

For further information on Polity, visit our website: www.politybooks.com

Contents

Preface

Facebook, now in the sixth year of existence, has overtaken Google to become the most visited site on the internet. According to the company's statistics,[1] there are currently over 500 million active users, of whom half log on during any given day. Every month sees three billion photos posted and every day sees 60 million status updates. The average user has 130 friends and spends just under an hour a day on the site. These are about the last figures you will encounter in reading this book. While we can all sit amazed by such statistics, this volume looks to the other end of the spectrum – the particular individuals, their friends and their families who use the site. It is an anthropological enquiry into the consequences of social networking for ordinary people. How have their lives been changed by the experience of using Facebook? What impact does it have on the relationships they really care about? Does Facebook approximate some kind of community? How does it change the way we see ourselves? Why are people seemingly so unconcerned with this loss of privacy?

One problem is the tendency to assume the origins of the site will necessarily dictate its future. We know that Facebook was invented for use by students in colleges. Yet that fact barely impinges upon the contents of this book. 2010 was the year in which we could start to see why Facebook might eventually have more importance

[1] www.facebook.com/press/info.php?statistics (accessed 27 July 2010).

for an elderly person who is housebound, and has no other means of effective socialization, than for a student. So the focus will be on what Facebook seems to be becoming rather than what it initially has been. Because Facebook started in the US, most of the research on its impact has been within the US. But today it is a global site where over 70 per cent of its users live outside the US and research needs to encompass this increasing diversity.

There are good reasons to view Facebook through an anthropological lens. After all, one definition of anthropology might be that while other academic disciplines treat people as individuals, anthropology has always treated people as part of a wider set of relationships. Indeed, prior to the invention of the internet, it was the way the individual was understood in anthropology that might have been termed a social networking site. So a new facility actually called a social networking site ought to be of particular interest to an anthropologist. On 21 April 2010, Mark Zuckerberg, the founder of Facebook, announced at the F8 conference a new phase in the development of the site. The words he used were 'we are building toward a web where the default is social.'[2] Given that for a century we have imagined that participation in community and social relations was in decline, this reversal of previous trends seems both astonishing and particularly relevant to the premise and future of anthropology.

Anthropology has a rather peculiar way of engaging with global phenomena. As Facebook has spread, it has also become increasingly diverse. So, from an anthropological perspective, it could be said that there is no longer any such thing as Facebook. There are only the particular genres of use that have developed for different peoples and regions. This volume is set in Trinidad, a place chosen specifically to dislodge the assumption that however people in the UK or the US use Facebook, that *is* Facebook. Trinidad is sufficiently distinctive to force us to engage with the comparative dimensions of Facebook's emergent heterogeneity. The intention is that for most readers this displacement from their usual setting will actually make this book more, rather than less, effective at helping them consider the impact also on their own lives. Although Trinidad is the setting, the focus is on particular individuals whose dilemmas and concerns will be familiar to most of

[2] http://news.bbc.co.uk/2/hi/technology/8590306.stm (accessed 22 April 2010).

us. They help us to appreciate the effects Facebook can have on a marriage, understand what teenagers do all day long and how we decide whether information on Facebook should be regarded as a kind of truth about another person or just a facade.

Trinidad is a Caribbean island within sight of Venezuela. It is one of the two islands that make up the state of Trinidad and Tobago. Since this research is limited to Trinidad, it refers to *Trinis* rather than the common local expression of Trinbagonian. Trinidad is just under 5,000 sq. km, i.e. you can drive around it in a day. The indigenous population was largely wiped out by Spanish colonialists. After subsequent French and British rule, it became independent in 1962. The population of around 1.3 million is composed of around 40 per cent descended from former African slaves, 40 per cent descended from former South Asian indentured labourers, with the remainder having widespread origins, including China, Madeira and Lebanon.

I have been carrying out fieldwork in Trinidad intermittently for over twenty years and have written three previous volumes about the island. This book is based on a year's observation of Trinis on Facebook itself, in addition to spending two months in December 2009 and January 2010 carrying out fieldwork within Trinidad. The study of Facebook arose alongside a larger research project, carried out with Mirca Madianou of Cambridge University, on the impact of new media on long-distance communication. Current figures[3] give a Facebook penetration in Trinidad of 26 per cent, of which 54 per cent are female. One analysis of these figures[4] suggests that, taking users as a proportion of persons with internet access, Trinidad may be second in the world after Panama. During fieldwork, Facebook was found to be ubiquitous amongst those of high school and college age, with the exception of very low income areas.

The first part of this book consists of twelve portraits. These are all based on research but, with one exception, I have made extensive changes in detail and combined materials from different participants within individual portraits in order to protect the anonymity of those who participated in the study. The writing style

---

[3] www.facebakers.com/countries-with-facebook/TT/ (accessed 2 August 2010).
[4] http://thekillerattitude.com/2008/06/facebook-statistics-and-google-motion.html (accessed 29 March 2010).

is taken more from short story composition than from academic genre. It includes an element of travelogue and is intended to be an enjoyable read. For those who are engaging with this book largely for academic purposes, this may require some patience. The second part of the book is more analytical and uses the material from the first part to draw academic conclusions, though I hope this part also remains both readable and of interest to a non-academic readership. This section starts with a brief discussion of what makes Facebook Trinidadian. There follows an attempt to address Facebook in its more general and global aspects through 15 tentative theses about what Facebook may be turning out to be.[5] Finally the book ends with a more theoretical excursion, an extended comparison between Facebook and a classic anthropological study of an island off the coast of New Guinea. By the nature of this social networking beast, we can assume that these observations will become outdated as Facebook evolves or is replaced. What remains is an anthropological study of people as social networking sites.

Why Trinidad?

On opening the pages and realizing that this is a volume principally about Facebook in Trinidad, the casual reader might be forgiven for assuming that it must therefore also be a book about some version of globalization or Americanization. That Trinidad is some poor peripheral island buffeted by the storms that emanate from the great powers. So the 'real', the 'proper' Facebook is that which we find in the US, where it was invented, while other places are reduced to inauthentic copies. This is a common perspective, especially in cultural studies and sociology, but I have always viewed anthropology as a place where things could and should be seen differently.

My own stance was made clear in the previous books I have published about Trinidad. The most obvious precedent was a book about the internet.[6] Our starting point was that there is no

---

[5] The focus remains on users. For a study of the company itself and a history of Facebook, the most authoritative guide to date is Kirkpatrick, D. (2010), *The Facebook Effect*. London: Virgin Books.

[6] Miller, D. and Slater, D. (2000), *The Internet: An Ethnographic Approach*. Oxford: Berg.

such thing as the internet. Different people were using different combinations of web-surfing, emailing, instant messaging and so forth. The internet was whatever any particular group of users had made it into. No one population was more 'proper' or 'authentic' than any others. For an anthropologist studying in Trinidad, the internet itself was something created by what Trinidadians do online. From which point we then try and understand why each place produces the internet that we find there. My starting point is that Trinidad is the centre of the world, not some inauthentic periphery. Similarly, I once published a paper called *Coca-Cola: A Black Sweet Drink from Trinidad* because the meaning and connotations of this drink, how it is mixed with rum, how its distinction from red sweet drinks reflects the local ethnic differences within Trinidad – these are what makes the drink significant for Trinidad, not its origins in the US. The advantage of this approach is firstly to contest overgeneralization. In another book,[7] I showed how even business itself operates in quite specific ways in Trinidad that are not exactly as predicted in business-school models. But this also showed that the word capitalism is used too glibly. That various forms of business and finance often work in ways that conflict with each other. The book also made the point that the biggest transnational companies in Trinidad were in fact Trinidadian and dominated much of the Caribbean, even selling into Florida.

These are the reasons why in this volume I will often refer to *Fasbook*, the local term, rather than Facebook. While Mark Zuckerberg may have created an interface called Facebook, it is the creativity of Trinidadians that produces *Fasbook*. As it happens, I have always been in awe of the creativity and intelligence of Trinidadians. The conversation between two Trinis strikes me as likely to be more articulate, funny and profound than in any other country I have been in (Trinis are not modest, a lot of them would say just the same thing). When Trinis migrated in recent decades to the UK, it was almost invariably as lawyers, doctors and other professionals. They expect to be more successful than the local population and they usually are. This too can be misleading since there are really two Trinidads. There are those Trinis who pass the early highly competitive examinations and are trained in one of the prestige high schools. These children

---

7 Miller, D. (1997), *Capitalism: An Ethnographic Approach*. Oxford: Berg.

generally score so well in exams that they expect to be offered a full scholarship to a US college of their choice if they should want one. Most of the extraordinary array of internationally known Trinidadian intellectuals, such as C. L. R. James or V. S. Naipaul came from such schools and, as those names show, they come equally from the populations of African and Indian origin. The majority of the population, however, do not make it into these schools and don't have the same opportunities in life – although, having spent much time working in low-income communities of squatters, I still find them more impressive in terms of general knowledge and entrepreneurial activity than their equivalent from any other country I know.

This is one of the reasons I tend to study new communication technologies in Trinidad. I anticipate that Trinidadian usage will not just be distinctive but also in some ways ahead of the game. That while innovation in Facebook as infrastructure will come from the company, ideas about what one can do with Facebook may arise first in a place such as Trinidad. There are historical reasons why Trinidad has a particular grasp on the possibilities of being modern. This is partly because the very rupture created by slavery and indentured labour created a subsequent sense of freedom that was different from the conservatism that emerged from more gradual changes in class and the peasantry in other regions. It has also done no harm that Trinidad was not just one of the world's first oil-producing countries but used the money to invest in educational infrastructure. So, to conclude, I am hoping that, given the time lag it takes for publishing a book, some of the already apparent trends described here for Trinidad may well match those starting to become evident in slower-moving places such as London or Los Angeles. We shall see.

Acknowledgements

First and foremost I would like to acknowledge the time and information given to me by all the Trinis who participated in this project. There must be upwards of a hundred individuals who have either been formally interviewed, chatted informally or become a key Facebook friend. I have made considerable efforts to ensure the anonymity that was promised them when I conducted the research, and I hope that everyone will respect this if they should nevertheless recognize someone or themselves. For this reason, I have also had to subsequently defriend them on Facebook. I apologize if I have failed anyone in this respect. Preserving anonymity also means I cannot acknowledge any of these individuals in person. That includes our excellent transcriber.

Happily I can, however, acknowledge the contribution of Mirca Madianou who jointly conducted many of these interviews and participated in the wider fieldwork. She has also been very tolerant of my building this project on the side of our joint research into long-distance communication in Trinidad and the Philippines. I am indebted to Simone Mangal who organized our accommodation, food and transport, as well as introducing me to some additional informants. Also, for discussion within Trinidad, hospitality and contributions to 'liming', I would like to thank Moonilal Das, Gabrielle Hosein, Francesca Hawkins, Kim Johnson, Pat Mohammed, Burton Sankeralli and Dennis Singh.

For commenting on the manuscript itself, many thanks to

Heather Horst, Gabrielle Hosein, Mirca Madianou, Simone Mangal, Anna Pertierra, John Postill, Jolynne Sinanan, Rachel Singh and the anonymous reviewers provided by Polity. Thanks to Ilana Gershon for sharing unpublished work. I would like to thank Lucia Neva for once again providing my cover design, and Polity for their help in seeing through this process of publication. Above all, thanks are due to my wife Rickie Burman for consistent and constructive criticism and editing.

Glossary

This provides approximate meanings of some common terms in Trinidad and Facebook. It does not deal with the examples of current youth dialect found in the volume. I have also tended to exclude terms that are clearly defined when first encountered within the text.

bacchanal: Disorder that derives from scandal and gossip. A word often used to describe Trinidadian culture in general

boi (boy): Hey you (male or female)

boldface: A kind of expressive bravado. Don't just misbehave, flaunt it

comment: A facility in Facebook where an individual responds to another's posting

calypso: Traditional Trinidad songs often based on social and political satire or protest

cuss: To swear at or curse

David Rudder: One of the greatest calypso singers

East Indian (Indo-Trinidadian): Around 40 per cent of the current population of Trinidad who came from India, originally as indentured labourers, to work the sugar plantations after the abolition of slavery

Eid: The most important Muslim festival of the year

FarmVille: The most popular game within Facebook

fete: The main term used for parties, especially the pre-Carnival parties dominated by Soca music

fas: Trying to find out about another person's business with inappropriate speed

friending: To ask someone to be a Facebook friend. But traditionally in Trinidad to be having sex with, or to be in a visiting, i.e. non-cohabiting, relationship with

'Go Brave': 'Just Do It' (without the Nike)

gyul (girl): Hey you (definitely female)

horning: Adultery

IM (or instant messenger): A means to engage in private, text based, turn taking, communication

lagniappe: A little extra one gives to the customers . . . just because

like: On Facebook when a person posts a status or news update, a friend can either choose to comment or press the 'to like' button signifying their approval

lime: A characteristically Trinidadian form of socialization, originally often based on hanging around street corners and implying spontaneity in both social composition and subsequent trajectory

LOL: Internet speak for 'laughing out loud'

maco: To be nosy or to spend time finding out about other peoples private business. So also a 'macotious' person

mas: Being a masquerader in Carnival. Also Mas Camp where carnival costumes are made for each band

mash up: To destroy

maxi-taxi: A small bus that travels on set routes. The most popular form of public transport in Trinidad

MSN: Windows Messenger Service, a popular form of IM

MySpace: One of the most successful social networking sites prior to Facebook

netiquette: The norms of behaviour that people come to feel appropriate to internet use

palance: Partying and having a good time. Massively over used in 2009 because of a soca tune with that name

pan: The music of steelband. Panyard – the place where they practise

parang: The Spanish-inflected music associated with Christmas

PNM: The People's National Party, the party associated with Eric Williams, the founder of independent Trinidad. In power during the period of fieldwork, and generally more associated with the Afro-Trinidadian than the Indo-Trinidadian population

posting: In 2009, the two main kinds of textual posting, that is, the 'status updates' and 'news items', were effectively combined

profile pictures: The picture that appears at the top left of an individual's Facebook page and accompanies their postings and comments

remediation: The way material in an established media becomes reconfigured as content in a new media (see Bolter, G. and Grusin, R. (2000), *Remediation: Understanding New Media.* Cambridge, MA: MIT Press.)

slight pepper: Some pepper sauce, but not much

soca: A blend of calypso with various forms of popular music

steups: A disparaging sound made by sucking your teeth between drawn cheeks

tag: To put a name to a Facebook photo image such that everyone linked to that name becomes aware of the photo. Thus to detag is to de-link the name

TT$: A Trinidadian dollar. At the time of fieldwork, the exchange rate was approximately TT$10 per £1 or TT$7 per US$1

UTT: The University of Trinidad and Tobago, founded in 2004

UWI: The University of the West Indies that includes a campus in St Augustine, Trinidad, established in 1960

wall: The place on a Facebook site where status and news updates are posted

wining: A dance form, based on gyrations around the waist, associated with soca music. Typically men (try to) wine behind a woman

Part I

Twelve Portraits

1

Marriage Dun Mash Up

For a moment my eyes are diverted from the screen to glance outside the window where, in the middle distance, hovers a red bird-feeder like a mini-spaceship. The movement that caught my attention was the ubiquitous bananaquit with its yellow belly. It was soon followed by the even brighter green honeycreeper. These feeders are common in Trinidad and if you are lucky in the morning you may spy the iridescent purple-blue of a humming-bird. The birds here rival a coral reef in their strong palette. It's hard sometimes to concentrate on the screen in front of me since this office is set in the midst of a cocoa estate near the centre of the island. The large clear windows are intended to give a pano-ramic view of the surrounding environment. Earlier in the day I spotted an iguana, complementing the sighting the day before, in the forest, of an agouti which looks like a cross between a rat and a hog.

These days I am more likely to examine such wildlife through my television screen in London, viewed on nature programmes where the content typically oscillates between one species eating another alive and two of the same species mating. Today, by con-trast, the natural environment is looking quite tame and sedate, while here on the screen I was about to bear witness to the fero-cious tearing apart of something else. Sitting here, I was to watch unfold in front of me the evidence that Facebook can destroy someone's marriage. As time went on, I was to become increasingly convinced by the person seated next to me that it was not just a question of Facebook revealing or portraying this destruction, but that ultimately it was Facebook itself that was doing the deed. Facebook was separating him from the mother of his child.

None of this was in the least bit anticipated when I turned up that morning. The conversation was supposed to be about the role of Facebook in the marketing of the cocoa estate. This was part of Marvin's job as project manager, until the estate could earn enough to appoint a full-time marketing manager. Marvin had been explaining how in the last two years the estate website, which had been up and running for some years, was being steadily replaced by a focus upon Facebook. This was not always a simple progression since Facebook had its limitations. It was a poor medium for viewing a newsletter since you still can't upload a pdf. So at present he needed these Facebook friends of the estate to migrate from Facebook through to the website and thence the newsletter. But at least for the Trini friends, contact increasingly came through Facebook itself. As he explained it, for Trinidadians, Facebook seemed to be replacing the entire internet as the only channel they were likely to actually use for either commercial or personal purposes.

That was fine for Marvin. He liked the idea that someone would 'friend' the Facebook group site he had set up for the project and would immediately be registered on his computer. He could then quickly respond more personally, sending messages to see if the new friend was willing to have a little chat. Mixing the personal with work was often the most effective way of promoting the business, since Marvin, aged around 30, was very personable. I am not a great judge of men's physical appearance, but I would have guessed that most women found him highly attractive. His face was a mixture of friendly with intense. When he contacted a new Facebook 'friend', especially a woman, he would display his best profile photograph and start to chat with them on the IM (instant messenger) facility within Facebook or alternatively on Windows Live Messenger (MSN). For international friends whose decision to friend the site indicated a keen interest in chocolate, he would suggest a visit to the estate, explain about accommodation, travel packages. This tourism side of the business was starting to become a serious complement to cocoa production. Even if they never came to Trinidad, it gave them that personal relationship to the product itself. He had so far put up six photo albums and a video clip and was encouraging visitors to send in their favourite photos to add to the website.

So what was I doing there? I was in Trinidad researching the impact of new media on international communications, especially divided families. Together with my colleague, Dr Mirca Madianou, I had already been to the Philippines to look at how domestic workers in the UK parent their children across the other side of the world. Trinidad was our comparison site. Mostly, we were becoming interested in the way people used a multiplicity of communication channels that we call 'polymedia' and in the relationship between these. But I had reached a point in my research when I was beginning to be tempted by a separate research project, devoted solely to Facebook. One reason lay in the number of times I had heard recently that Facebook was starting to become an important component of economic activity such as clothes retailing. My conversation with Marvin seemed to confirm this buzz in the Trinidad air. I recalled being in Trinidad ten years previously. Then, too, everyone was convinced that, whatever you were in the economic food chain, you should be present on the internet. Otherwise you were bereft of an essential sign of modernity. That commitment to the future was a necessary part of the public image of a successful company. Today, Facebook seemed to have that same quality. You needed to be there; it was the first place Trinis looked to.

There were other grounds for being here in particular. It was after all a cocoa estate, and I am passionate about high-quality chocolate. As it happens, central Trinidad is established as amongst the highest quality cocoa producers in the world, especially the nearby Gran Couva estates, famous for the French fine chocolate maker Valrhona. Trinidad cocoa is usually mixed with lesser blends to improve them. It is expensively available in pure form. I had been in a hugely pleasurable relationship with this stuff for years. But you cannot actually buy high-quality chocolate in Trinidad. The final processing tends to happen in countries such as France which is also where it is marketed. What you can see here is the process of cocoa production, collecting and roasting. Then there is 'dancing the beans' to help remove the outer coverings, analogous to the better-known traditions of treading grapes in the

Mediterranean. A little video clip of dancing the beans was one of the highlights of the estate's marketing strategy. Since you couldn't actually buy chocolate there, it was another culinary indulgence that drew me back to the cocoa estates. My favourite fruit in the world, a fruit which, to the best of my knowledge, has never even been graced with a name, is the white pulp that surrounds the cocoa beans within the pods. Slightly acidic, a bit like mangosteen. I completely adore the stuff. But the only way one can find it is by breaking open a fresh pod at a cocoa estate, where it is merely regarded as a waste product from the process. An encumbrance to getting to the bean itself, it is something to be danced off.

So having gorged myself on cocoa pulp, I had turned to the research that was justifying my presence there. I had been happy to chat at length with Marvin about Facebook and marketing. It was just happenstance that being there for such an extended period meant that I was also able to observe a quite unexpected occurrence. It had been lurking in the background but was increasingly coming to my attention as Marvin appeared more and more distracted. Eventually he reached that state where he wanted and needed to discuss what was happening, even to this perfect stranger who was sharing his office and admittedly prompting and encouraging the exchange.

Marvin was one of those for whom Facebook is almost co-terminous with the working day. In the evenings at home with two children, he has little time to go online, but his job and the emphasis on online marketing means he remains close to the internet whenever he is at work, either in his office with a PC or another part of the site with a laptop, or even when travelling between them or around the estate, generally thanks to his BlackBerry. As long as he is at work, he has this compulsion and excuse to never be offline. And while he is online, Facebook is always either in the foreground or background. He has 620 friends and, unusually for a Trinidadian, relatively few of them are family. This is partly because he comes from a nearby village and is the first from this background to go to university. Most of his family don't have computer access, let alone the additional laptop. Most especially, they don't have a BlackBerry which is *the* accessory for wealthier Trinidadians these days. The core of his extensive friends list is the women who used to go to one of the same series of schools he attended. He claims that this is because women in Trinidad are more avid users of Facebook than men, which was already becoming clear from my research.

From that perspective, there was already something distinctly odd about Marvin's usage. He just never seemed to employ his phone for voice, but almost always for IM (instant messaging). Similarly, the most active part of his computer is MSN where I could see around 50 people on his list whose simultaneous presence online was automatically indicated. He isn't texting either. I had rarely noted such devotion to IM as a medium. It bugs me until, just before we finished, the penny dropped.

However much time Marvin spends on Facebook, there is one person he knows who spends even more time on it, and that is his wife. What's more, she doesn't just spend this time on her account: she spends much of it on his Facebook account. She monitors everything he does. She wants to know who this new friend is, how he knows her and what she means to him. Of course he comments on their photographs, everyone in Trinidad does, but she interrogates all such comments. The problem is that he is a man who spends much of the day on Facebook. He is frequently engaged in communication with women, and nearly every single such act is an inscription, something she can trace, interrogate and become anxious about. To his mind, this is now tantamount to being stalked by his own wife, leading to endless repetitive justifications following accusations, day after day. This has turned into an obsession, a relentless pursuit that has worn him down. Recently he has been thinking seriously about calling it a day and separating from the woman who, however much he loves her, is driving him to distraction. But today was the day when she pre-empted any such intent.

He has tried to deal with this stalking in various ways. On occasion he has even gone through the call log on her phone just to show her what it is like to be on the receiving end of such intrusions. But that doesn't work: 'I have nothing to hide,' she snorts. He responds 'Well, I have nothing to hide either.' It doesn't help. Neither does the idea of privacy settings or passwords. So far from keeping him distanced from her prying, such actions are taken as incendiary proof that he *does* have something to hide, that there is a crisis here. Inevitably, it just makes the situation worse.

Marvin's take on what is going on is quite clear. He has two children, one by a previous 'babymother', another by his wife. He doesn't want this relationship to end; he claims he still loves her. He claims that the problem that is defeating them both ultimately rests in the technology itself and, most especially, in Facebook. This is Trinidad, partners will be jealous, and, in truth, partners will often have reason to be suspicious. Fears and anxieties about what Trinis call *horning* are part and parcel of relationships in Trinidad. But that's the point: they always have been; there is nothing new in that at all. For an anthropologist to say it is part of a culture is not to make any judgement. It is simply to acknowledge that this has been a constant aspect of people's lives and expectations for generations. But, prior to Facebook, these other men or women generally lurked more as vague threats in consciousness. They were not visible as they are now, sitting there with their provocative photographs, their innuendo or even more explicit flirting in their comments. Then there is the extent of their own sites that seems to invite stalking. Now they surround you, present in their hundreds, sending 'gifts' of flowers and puzzles, adding ambiguous status updates and news items. Facebook puts these other women in your face. It creates this world in which you can so quickly and easily do more than just obsess about them. You can act on your obsession by hunting them down, scrutinizing their profiles, looking for clues that link them to your partner. It is just too easy, too relentlessly present. One click takes you from your friends to his friends. And the results can never be reassuring, an end to anxiety. Each scratch of the screen's surface creates more irritation and the desire to scratch deeper, and around you are further swarms that threaten.

Nor was it at all difficult to understand Marvin's wife's particular concern. I had already picked up on the way Marvin used himself to embody chocolate in this marketing. As a result, yes, there did seem to be a whole lot of women out there in Sweden, Canada and the UK who would be in IM contact with him about chocolate, and then maybe about travel and accommodation. I couldn't say or know what might follow. On the neighbouring island of Tobago, sex tourism by white women looking for black men was overt and common and seemed to have easily taken over from previous times when the gender relationships were reversed. But then was I just following the rather febrile logic of his wife as he portrayed it to me in detail? I have no idea to what extent there was a sexual aspect or intention here, either on these foreign women's part or on his. It's just that I could understand why his wife might become obsessed by this.

What was rather more evident was the underlying issue of friending with respect to his Trini contacts because this was taking place in front of my eyes. However concerned Marvin was with his work and with his marriage, he was still carrying on IM conversations with persons who popped up on the screen as we talked. True to the picture that was forming, the main IM conversation taking place at this point was with a glamorous young woman – as it happens, not one of those he went to school with. Currently, she is a flight attendant and is chatting from her hotel room in New York between flights. There is no mistaking the flirtatious undertone to her conversation. It's so cold there in New York. She is so looking forward to seeing him again; she needs some warmth. She is mocking him: 'Oh, you won't have time for me when I come back to Trinidad next month.'

Still he proclaims his own innocence, he blames Trini women:

'Yeah . . . and that is true because she has been asking me to take her out; she has been asking me to see her. And because of the relationship, I don't want to do it. But at the same time, I don't want her to get totally annoying. Because a lot of girls, if they are not getting through to the guy they like, they would totally sever the relationship. They don't . . . being friends alone is not good enough. If they like you, in that way. If they like you more than a friend, being a friend with them, or attempting to be a friend with them will not work. Happens all the time with me. They find me attractive. They want to get with me. They want to at least explore the option. If I keep turning them down, which is what I have been doing. And I don't think this is going to last long with this girl because she seems to want to know – what have I been doing? When can I see you? Nothing happened, I mean can't we just be friends? But a part of me wants to see her. I don't want to compromise my relationship with my wife.'

The trouble is that, at the same time he is spinning out this defence of his behaviour, it's still pretty clear that the man is also flirting. By this stage, I had realized why it was that he had this phone which never rang to voice because he had just admitted this to me. IM is the only medium his wife can't check up on, that isn't logged in the way voice calls are, or texts are, or Facebook updates are.

There was a critical question in my own mind, one I simply couldn't decide upon. Was Trinidad in some ways doomed to this very problematic consequence of Facebook, by comparison with all other countries, by a mere happenstance, a semantic coincidence? A mix-up of words that in and of itself was perhaps contributing to the breakup of this and other relationships? The issue lay in the meaning of the very word *friending* or *to friend*. Because Trinidad is the one country where this is a very old and much-employed term, used a century before anyone had heard of Facebook. In Trinidadian dialect, *to friend* means to have sex with someone, and most of all it meant that one was in a relationship other than marriage. As with other Caribbean islands, much to the despair of the church, people rarely married until they could afford a house together. Prior to that, it was expected that a girl should have a baby to demonstrate her adulthood, and that a man should be a babyfather for much the same reason. The children of these children would be looked after by the older generation, typically their grandparents or great-aunts. The system had always worked well. Young, biologically fit girls, gave birth. Older women, who had done with partying, looked after the children. In some ways there was a better logic to this than the assumption in Britain that the biological mother had to be the cultural mother. But such young, unmarried couples would typically be described as in a friending relationship.

Friending, though, did not necessarily end with marriage. There is also a rich vocabulary in Trinidad for what the French call a mistress but in Trinidad is called a *deputy* or an *outside woman*. The issue with Facebook is less whether it increases complex and multiple relationships than whether it makes them more visible. Reading the novelist Emile Zola, it is clear that, even in France, there was a historical difference between having a discreet mistress and having her live openly in one's house.

I suspect that for the more sophisticated urban Trinidadian today, none of this ambiguity followed. They had largely ceased using the word 'friending' in that fashion. But both Marvin and his wife come from villages near the cocoa estate and represent unusually successful children from such rural areas. In their milieu, the word 'friending' is still employed in its traditional guise. Every time his wife notes that a woman has friended him on Facebook, there is this ambiguity in the language itself.

Within Facebook, there is a parallel form of semantic ambiguity. It lies not in the words *to friend* but rather in the term *relationship*. That word has changed its connotations in pretty much the opposite direction. Previously relatively innocuous – but now? Is it possible to say one is in a relationship with someone without implying a sexual content? Has this too become simply a coy way of saying you are having sex with someone? And is it any surprise that when people look at each other's profiles in Trinidad, the thing that they are always alert to is any change in the relationship status that is posted so conspicuously on the profile of every Facebook account?

So the drama of my encounter with Marvin is summarized by what happened just before I walked into his office. He had seen that his wife had just changed her relationship status on her own Facebook account. It still said that she was in a relationship, but no longer made clear just who she was in a relationship with. He had got angry at this and, in a tit for tat, as he put it, he had removed all information about his relationships status. Once I realized what was going on, I was amazed that he had been calmly chatting to me at first about such extraneous things as chocolate and Facebook marketing. But eventually he dropped everything else to explain the dilemma of the moment. While we had been talking, the first comments were being posted on Facebook from his and her friends respectively. He knew this was just the start of what would become a flood of comments, some genuinely concerned, some probably just stirring or voyeuristic. The shock was that he had been gradually moving towards a sense that he might need to leave his wife as the only way to escape her daily interrogations but by this one action she had turned the tables and seized the initiative.

As he put it:

'This is where Facebook becomes dangerous because everyone is seeing this. Everyone on our friends list is seeing this. Everyone is seeing this. She had 799 friends up until a couple of hours ago. What I told her is she does these things to provoke a response from her friends. And of course some of her friends, who don't want the relationship to work, will reply and comment on things that are not healthy for the relationship.'

Marvin is actually even angrier at this point with Facebook than
with his wife. It's not just that Facebook has made his other friends
so visible, thus constantly tormenting his wife with their presence.
But that her response creates such an immediate public airing of
their dirty linen. Things that could have been aired, exhumed,
reconciled and then buried in private are now too concretely in
the public sphere. Once on Facebook, they have to be acknowledged in relation to potentially more than a thousand other people
between their two sites.

For Marvin, Facebook had turned everything into confusion,
into public slavering and gossip, into the prospect of endless
explanations and legitimations. The natural transient anger and
quarrels of the world no longer blow over in the next wind, to be
suppressed by the romance of a gesture or good sex. Now they are
impressed in the Facebook of life, part of fate, of legacy, history
and biography. Even if things turn out well, everyone still knows
this happened; it's deeply inscribed onto their computers, etched
into hard discs. And that sours the relationship itself. It has lost
its protection of intimacy and shared secrets. You can no longer
know who is going to bring this up again and against whom and
when. It is tiresome and tiring, adding its own momentum to the
desire to simply extricate oneself from the relationship itself, so
that this quarrel becomes the last quarrel – to seek some refuge
from exhausting cycles of blame and shame in permanent separation.

It's not hard to take up cudgels for the defence, to attempt to
exonerate Facebook from this accusation of breaking up Marvin's
marriage. After all, this is a man who can't help flirting with some
woman in New York at the very moment he is casting aspersions
on the technology, who is openly discussing with me a sexually
charged field of gender in which he readily states that both men
and women look at each other's Facebook profiles with an imagination of, to use his words, *trading up,* irrespective of the relationship they are actually in at that time. But I also understand that he
is right to blame Facebook because the gender relations he reveals
are nothing new. They were just the same when I was first writing
about Trinidad. People imagined alternatives, but this fantasy
of trading up, and the alternative of having a deputy, was more
often just a fantasy. As fantasies they are not specific to Trinidad.
It didn't seem so different to the way a man in a London office

might think about the secretary doing his photocopying, or what she imagines on her way home about the guy sitting opposite on the underground train. Nevertheless, most core relationships in Trinidad I had encountered were pretty much as stable as those of London, with strong commitments born of love for children, care for long-term partners, wider bonds developed with extended families and affections deepened with trust and time, even if sometimes they had lost some of their original romance to inertia.

When Facebook invaded this terrain and interposed itself 'twixt man and woman, and woman and woman again, things changed. At least in some cases, such as Marvin's, the sheer visibility and presence made that extra difference. It made that which was problematic, but bearable, into intolerable and unbearable. This daily checking of every name, every action, every ambiguity, wore them both down. I was later to meet women who entirely confirmed this feeling about Facebook. Caryn, for example, someone I knew in an entirely different context, when talking about the breakup of her relationship, confided:

'It just seemed like the only friends he could make in the world were females and they just always seemed to have a lot of stuff to say on his wall. And he just never seemed to be able to draw a clear line as in "I am actually in a relationship so maybe this is not an appropriate conversation a guy in a relationship should be having." So, yeah, it just, I think it makes you more paranoid. Because you see all these things and then you think, OK, how does he know this person and why is she saying thanks for the good night last night? What does that mean? . . . You can almost get obsessive about it.'

If you read the newspapers, you know that worse happens. The British *Daily Mail* (19 February 2010) reports on a Trinidadian murder. Paul Bristol, aged 25, an IT technician for the Trinidad and Tobago Ministry of Administration, travelled to London and stabbed his lover Camille Mathurasingh twenty times in a frenzied attack. She died on the floor of the kitchen. All of this was said to be the result of seeing her on Facebook with another man. There are other murders and fights also said to have been caused by Facebook reported within the Trinidadian press. There is nothing new about murders caused by a jealous rage, and it seems glib and simplistic to blame this on Facebook. But what I have just witnessed with Marvin suggests it would be equally glib and simplistic to dismiss the idea that Facebook as a technology had some role to play here. No doubt one day some lawyers will make a good deal of money arguing such things to their illogical limits.

Of course, when Marvin himself blames Facebook for the ending of his relationship, he also senses that this is not just a pure technology that acts in some robotic fashion. Facebook responds to circumstances and it's just that his circumstance turns Facebook from friend to villain. There is the fact that he has to be on Facebook for his work. And there is also the fact that he is alone in an office and thus the temptations of endless IM chats with women matches him to Cherryl, alone in her hotel in New York, with nothing better to do than flirt. It might not have been so bad if he had stuck to IM since, as we have seen, this is invisible. But then, as we are talking, he notes that he has just added Adelaide to his friends list. He kicks himself. Someone called Adelaide had asked to be his friend and he had agreed. But then he has not the least idea who she is. Unusually, they have no friends in common; she doesn't seem to be there as a fan of the estate. All of which means that if his wife asks him who this new friend is, he won't be able to give any kind of account – and that is the worst explanation of all. Just what constantly incenses her. And yet he can't stop himself from adding her: the curiosity, the fact that she is female, the fact that he so easily can. The compulsion of the technology is welded to the compulsion of desire. It's a deadly combination. I see only these snippets – a morning extending through an afternoon – but it's enough to witness their destructive power. Maybe if his wife had been different, someone more passive and submissive? But as he himself says, he would never have found such a woman attractive. He likes the fact that she is strong-willed and headstrong. But then things cycle back again from personality to technology because he ends by saying it's just that you need boundaries: 'And not every time that you get upset with me you go air it on the internet.' Facebook may not originate the problems but it's obvious that it has the power to exacerbate or refine traits, tendencies, foibles which can tip some balance that leads its victims to slide off the scales and towards destruction. That last-straw woman that broke the couple's back came from Facebook.

I sense this is about to happen, that today's public airing is a final straw and they will separate. Marvin will forever blame Facebook for this. He says there and then that he wishes he could end his relationship. He doesn't mean his relationship to his wife but rather his relationship with Facebook itself. But he knows he can't. Facebook is one of the most successful things he has ever provided for his work, this highly responsible job which is visible evidence of his success to the neighbourhood, to his family, to his peers, not to mention those 620 friends on his own Facebook page. In the tussle for relationships, Facebook has won. He might as well re-designate his profile 'in a relationship – with Facebook'. And it seems that ultimately the jealous owner of them all is the technology. S/he, who will brook no other, has destroyed and severed him from the woman he says he still loves and would have found a way to reconciliation but for . . . In the end there is no way one can separate out the relationships we have through Facebook and the relationships we have to Facebook.

Suddenly all conversation stops. There is a screaming and a screeching at such a pitch and intensity that makes all communication between us impossible. High, high up in the sky, is another pair of eyes that observes all with a destructive intent. Twice a day the hawks are released and immediately this unleashes the panicked screeching of parrots. The parrots and I have something in common: an insatiable fondness for that white nameless pulp around the cocoa bean. But to reach it the parrot also breaks apart the pod and destroys the crop. Not wishing to use pesticides, the estate needs a solution compatible with its ecotourism. So it leaves it to the hawks to keep down the predations of the parrots. In this new Facebook world, the all-seeing hawks are in the ascendancy.

2

Community

One of the problems in teaching anthropology is the awareness
that so many people come to study this discipline because of some
romantic idyll of kinship, the village or community. These seem
to be imagined as some kind of paradise lost, remaining only in
these enclaves studied by anthropologists. This romantic other-
ness is largely used as a stick to beat ourselves with. All sorts of
faults and deficiencies are assumed to exist in our own society as
against these others. One of the reasons I try to conduct research
in areas as varied as London, Manila, village India or Trinidad is
in order to contest such assumptions. We all live equally in the
present. Peoples studied by anthropologists in tribes or villages are
not some evolutionary remnant of our own past. Anthropologists
themselves can be in thrall to the marginal and to the critique.
So it seems almost heresy to want to use anthropology to affirm
positively that which we can accomplish within the contemporary world we actually inhabit, rather than use it as some kind of
lament and regret. But that is my desire and intention.

Having said all this, although I barely know Alana, sitting in
this quiet rural hamlet, it is quite hard to entirely escape from
this romance of community. I can just feel sentimentality creeping up my spine, softening my resolve, despite all my attempts to
disown it. I blame the palm trees. But if I have let my guard slip,
it is more because Alana herself seems incredibly nice. There is
something about her that is warm and gentle and considerate and

seductive. Although she is twenty-five and good looking, this is not an erotic attachment. Actually, it's more the feeling that you want her to be your mother, to comfort you when you get hurt, to keep your innermost confidences and protect you from horrible people.

This sentiment naturally extends to her family who seem just as benign. Each of them seems to have a kind of maturity of vision of how to care for others, that natural sense of the balance between order and freedom, concern and autonomy that makes parenting work but is so hard to explain or achieve. It is conservatively gendered. The mother cooks while the father pontificates wisely about the future of the world and local politics. Both seem strong in the appropriately gendered fashion for Trinidadians. I confess I tend to be more drawn to the woman's world, especially as it turns out that Alana's mother is preparing a Christmas drink I adore called *punch à crème*. Now, the problem when I want to prepare this drink at home is that my own family is a bit fussy about downing raw eggs, which I had assumed was essential to this delectable concoction. But Alana's mother has a recipe using cooked eggs. Basically mixing six tins of condensed with four of evaporated milk, heating this up with nutmeg, the rinds of three limes and other spices (unspecified – I can't give away all her secrets) and then whisking a dozen eggs into the hot milk. Finally adding two and a half litres of strong rum and leaving at least overnight. Fortunately, this was one of those 'here is some I made earlier' cookery classes. But I honestly don't think that my three glasses of *punch à crème* were the only reason I felt this benign glow in the company of Alana's family. They all seemed to embody an ethical sensibility of concern for others' well-being, but never as a matter of abstract principle, always with a touch of humour, and with those allowances for slippage and spoilage that are realistic about the actual world and its foibles.

This attraction first for Alana and then her family leads back to that romantic ideal of community, since Alana lives in the kind of settlement which has become quite rare in contemporary Trinidad. Modern Trinidad is a pretty mobile place and one meets relatively few people of any age who live where they were born. But as one moves along the main East–West corridor where much of the island's population live, there are roads that lead out to the north, where, if you travel for a while, you can hear the forest echo with the last voices of the original Amerindian populations of this land, where there is a sense of continuity and history.

Santa Ana is known as a Spanish village. *Spanish* is a curious Trinidadian term, in that it can apply to a person who has absolutely no claim to any lineage that comes from Spain. Rather, it tends to imply a mixed descent, often a very mixed descent. You can have a bit of Chinese, *Syrian* (who are actually Lebanese), *Portuguese* (who are actually from Madeira), Indian, African and *French Creole* (some of whom are British), the combination of which makes you quite clearly Spanish. Some dispute this, but my reading of Trinidadian history is that there are no people in the island today who can claim pure descent from the pre-colonial population. For a long period, Trinidad was under the titular rule of Spain, though it was pretty sparsely inhabited by either Amerindians, decimated by disease, or indeed Spanish. Both of these groups largely disappeared through the pores of later French and British colonialism. In the middle of Trinidad, there are Spanish settlements founded by people who migrated from Venezuela, but in most other areas Spanish really just means mixed and old.

Santa Ana is quite small. There are around twenty-five houses straddling a ridge in the foothills of the mountains that form a spine pointing north into the hills. These houses, with only two exceptions, represent the descendants of the same three or four core families. So by now pretty much everyone in the village is related to pretty much everyone else. When it comes to any kind of significant event, such as a wedding or a wake, then any remaining lack of relationship is ignored. To all intents and purposes, this village is a family writ large. All of which makes this the kind of place one imagines to approximate that romantic idyll of community. And Santa Ana has that feeling of common identity, of solidarity and reciprocal concern. Working back downwards, this is the solidarity and common care that seems to be channelled through Alana's exemplary family and thence to Alana herself.

None of this means that everything in the village is actually peace and goodwill. Alana's family has a running feud with their neighbour that has gone on for years. Every time a pause arises that might have led to a rapprochement it gets extended by disputes about where children shouldn't be playing or when dogs shouldn't be barking. They even have a classic confrontation as to where exactly the boundary lies between the two houses, and who last moved the fence late at night to their advantage. If we stand around the village for an evening and gossip, it's not going to be long before there are whispers about who has slept with who and really, really shouldn't have. This is a real village. Was there ever a community so ironclad that you couldn't find pockets that have been corroded deeply by illicit sex? If the newspapers regularly find this in communities of monks and ascetics, what hope for a Trinidadian village?

Within this actual community, with all its troubles and potential claustrophobia, Alana has in fact thrived. She didn't get to one of those elite secondary schools which are so often a passport out to other lands. But she did just fine at the local school. She worked hard, is naturally bright, and achieved the A level grades to take her to the University of Trinidad and Tobago (UTT). This is the new university that was set up six years earlier to try and expand tertiary education beyond the hallowed, impressive, but also now somewhat musty halls of the University of the West Indies (UWI). UTT, being less pretentious and more sympathetic to the applied side of academia, suited Alana perfectly and she has flourished there, doing well in her first degree and now embarked upon a master's course in occupational psychology.

Alana explains almost nothing about herself, as being simply an expression of her own individualistic whim. Everything around her is understood as connected to the networks she lives within. She was reluctant to come onto Facebook in the first place. But pressure from her younger cousins forced her to give in. And once on, she loved it. Today her main usage follows naturally from the social circumstance of her day-to-day life. It works exceptionally well within the ethos of collective education. This has turned out to be central to her course in occupational psychology where the teaching has a strong background in social psychology and family therapy. Typically, part of the marking system depends upon group work. The teacher had intended this to be carried out as a group blog but Alana and her peers felt things worked much more smoothly when tasks could be integrated between studying and social networking more generally. So they have opted to do all their group work through Facebook. The teacher agreed. It's typical of the way the internet more generally seems to have become consolidated around Facebook over the last year in Trinidad.

This also fits in well within Alana's own networking. She has around two hundred Facebook friends of whom about forty are relatives. She has less than ten friends from outside Trinidad. This is unusual for Trinidad, which could hardly be more transnational. In a previous study, I found that the majority of the population is transnational even at the nuclear level, defined as having either parents, children or siblings living abroad. The bulk of her network are from her university and centres on her class. She logs on in the morning before she goes to class and spends much of her lunchtime on Facebook. There are computers available at college for use when she is not actually in lectures and she spends about an hour a day there on Facebook. But the real commitment comes later. Most nights, she goes to sleep around eight. Then, when the rest of her household is asleep, she gets up. From midnight to three in the morning is her core Facebook time and life.

Her reasoning is that this is the quiet period when she can concentrate on her studies without household disturbance. But there is more to it. Almost all her class have adopted the same diurnal rhythm. They have become a Facebook flock that roost together at night, setting up an incessant chatter that echoes through the branches. As a supervisor of postgraduate students, I learned a long time ago that the more learning is fun, the more that it is social, the more that individual students actually learn. I have rescued a few pasty-faced US students who have been to colleges where the ethos was that if the students ever lifted their noses from the grindstones they were poor students. Students need long weekends and evenings when they are forbidden from even thinking about their thesis and to learn that the best intellectual discussion tends to take place in pubs when infused with alcohol. After all, this is anthropology. If you don't like to socialize and make friends, you are in the wrong business.

Alana's group has discovered this quite happily for itself and without any such pedagogic prompting. Free of the delusion that learning is competitive or a limited quantity, everyone helps each other. If you are all on Facebook together, then researching homework and socializing are seamlessly joined. In the middle of chatting about boyfriends, you ask for clarification about a term you suddenly remember you hadn't understood in class. Conversely, as this guy explains patiently, clearly and with obvious knowledge about some nineteenth-century approach to the psychology of work, you start to see things in the man you hadn't previously acknowledged. By the end of the explanation, you find a reason to need some further point of clarification in person next time you are in class together. For the group as a whole, it provides a kind of general reassuring co-presence. As she describes it: 'Yeah, like seeing that, say if all of us up studying at the same time, we would log on just for each other to know that we there. So in the event that you come across something that you don't really understand, we would do it over Facebook or if it very necessary then we call.'

Yes, of course, this can be distracting and Alana reckons that only about 20 per cent of the conversation is purely discussion of homework. Mostly, this is a public set of encounters, but not entirely. There is nothing to say that you can't also have a few issues that are better discussed more discreetly, through Facebook's internal IM facility or message-sending service. Anyway, if you end up having a private chat through Facebook with your three best friends more or less every night, as Alana does, it isn't necessarily because things need to be more discreet. It's also just an affirmation that they are your best friends.

Within Facebook, one can have different networks that largely ignore one another. Alana probably wouldn't be that interested in *FarmVille*, left to herself. But she has a score of younger cousins who need her to be a good neighbour so they can progress in the game, which anyway she finds reasonably relaxing. She admits that this can add up to something like two hours a day online labour. But the consequence is a thriving online cousinhood that is effective in developing her extended family relations. It co-exists without much overlap with the network that forms around her class. Alana partly uses her diurnal rhythm to keep this separation. The *FarmVille* with cousins happens between six and eight. The exchanges with her class come when the cousins are asleep. There are other networks she refuses. She knows, for example, a group of her friends use Facebook extensively to discuss politics. But she is wary of the falling out that this brings and refuses to get involved.

Having this degree of sharing is also a way to leverage networks. Some, but not all, of those in the class may have the kind of links to people that everyone would quite like to have some sort of connection with, but have no means of achieving for themselves. So, one girl is a relative of a key soca star of the moment, Bunji

Garlin. Another was at school with a well-known Rasta singer. A third has a link with a guy who isn't just a member of the national cricket team but is also pretty cute. Much of the 80 per cent of communication that is not homework could be at least loosely described as gossip. So these little tit-bits of news and closeness to semi-celebs seem to add yeast to the general doughy gossip that bakes of a night.

Then again, research was never something that was confined within academic boundaries. A person does well in class because they know how to locate the latest journal articles and the most recent internet debates about the topic they will be examined on. This may be the same person who is first to know how to find out what is in fashion and where the cool places are to be seen. It's all research, and knowing how to know things first. Not necessarily new things. Alana has just been learning about an ideology that springs out of Rastafari. Called Bobo Shanti, it was founded in 1958 by Prince Emmanuel Charles Edwards who formed a kind of black trinity with Marcus Garvey and Haile Selassie. In Trinidad, they appear as more extreme than most Rasta, whether in what they wear or how they live. They also lean towards Jewish customs such as a Saturday Sabbath. Alana is no more than curious about them, but chatting on Facebook with someone whose close friend is actually part of the movement is a good way of satisfying this curiosity. She is someone who doesn't like to be ignorant about anything much at all. It may not have any immediate purpose but at this point it's hard to make a firm distinction between curiosity and research.

The other side of gossip, though, especially in Trinidad, is scandal, leading to bacchanal. At the fringe of their group is a photographer who tends to take pictures of people having 'scenes', such as a couple quarrelling at a nightclub. It seems OK when he managed to show a policeman verbally assaulting a driver, but what of an ordinary couple spotted after a couple of drinks who unintentionally bring their quarrel out into the public domain? And then he posts it on Facebook or YouTube? Even abstractly, this was a problem. But then recently this same photographer took a picture of one of Alana's classmates who was dancing with a guy when everyone knew she was engaged to another. It's not like anybody thinks that an engaged woman will never dance with someone else. But, once it was on Facebook, it was bound to cause problems in their relationship and to spread as the more insinuating form of negative gossip. There are also too many instances of women being malicious to each other, as recently happened to a girl who wasn't too worried about her profile since her boyfriend is not on Facebook. Then another woman put up explicit posts about how 'I thought you already had a man', causing her to defriend that woman. Trinidad is an island where there tends to be an assumption that women in general will maintain a certain level of simmering resentment and competition in relation to men. It goes with the myth that there are more women than men in the country.

Alana fully acknowledges this problematic side to Facebook. As she puts it, you might trust your ten friends but then they trust their ten friends and a friend's friend doesn't have the same trust and commitment to you. So before you know it, things get circulated that shouldn't. It's not usually so bad or so common in her age group, though even she finds herself often tagged in photos. Quite a few times, she has moved swiftly to untag them. After all, she has most of her family also as friends on her site. But then she also monitors what she does in public because she knows this could happen. Where she feels Facebook really causes havoc is amongst the teenagers. Partly they simply haven't learnt the self-discipline that this technology so evidently requires. But also they are the ones who play with taking risks; where the girls compete in trying to look sexy. It is also at this age when sometimes girls can be complete bitches to each other, especially when your best friend, who told you all her secrets, is now suddenly your worst enemy.

You could have this discussion with pretty much anyone who uses Facebook. But it is particularly significant to this research project to be having the conversation specifically with Alana, since who else could give a sense of what it means to call Facebook a community than someone who actually lives in a close-knit community? Listening to her talk about the use of Facebook at night, amongst her peers, there is no getting away from the conclusion that Facebook creates, maintains and constitutes some kind of community, whatever we mean by that term. And through this common internet life are emerging some of the values that make community so special. On the one hand, there is the deeper knowledge and experience of fellow humanity that breeds care and concern, friendship and reciprocity, in short an ethical sensibility. Yet at the same time there is the invasion, the devastation of privacy – the degree to which everyone knows everyone's business. There is the speed with which gossip surges through the network and spills as grimy foam through the doors and onto the carpets of those living far from its source. There are the quarrels and the suspicions and, as the first portrait has shown, the actual breakup of otherwise viable relationships. This looks like the very opposite of those same ethics. It is that which pulls people apart into suspicion and revenge, rather than unites them in common concern.

If we are ever going to understand these contradictions, we need to go much more deeply into what is meant when we talk about Facebook as some sort of community. The problem is that the word is used so easily by academics and others, almost none of whom have ever lived in such conditions. So the intention of this enquiry was to exploit the immediate juxtaposition in the lives of people such as Alana, who were qualified to compare the virtual community of Facebook with the rest of their lives. This is why much of my conversation with her was not about Facebook but concerned her wider experience. What was it like growing up in and continuing to live in Santa Ana? She is a student at university and is used to thinking abstractly about such comparisons and concepts. What does she think community is and what are its consequences? She hasn't the slightest difficulty in appreciating either the meaning or significance of this question. Her answer is clear and unequivocal. Everything I have said about Facebook is true for her and true to her. Yes, it creates these bonds that go well beyond those which you would normally expect from a bunch of classmates. Yes, it has a propensity for bacchanal and scandal and she has given me the anecdotes to back that up. But with respect to both aspects, Facebook is not a patch on the real thing.

However much one blames Facebook for malicious or ill-informed gossip, Alana feels it doesn't even start to approach what happens routinely in a small place like Santa Ana. She tells of how, in a community like this, people would look at how their friends' children are growing up, or criticize the youths in the village. They wouldn't take time to get to know them; they would just sit and talk about whether a child is neglected or a youth is into drugs. She says:

Yeh, it's much, much worse. I think people still have some level of respect on Facebook, well at least the people that I socialize with. They wouldn't blatantly put something very offensive. Whereas if you having a conversation with somebody, they would tell yuh what they think about someone else in confidentiality . . . With the older people you would just probably hear an exchange of words but the youths they would start with the words and end up with the fist-fighting and stuff like that. We recently had a stranger that came in. I think he dating a girl out the road and she girl, she pretty young. And she and a guy in the village always had an exchange of words. Like throw talk for one another and stuff like that. So he was passing and something she said and her boyfriend get up and try swing a blade at him. And he hold it and pull it away from his hand. All his ligaments and everything gone. He came out of the hospital about three days ago. His right hand, he can't do anything right now. He have strings and stuff on his hand trying to get it back . . . yeah, terrible.'

As far as Alana is concerned, Facebook is a much safer version of community, a whole lot less malicious and vicious than the real thing.

The point can also work in the other direction. People congregate online and help each other with homework. But that doesn't represent the kind of commitment people make to each other in the village. Santa Ana is a place where you can spend the whole day cooking something up for a neighbour who is hosting some communal occasion. There had just recently been a wake that is celebrated on the first year's anniversary of a death, with food cooked by many neighbours and the community playing cards into the night. In a village such as this, whatever the internal quarrels, there is still the foundation for deep and sustained solidarity in relation to any external threat. When someone is ill or in crisis, then you know instinctively what being in a community means, the responsibilities it gives you and the hold it has on you.

Alana notes the extent to which people in Santa Ana itself who used to lime together physically now do so through Facebook. Cousins still do lime by Alana's grandmother's house, although quite often they now sit and talk about *FarmVille* and then may rush back to actually be part of the game. Given, however, that *FarmVille* is all about helping each other progress and friendly competition, there is no sense that they are thereby becoming more individualistic or less communal even if they physically meet a bit less often. In any case, the main thing that Facebook is seen as replacing is not the physical liming together but television. Alana hardly ever watches television any more. Television-watching here was often quite sociable but had much less of the intense sociability that is integral to Facebook. Facebook often replicates relationships within the village itself.

When judging the nature of Facebook as community, Alana makes a profound observation: that it can only be assessed relative to offline community. She regards her situation, living in Santa Ana, as exceptional in contemporary Trinidad, precisely because she recognizes that she has always lived within community par excellence. In her case, some of the time she spends online is at the expense of co-present socializing 'in the sense that I would spend my free time on the computer rather than walk out the road or go to the beach or something like that'. But she contrasts her experience with a friend who lives in a much more typical settlement within Trinidad, near Tunapuna: 'it's more of a small town and you don't really see people going by each other. But she will keep in contact via Facebook.'

When you are living in a place like Santa Ana, the community is incredibly intense and her use of Facebook, however sociable, is a means to give herself some sort of break from this intensity. If people in Santa Ana lime together less than they used to and instead turn to Facebook as a kind of milder version of community, it is to achieve some sort of distance because the reality of living within such a close-knit community is simply too intense and invasive. Recently, a friend of mine who had lived for a while in London found the return to Trinidad unbearable because she felt there was just no privacy, no escape from an entire community that knew her business, and she wasn't even on Facebook. By comparison, many people in London, simply have no conception how thoroughly claustrophobic and sometimes downright nasty the reality of a community can be.

By contrast, for Alana's friend near Tunapuna, there simply isn't enough actual community. She is frustrated at how little she knows or interacts with the people who live close to her. So her experience of Facebook does the opposite. It helps create a bit more social intensity in a situation where people have an insufficiency of direct communication and contact with each other.

Facebook is not the dish. It is more like an ingredient that balances the other flavours to give you the best overall mix. In turn, it links with other ingredients in cooking up one's social media. For example, a couple starting to get into a more dating-like relationship will complement Facebook with the spice of texting which is more dyadic and personal and, if you were to see their texting, sometimes pretty hot.

When Alana talks about the group being together between midnight and three in the morning, she describes it as a *group lime*. This seems about right. A lime is not the same as a community, but without liming Trinidad would not be the kind of community it is. Even though most liming no longer actually has the spontaneity – the sense that you never know where you are going to end up, and who with – that the ideal of a lime stands for, still it has something of the frisson that comes with that ideal. That is what gives a lime its flavour, more relaxed, more uncertain and more fun than socializing in London by arrangement and with a plan and only with the group you originally set out with. Her Facebook lime has an agreed time but there is much of the same fun and spontaneity and mixture of different elements.

So for Alana it makes less sense to ask whether Facebook is in and of itself a community. Rather, she foregrounds the way in which Facebook is used to balance out the degree of offline community. Alana also confirms, as someone who lives in a community, that Facebook shares many recognizable traits. This makes it pretty extraordinary. At the start of the twenty-first century, we can see in Facebook a dramatic reversal of the general decline in community that had preceded it for a century, if not two. As a site of community, we can expect Facebook to have all the contradictions found in the kind of community that Alana lives in. You simply can't have both closeness and privacy. You can't have support without claustrophobia. You can't have this degree of friendship without the risk of explosive quarrelling. Either everything is more socially intense or none of it is. Alana is the expert voice here. She has the authority to pronounce on what, at least for her, community is actually like. She has no problem in seeing and articulating these contradictions and thereby understanding why the most important thing Facebook provides is a means to help complement the offline version and to live with those same contradictions.

3

For Whom the Bell Doesn't Toll

There is something about some East Indian men when they are around sixty years old; when their temples are greying but much of the rest of their hair remains black; when there are lines of profundity in the forehead but their face remains smooth. However they looked at other times in their lives, at this particular conjuncture they become almost peculiarly handsome. Terms such as distinguished, gentleman, guruji, father seem warranted, even if they were never your relative or teacher. They just exude a generic aura of wisdom, fronted by a bright smile and a kindly patrician air.

Actually in the case of Dr Karamath, this sense of nobility is not entirely unselfconscious. He has a very strong awareness of his own ancestry which was in some respects quite untypical for Trinidadian families. Most of the ancestors of the East Indian population of the country came as indentured labourers. We can assume that the primary cause was poverty, if not destitution, that forced them to face the passage of the black waters. Many of the Hindu families of Trinidad today claim descent from the Brahmin caste. But if one goes back to the original records, it seems probable that there has been a certain amount of 'status inflation' that has accrued over the intervening period. By contrast, there is pretty good evidence for the precise ancestry of Dr Karamath from an original migrant who appears to have come from the Lahore area and had some training as a civil servant. Certainly he had mastery over several languages, was cultivated in terms of the arts and letters and worked in a more senior capacity with respect to the British overseers of the time.

Even within the Muslim population of Trinidad, which represents around 6 per cent of the country, the Karamath family remains somewhat distinct. This is a community that has seen rapid changes in recent years. In some ways, it had traditionally been one of the quieter elements within Trinidad. It seems somewhat unsure of its own identity as part of the East Indian population but not entirely aligned with the larger Hindu fraction. Many had developed a close relationship with the government of the PNM, otherwise more associated with the population of ex-African descent, partly to differentiate themselves from the Hindu-led opposition. Nor was this just one homogeneous community. The most prominent cultural event celebrated by Muslims, outside of Eid, was the festival of Hosein. This is associated with the minority Shia faction of this population and takes place in the St James district of Port of Spain, quite distant from the rural majority. It has a unique atmosphere, backed by the incessant *tassa* drums, played at an incredible speed, which herald the procession through the streets of a series of large, sometimes quite precariously perched, models which look like mosques or mausoleums, obviously crafted from paper and tinsel with considerable love and devotion. Of all the celebrations in Trinidad, it is the one least tarnished by commercialism and advertising.

The situation among Muslims had become still more confused with the rise of radical African neo-Muslim elements that had been associated with an attempted coup. There was an uneasy relationship between this trend and the wider increase in religious observation. Today it is quite common to find women wearing veils in Trinidad, something practically unheard of some twenty years before. It is quite likely that, as well as reflecting wider trends, this was a means by which the Indo-Trinidadian Muslims felt obliged to demonstrate their own religiosity in response to this African participation. There is now also a full-time Muslim television station in Trinidad, though one representing the middle ground of Muslim identity rather than either an especially staunch religiosity or more fundamentalist politics.

None of this would, however, tell you much at all about the nature and culture of Dr Karamath. He has relatives who have occupied senior positions in the Trinidadian Muslim community and even include some prominent theologians. But, for himself, he saw his lineage as coming more from that deep reverence for education ascribed to his immigrant ancestor and those descendants who had always been much more orientated towards these same secular educational values. Dr Karamath has had a distinguished career as a human rights lawyer, having first obtained a PhD in literature at a prestigious US university.

In keeping with these values, Dr Karamath has had a lifelong commitment to human rights issues within the region of his birth. He might well have garnered still more fame and reputation if he had practised in other fields. But his specialization has tended to remain with legal issues within the Caribbean itself, especially countries such as Guyana, where human rights have sadly been of far more concern, for a far longer period, than anyone would have wished – though he and others have been gratified with the way more recently that Guyana has risen from the mire and now is in some ways moving towards an exemplary concern with issues of the environment, political rights, and the status of the Amerindian population.

As befitting the needs of his work, Dr Karamath became a consummate cosmopolitan. He was known as something of a raconteur, with a glass of whisky in hand, an insatiable appetite for knowledge, a deserved reputation for personal integrity and a solicitous manner. These attracted his own little circle of younger admirers and conversationalists at parties. He had developed sustained links with international bodies such as the UN and with Washington. He was a regular participant within the 'Caribbean' representatives to such august bodies. All of this has meant that, as the years went by, although he remained largely within the Caribbean, his links to Trinidad itself were sometimes somewhat attenuated.

The fact that he seems to look still more distinguished and handsome with age makes it more, rather than less, difficult to reconcile himself to the process of ageing itself. But still this might have been managed appropriately if it had followed the natural course of gradual adaptation to frailty over many years. Sadly this was not the case. Eighteen months previously, he had been diagnosed with a serious condition that within a short time meant he had become wheelchair-bound and afflicted with other weaknesses, one of which affected his speech. Although these disabilities had now stabilized, they were almost certainly a permanent condition. Suddenly this gregarious man who had never been without company, and who had spent his life cultivating a public persona, who brightened a party or cast a spell through conviction and rhetoric, found himself almost entirely housebound. Now he was only able to speak in a voice that had descended from sonorous to ponderous.

Dr Karamath is determined to both acknowledge and confront the nature of this curse that has been laid on him by fate. He is well aware of the way other people have responded when, having climbed all those ladders, they fall precipitously down the grinning snake just a few throws before the end of the game. He has seen people decline into despondency, despair, and worst of all malevolence to those about them whom they 'blame' somehow for not saving them from this undeserved loss. He has seen good people shrivel up and become a kind of living ghost that haunts their relatives and friends, when their only concern appears to be with their own health and misfortune. In particular, he remembers one relative from the past who had been something of a matriarch and a figure of great generosity to her descendants until she became elderly and stricken with illness. At this point, she seemed to lose all her concern with the welfare of others and became completely obsessed by her own medical condition. She used to ring him in New York or Georgetown to tell him she could feel a heart attack coming on and if he didn't come home immediately he would curse himself for ever because he had been absent at her death. Despite being able to reassure himself, in every case, that this signified heartburn rather than a heart attack, these calls were still incredibly distressing.

So Dr Karamath knew what could happen in such circumstances and was determined that this was not the road he would ever travel. Yes, he was practically housebound and no, he was not going to entertain the world ever again with his jokes and innuendoes or his rhetorical dismantling of corruption and exploitation. But he still possessed that positive energy, still had the same desire to help the world rather than hinder it. And if there were any vehicle that he could still ride to assist those around him, he would still want to lead a charge, though a wheelchair didn't really seem to offer much promise. So when, at just the right time, a magical white horse appeared in his doorway, there was no way he was going to look this gift horse in the mouth. Dr Karamath saw his opportunity, swung his lame body into this Facebook saddle and prepared one more time to engage the world.

The timing actually was perfect, just when he was feeling at his lowest ebb and closest to despairing of his fate. But Dr Karamath was exactly the kind of person to recognize Facebook, not for what it was, but for what it could become. At that time, more or less everyone around him just saw Facebook as something that students in college used to organize their social lives so they could 'party hard' and regret the degree to which the consequences entered the public domain. Most people in Trinidad were fixated on its potential for bacchanal and 'macotiousness'. Dr Karamath saw something entirely different: that Facebook was going to become, in the longer term, a far more important instrument within an entirely different segment of the population: the elderly, the infirm, the housebound, the frail and those whose faculties were in decline. It had a potential to ameliorate loss and give new life where there had been little hope. Dr Karamath was not just going to seize this opportunity for a personal resurrection. He was going to exemplify thereby this brave new world of Facebook and the way it could serve a brave old world.

So, bit by bit, Dr Karamath replicated exactly the kinds of networking relationships that he had fostered before his illness, but this time within the virtual world of servers and software and their manifestation in the connectivities of persons. He soon found that, even for someone with as international and cosmopolitan experience as himself who had met so many people in so many lands, Facebook could take this whole operation up a gear. He could now be in contact with yet more people in yet more countries and far more effectively than had ever previously been the case. Before, it had mattered that this friend was in Washington and that one in Toronto, and there were weary overnight flights and the cold alienating waitovers in airports to negotiate. Not any more.

This facility with Facebook did not spring *sui generis* from the ether. It was the culmination of Dr Karamath's quick comprehension of each new genre of internet-based communication that had preceded it. He was previously an inveterate emailer and quite prepared to use IM or the cheap rates on phones and texting. Given his own fluency, his bias had been towards the phone and long voice conversations, affordable at first only from the phones of organizations he was working for but later more generally, when international calls became relatively inexpensive. But he also had both the education and the need to become an 'early adopter' of any new communication facility offered by the internet, whether text or voice.

There was some ambivalence. In particular, he recalled an early appreciation of long emails. He had seen in these a potential for reviving a still earlier genre of the love letter. But his deep emotional investment in these had been terminated by the way in which the woman he had addressed them to had betrayed him in love. So it helped that soon afterwards the genre itself shifted and emails tended to get shorter and much closer to the world of work. He adapted to the new genre, where he, as so many others, found email a means to become more efficient in carrying out his work but also a way to allow personal communication to fit within his day-to-day routine. Alongside many of his colleagues whose work took them on long journeys to foreign sojourns, he had come to appreciate how each new internet facility had increased his ability to compensate for his absence by helping him retain a continued co-presence with family and friends.

But none of these proffered the same kind of ever-present and instantly effective networking that he saw in Facebook. He watched as people representing a variety of particular interests from various parts of the world formed themselves into Facebook groups. Facebook replicated the way that, for individuals who had a shared concern with the work of Amnesty International or Greenpeace or Caribbean democracy, it didn't seem to matter if they were living in a diaspora, or in their place of birth, or in some part of Scandinavia. (Dr Karamath has been impressed throughout his life at the way there always seemed to be an abundance of dedicated activists from Scandinavia). Wherever they were based, they could exchange information and debate about how to move the world forward. There were precedents, but all this activity seemed to become that much more natural and unforced when it came together under the auspices of Facebook.

The beauty of this was that when it came to having an opinion on the aluminium smelter in Trinidad, on Gore's position on climate change, or on political changes in Cuba, it did not matter one jot that he was wheelchair-bound or that he could no longer be articulate through voice. None of his Facebook interlocutors were any the wiser about his health or physical faculties. Within the land of Facebook, he was just as mobile and just as articulate as any of them. He could note a new finding within one of these groups and instantly recognize that these were important data that needed to be brought to the attention of another such group. He could once again become the person to whom everyone was beholden and feel that he was still playing his small part in raising, maintaining and keeping to the fore issues that mattered.

One of the most difficult changes for Dr Karamath to confront was that these days the doorbell rarely rang for him. For someone who had been the life and soul, there could be days on end when the only human company was the cook/cleaner. He almost couldn't imagine what he would have done without the consolation of Facebook. There were yet more Facebook blessings to be counted, unforeseen consequences of this almost obsessional devotion to social networking. The sheer quantity of his postings revealed his political convictions and passions, and he was able to frame them within interesting cultural allusions. This meant that even more casual users of the site, who happened to friend Dr Karamath through a common interest in a particular issue, very quickly came to share a density and depth of material that gave them considerable insight into the nature and the personality behind it.

It would have taken quite a few cocktail parties to have reached the same level of knowledge regarding the man. Facebook provided a more direct link to some of his more attractive features, without the banter and play that didn't appeal to everyone. On Facebook, Dr Karamath stood out as a particularly interesting individual, very different from the mass of postings and posturings that people otherwise came across in news and status updates. They might then start to comment on his postings, and be curious as to his replies, and this could lead to a deepening of the encounter. Dr Karamath is not quite sure how exactly this evolved into his present situation. But today he seems to have developed a core group of three or four Asian women friends, currently domiciled in London, who became attracted both to him and partly through him, to each other. They are all deeply interested in the relationship between politics and art and all have a further sense of some spirituality that, as they have got older, they feel has to be integral to both the politics and the art. This became the focus for much deeper and more sustained dialogue, both dyadically and through group postings.

In the midst of this has developed a special place for artwork. His was the legacy of a sixties generation that developed much of the modern aesthetics of political activism, a culture of posters and agitprop that dominates the way he decorates his environment. He has paintings, some by himself, and affection for ethnic art but also for art with a message. His age group formed part of the particular taste epiphany in which even quite brutal issues tend to be represented through posters and prints that try to gain attention for the cause through aesthetic devices. It was clear that, even though they had never met, thanks to their facility with a webcam, this little coterie of friends had a good knowledge also of the artworks, prints and paraphernalia of their respective homes. It seemed as though Facebook with its complementary cousins, Skype and webcam, had managed to somehow replicate the older circuit of cocktail parties in which each had in turn hosted the group. So the decorations of the home could still create an ambience that helped generate productive conversation and friendship.

This was a group who would recognize the sharp black, white and reds of Soviet constructivism, modernist appropriations of popular culture motifs, such as ironic collages of Indian miniatures by the Singh twins of Liverpool, or the retrospective of the Trinidadian-based artist Chris Ofili at the Tate Gallery in London. This was reflected also in the way each of them created something themselves by way of weaving or ceramics or painting. It somehow worked rather well that the distinguished Dr Karamath, with just the right amount of grey in his hair, was present in virtual valorization for this arts world. It added something to what otherwise might have been just another of those London diaspora groups and very female South Asian sisterhoods.

So Dr Karamath has become part of a vibrant, mature and sophisticated circle of close friends that exists in the transnational space facilitated by Facebook, comprising individuals, none of whom previously were friends with each other but who had networked through one of the various Facebook groups that shared political or activist interests. They had developed a particular kind of online friendship that had never needed to give itself a label or be concerned at all with the degree to which Facebook friends were *real* friends. Rather, they had just grown organically through the medium of Facebook itself. They were not confined to Facebook, as there are now certain blogs they all refer to, but Facebook was the core.

This representative group of sixty-somethings, who had emerged from the sixties, had never seen politics as an isolated area of abstract governance. They had their consciousness raised as much through Bob Dylan and Bob Marley as through reading texts. So it seemed equally natural that their discourse today moved freely between exchanges around their favourite music, radical arts and culture, theatre and performance. Dr Karamath might decide to send them a little local Trinidadian parang, or some gypsy music, with some comment about how they must be freezing up there given what he has seen on screen about the weather in London. And perhaps if they would like to get up and dance to some of this music it might just warm them up a little. Sadly, he was unable to take this advice himself, but then Trinidad was a good deal warmer.

In turn, these exchanges in substance could migrate to exchanges of sentiment. Nowadays, this could certainly include sympathy over the loss of a friend or relative whom they have come to know about through their more personal exchanges. Finally, they seemed to have developed an increasingly common interest in these new technologies themselves. Many of their more recent discussions were about new media, and, unlikely though it had seemed at first, they were finally developing a little bit of 'geeky' knowledge. They had developed a keen interest in the latest Google phone or nil-cost transnational communication devices. Looking at these conversations and the excitement over some new gadget, you would think they were techies in their twenties. This was the same Facebook that had such paraphernalia as *FarmVille*, silly gifts and virtual presents. Yet such things did not impinge at all on their online lives. They had found quite another niche. But they were not at all averse to discussing the medium as well as the message. Was Facebook itself too controlling? Should there be an open-source alternative?

Apart from these transnational contacts, Dr Karamath has encountered yet another unintended consequence of his devotion to Facebook. He has become more deeply involved in local Trinidadian politics. Previously, he had been mostly orientated to the wider Caribbean, almost at the expense of his own Trinidadian

roots which somehow seemed too parochial. Given that he is practically housebound, he has little direct involvement. But nearly
half his Facebook friends are Trini. As well as their shared concern
with human rights issues, they tend to have a strong commitment
to the specifics of Trinidadian politics which has increasingly
rubbed off on him. So he has ended up more knowledgeable and
more involved in recent Trinidadian politics than ever before;
issues such as the anti-smelter movement and 'Axe the Tax' which
opposed a recent new property tax. He also shares the despair at
the increase in violent crime and its appalling consequences for
this small island. Indeed, much of his discussion is about how in
the future Facebook might be more effectively mobilized to get
people out on the street and create a bigger protest movement
than is typical today. Like many of his generation, he bemoans the
decline of street action as part of political protest.

Facebook is not just a mode of communication: it's also the
conduit to magazines, various online sources of information and
thereby news generally. It is no surprise that Dr Karamath is something of a news junkie: 'Well, I've always, you know, as colonized
people, you always learn about the other – as a child we all rushed
to the radio for the 7 a.m. BBC news as we were having breakfast,
and the 6 p.m. news. So the BBC and British news was always part
of our lives. And I am talking more than 55 years ago.'

For Dr Karamath, at least, Facebook facilitates this desire that
being involved in the politics of his small island is never at the
expense of being an informed and active citizen of the world.

In general, Dr Karamath is happy with the seamless relationship
between his work, his friendships and his family created through
Facebook. While others were disconcerted by this forced juxtaposition of incompatible networks, from his perspective this was
a positive consequence. He has one child living in the US and a
sister in London and is looking forward to grandchildren whom he
hopes will be imminent. It is wonderful to him that several times a
day he may also see more personal 'news', concerning his immediate, and extended, family: the relative who incessantly posts pictures of her pets, or the younger generation enjoying themselves at
college as they should. Instead of having to close one application
and open another, this constant awareness of his family comes up
in the midst of his activist or political networking and the maintenance of friendships. It all comes together quite naturally as the

life he cares about and is concerned with. At this point he has no desire or reason to compartmentalize his life into discrete areas. He doesn't mind in the least if his research on human rights within the fractious politics of Jamaica is interrupted by some photos his child has posted online. He rather hopes that his relatives also read up on and are influenced by his politics.

On the other hand, it took him a while to work out how to deal with some issues raised by the technologies of Facebook. While he doesn't mind mixing family and work, he has no desire to compromise what he sees as his basic privacy. So, for example, when he first took to social networking, he tried putting up a photograph, but ended up accidently posting a whole album. He quickly resorted to ringing around desperately looking for someone who had the technical skills to remove them. Looking young for his age and quite distinguished, he was still surprised to get some rather forward enquiries from a younger woman in the UK with some surprisingly explicit suggestions and photographs, accompanied by a deluge of virtual gifts. He politely asked her to desist. Even more shocking was being approached by a 17-year old:

> 'So I wrote to her and said "ok, do you know I could be your grandfather, and my picture isn't really hot and sexy, so I don't think we should be friends." So she wrote back and said "ok, ok but I am not discriminating, maybe I was rude, I am sorry for that, but I would like to learn about other people in the world and age doesn't matter, so would you mind?" Oh, yes there was also that gay proposal . . .'

He refuses far more friend requests than he accepts but is more bemused than affronted by these occasional revelations of the wilder side to Facebook friending. After all, this is more than compensated for by the incalculable benefits that he feels Facebook represents in a situation such as his own; its ability to give him back the kind of role in life that is the foundation of his own self-respect and of dignity. He has ended up with far more time on his hands than most of his peers, but instead of frittering this away, or becoming maudlin about his own fate, he has carved a niche for himself. He now sees a role that could be termed a personal human rights news aggregator, whose job it is to recognize that there is a vast amount more information coming online day by day than anyone can really cope with. What the world needs more of are people such as himself, who have the time, patience, confidence and knowledge to read, select, edit, and re-send from one sphere of interest to another. Dr Karamath had seen how Facebook could grant him back his own social life at a time when he seemed destined only for loss and loneliness. But equally he was able to transform Facebook from a machine for replicating trivia and gossip into an effective and efficient means for spreading information, creating networks and even galvanizing them into action.

4

The Book of Truth

'i wish all my friends Peace, Luv, Health & Happiness. blah blah blah. Fuck that shit!i wish u sex, alcohol, orgasms and hope u win the fucking lottery. have a great 2010!!!'

I confess I was pretty startled when Vishala posted this at the start of the year. My immediate thought was that this merited one of my favourite Trini expressions, which is 'Go Brave'. These two words were the title of a recent calypso CD whose front cover consisted simply of a photo of Michelle and Barack Obama. For a Trinidadian in 2009, that photo would have said everything that could be said about why a black or Asian person should 'Go Brave'. What I didn't appreciate at the time was the way this posting also contained a clue to something that was going to become central to my research. Partly because it never occurred to me that Vishala, of all people, was going to emerge as a key philosopher informant with respect to the fundamental relationship between Facebook and truth. But, in retrospect, that is exactly what this posting is commenting upon. It was just that I simply couldn't see beyond the drama and the gesture to the deeper implication.

My excuse for this lack of perspicacity was that in pretty much every respect Vishala came across as the diametric opposite of what we might think of as a philosopher, contemplating rarefied abstractions. She was rather the quintessence of a regional stereotype – the highly pragmatic, tough, independent and loud-spoken

Caribbean woman. This didn't seem to be just a myth of stereotype because there were many women who seemed to accord well with these generalizations. In the academic literature,[1] they tended to be associated with Caribbean women of African descent. This would have linked them with a particular cultural trajectory, against which women of East Indian descent were seen as relatively quiet and submissive. But the same literature contained other arguments that associated this stereotype with the experience of poverty and the need to develop such traits as a means to toughen out the hardships of life. An emphasis upon this association leads to a rather different explanation for its emergence. I favoured the latter version since, during my original year's fieldwork in Trinidad, the women I encountered who seemed loud, brash, pragmatic and forthright were as likely to be of South Asian origin as African. What they had in common was this experience of poverty.

Vishala seemed clear confirmation of this argument. She may be of Indian descent but she is every inch the stereotypical strong black woman. Her biography was a litany of hardship. One of her parents was an immigrant from Guyana, a group who tend to have a hard time in Trinidad. Her father was abusive both to her and to her mother, before ending up in prison on a drug charge, after which her mother took up with an alcoholic. Vishala started working at the age of eleven at a supermarket. She met a man when she was sixteen, who by eighteen she had married and had a child with, partly because moving from her house to his house was a major blessing in itself. It didn't work out and after a while they divorced. But Vishala is still in her early twenties and feels there is time to develop her own life, which she is now trying to do.

For reasons that will soon become apparent from her own account, it makes sense to first encounter Vishala in the guise she appears in on Facebook itself. The front page of her profile is dominated by one particular theme. She has presented a series of tests on topics such as 'How good are you in bed?' or 'What kind of lover are you?', not to mention 'What sexual position are you?' and 'Do I look single?' Since the answers to these quizzes are typically revealed as 'hardcore lover' with accompanying lurid photographs, it is clear that this is one of the idioms through which

---

[1] For an example of this literature, see Senior Olive (1991), *Working Miracles*. London: James Currey.

Vishala has decided to 'Go Brave'. You are left in no doubt from her profile what Vishala could do, if she ever chose to do it with you – and that it is she who would do the choosing.

She has 504 friends who are active in showering her with typical Trini Facebook gifts such as a memory pillow, a Hindu god, a pet dog, a cherry cupcake, bottles of vodka or a blingee postcard. She also has a daily horoscope posting. She is happy to try out many of the other regular quizzes that circulate on Facebook. So if you go on her site you can uncover illuminating personal attributes such as 'If she were a pizza topping, which one would she be?' Much of her profile is concerned with her music tastes, including a fair range of heavy metal with names like 'Louder than Hell' or 'Cirith Ungol' and some electro music. There is also some fashion interest and the odd swipe at the government. She belongs to over 80 groups in all. I try to ignore the link to Manchester United (I support Arsenal) but Man U is big in Trinidad since Dwight Yorke, an excellent Trinidadian player, was based there for many years. She links to the pages of various well-known nightclubs, some clothing and cosmetics shops and outlets, athletes and movie stars, and the most quintessential and by now traditional Trinidadian food – Kentucky Fried Chicken. Trinidad is an island where people will insist that they live in a real town since it has two Kentucky Fried Chicken outlets. There are also a few religious links, such as Devotees of Maha Kali Bhavani Maa.

Vishala posts a status update about every three days. These tend to attract an average of around three comments each and a couple of other people ticking the 'like' button. Her comments can be pretty honest in presenting equally a negative or positive front. For example: 'Another lonely Christmas ahead, another new yrs to break being single . . . i wonder if i will be lucky next yrs?????????????' and, even more poignantly, 'i must say today i feel i dont have the answer i feel inside of my body crying so hard and i just dont have the answer . . . god show me the way please . . . for the first time in my life i feel i have to question my parenting skill.' There are general reflections on life such as 'Happiness is not a destination but a day by day journey . . . so get with the times.' They could also be small personal comments such as 'cant wait to put up my christmas tree this weekend . . . with my loving son . . . Joseph'; 'hangovers are the worst. . . . i think i drunk a bottle of tequila by myself . . . but i must say i really enjoy being drunk . . . its felt good.'

There is nothing naive about this. She knows what she is posting and why she is posting it. As she herself says:

'Yeah, like at the moment, like yesterday morning, I get up and I was feeling for some strange reason, I wasn't feeling bright, which I put up on Facebook. For some reason, I don't know why today I am feeling a bit uncomfortable, something like that. But why I put that up? I could have called a million people and tell them why I feeling uncomfortable, but I didn't do that. I put it on Facebook, and then people commented. You're not feeling great, so you want people to respond and give you some kind of . . . support or something. My friends and them who living away, they would um, normally say something to cheer me up.'

One of my PhD students, Razvan Nicolescu, wrote a Masters thesis examining why teenagers, who are surrounded by more things they could be doing than at any time in history, constantly moan that they are bored. His answer is very much in keeping with Vishala. They do so because this tells their friends that they want company and attention.

Someone following Vishala's site would also have a pretty good idea of her relationship status without having to look at her official designation. One could quickly decode 'Tobago was the best i finally broke the rules after 5months thank u god . . . it was the best i taught u would never send me some love . . . Rafique and dennis dont comment . . . lol,' followed a few days later by 'funny how u coud meet someone like less then 24hrs and u give in easy then turn around and ask yourself what ever happen to the rules . . . lol . . . weird.' Nor would there be much doubt as to who the man implicated in this was since, a couple of days later, she posts 'next week is a bill paying week . . . but im ready to face it . . . cause i had the best weekend ever . . . thanx to my roommates.' And there, in the comment section, is found the man himself complaining that he is not her room-mate and gets no credit for her wonderful weekend; which she then acknowledges in her reply. It is no great surprise, given the way Trini men often publicly cultivate their sense of reputation, that through this and other postings a man makes quite sure that people end up knowing who it is that she had her holiday fling with.

One of the characteristics of Trinidadian Facebook is the heavy emphasis on photographs and making comments on photographs. When watching people using Facebook, it emerges that the first priority is usually not the new texts, such as status updates, but largely any new pictures posted by friends. If you turn to the picture albums, you can see that people are often also more ready to make direct comments on these pictures than on status updates. This makes the photos themselves often a key medium for communication between friends. Vishala puts up quite a few of the kind of pictures that will attract comments from men, such as 'dam girl u look so sexy is to much to handl' or 'well yes miss hot sexy and divalicious!', 'hoooooooooo OMG ur so hot . . . lol.' But she also has plenty of pictures of her child which attract comments such as 'This is a cute pic' or 'Nice pic . . . Mr is growing up!' She has forty potential profile pictures. Most of her albums are dominated by Carnival-related parties, by her trips to Tobago, which is where Trinis often take their holidays, and by her child, such as his pre-school graduation.

For Vishala, looking at other people's photos is simply an obvious source of information, not only for telling her what her friends are up to, but also as a research tool. It is the photos that inform her as to what people are wearing these days when they go to fetes (parties). This will help her decide what to choose or buy when she goes out partying in her turn. Posting photos also serves as a kind of online accessorizing for the individual who thereby gets to choose the background they want to be pictured against. Photos tell you the cars they want to be seen with, the people and the places. Vishala is entirely open about this. Most especially she likes to 'dress' in Tobago. This is the setting against which she most likes to post photos of herself, the place where she feels she looks good and feels good. It gives the right message as to who she sees herself to actually be as opposed to the person she is generally constrained into being now. She feels having Tobago as her background reveals her truer self, the person she would be if she could.

As many Trinidadians, she poses in many of her photos. It's quite clear after a while what kind of smile she prefers to adopt when someone says they are about to take her picture. But while her photos display a good range of clothes and backgrounds, she is not just a mannequin. In a way that is very typical of Trinidadian

Facebook, every now and then there is a photo in which she just looks plain silly. A photo taken unawares in clothes she probably doesn't see as her best, photos which show that, for all her ability to groom herself for a pose, she doesn't take herself and her looks too seriously. She is quite ready to expose a lighter, less posed and unglamorous side to who she is. She has never untagged a photo on Facebook.

The significance of photos on Facebook has become blurred in recent years with the rise of a new kind of photojournalism associated with the feting side of Trini culture. It is no surprise that Vishala's current profile picture is not one she took of herself. It is lifted off the pages of one of the two key online sites, triniscene. com and trinijunglejuice.com. These sites specialize in posting pictures of people enjoying themselves at fetes. They tend to be heavily repetitive. They will group a few friends to pose for their photo at the event, all with the correct smile, drink, arms around each other. They ensure that everyone sees that they were having a good time, what they were wearing, and above all simply that they were there. The hope of being posted on one of these sites has become for some the single main motivation for actually going to the fete. Vishala is more than a little pleased that she has been seen at a couple of the more exclusive fetes. One of these was right out of her price range, but fortunately some distant relatives paid for the ticket, feeling safer if they had a genuine 'party girl' to accompany them while they were there.

It is easy in the UK to come to hold quite problematic prejudices in the face of poverty. I have carried out much of my London field-work in run-down housing estates, often with people who seem, by now, to have little by way of initiative or drive or ability. One can see why casual visitors from the middle classes start to see the impoverished as responsible for their own fate. In fact, this has more to do with the impenetrable nature of the British class and education system and the difficulty of breaking through. Trinidad has always made the opposite impression on me. When I was working in squatting areas, amongst desperately impoverished people, many of them came across as among the smartest people I had met anywhere in the world and the most enterprising. They were articulate, knowledgeable and ingenious. What this demonstrated was that a person could have all these qualities, but, without the initial capital to develop that entrepreneurial ability, official preferment or at least luck, you could still remain at the bottom of the pile, for life.

My guess, though, is that Vishala will be one of those who will break out of her situation. There are already positive signs. Her main job is working for a firm that hires out music equipment, sometimes just for the night or sometimes for a week or longer term. The neat thing about this is that much of it can be done by phone, especially with customers who are becoming her regulars. Once she had hired out all the equipment the firm possesses, there is nothing else for her to do. As with many Trinis, she also has other jobs concurrent with her main work, including helping in security. Most weeks she now hires out all her boss's equipment quite early on in the week, which was not true of his previous employee. He is sufficiently impressed to be thinking about expanding the business and giving her a greater, more formal role, perhaps a percentage of the profits. It seems that once Vishala has two feet on the ladder, not a lot is going to stop this woman rising. In her mind this is not if, but when.

She has no sense that technology is a struggle or needs to be learnt. Once there is an awareness that something exists in the world that can do something for her, she doesn't need to be told twice. Facebook is obvious:

> 'It keeps you connected, it's cheaper, you don't have to call somebody and if somebody is on Facebook that means that they have time. If you call them on their phone you don't know if you catching them at the right time, if they are in a meeting, what going on . . . But you know once you see somebody online that means they are surfing the net so they have time to chat.'

She is also aware of what the technology does to her and how she could lose control. For example, she doesn't like to use a webcam. She thinks that men are only ever going to use them with one thing in mind, but her problem is more the other way around. Vishala is clearly not shy about her own interest in sex. She readily talks about surfing for pornography on line. But that's the trouble. If a man has a webcam and she is sitting there watching him move, she feels she could get too interested in him for the wrong reasons and thereby lose control of the situation. If she wants to remind herself what he looks like, then she can gaze at his profile pictures on Facebook. With a webcam, she recalls looking at this guy cleaning his room in his boxers. And he was just too *hot*. As she put it, 'You know women; when we want something we make sure and have it.' It was better not to allow herself a webcam to drive this desire.

'Go Brave' describes Vishala's reaction to Facebook. She is fearless in the face of its capacities. Facebook now has the facility to chat with people who are simultaneously online. This involves opening up a little chat window that looks somewhat like a Post-it note. Within this, one can IM (instant message). The more conservative, such as myself, see this as something that is only engaged in with one person at a time, but many Trinidadians will simultaneously chat to several people at the same time, responding to other people's comments when they pop up. Vishala is scornful. Once some people are around to chat and she feels like chatting, she will open up often more than twenty at a time and sees no problem in doing this:

> 'Yeah, because when you go back onto the person you would know what you was talking about, and when someone else pop up you see what they ask and you respond . . . like I was doing that last night actually. My friend Dennis we were talking about the all inclusive fetes, my friend Rodney was talking about his baby. My friend Radikha was talking about what she ate, um. This fella was tracking me, Sonny, trying to figure out how he could get to come home and spend the night by me. And I was actually having a conversation with everybody. . . . Somebody was even trying to get my attention to help them get some music equipment for their recording . . . Yeah, it's the only thing entertaining other than nothing . . . I mean when ya at home, you don't have anything to do. I mean if I have nothing to do, the only thing to do is go online and chat with somebody. I think it's better than being in a chatroom with people you don't know and you can't see . . . you know.'

For Vishala, this activity of talking to twenty people at once is experienced as something directly analogous to being in the middle of a crowd at a party. She is having fun, much as she would at a party. But the key difference is that at a party, with so many people milling around, an individual might be more afraid as to what they say to you. But the situation on Facebook is different:

> 'Maybe at the point in time I have a group of people around them, that they can't say what they want to say. So it actually takes you out of the box where you and somebody could have a conversation

alone, even if there is a million people behind. You could have a silent conversation on the internet . . . Silent, meaning if I am in a group with people you wouldn't want to tell me anything because you would have to say it via voice. You wouldn't want to take a piece of paper and write it and hand it to me, because everybody would see . . . Whereas if you are on the computer and there are people around you, and I am on the computer and there are people around me . . .'

With IM on Facebook, no one else knows what you are saying to each other.

So Vishala finds that people are much more ready to say things, personal things, more reflective things, deeper things about themselves, on Facebook than in everyday life. But then she goes further and claims that it's not just easier to tell the truth, Facebook is in itself more truthful as an encounter with people. She contrasts the Vishala that people come to know on Facebook with the Vishala they might meet otherwise.

'Yeah, because if they don't know me and they just seeing me passing on the streets they could think all the negative things that people say about me or whatever. But when they add me on Facebook and they view my profile, they see well, alright I have a son. Nobody doesn't see me with my son, because I am always at work but nobody don't know what I would do with him.'

People she just meets casually understand very little about her. But if they go carefully through her Facebook profile, she feels they would have a very reasonable understanding of who she actually is:

'You know, if you write something, they will know what was going on in your head or what I was thinking or why you so busy . . . like if you put up, so today I decide to go shopping, or today I have a million things I have to go do grocery you know. I might pass somebody and they don't know that I busy you know, but if they check my profile they might see – oh, so she had stuff to do. That's why I believe in the status thing. Yes everybody's status is always about them, it's always something that comes from their mind.'

As an example of this, she actually encouraged her ex-boyfriend's current girlfriend to friend her on Facebook, rather than have her pass on the street and think whatever bad thoughts she might have had about her.

'She probably thinks if she saw me, she might think insecure, you know women. But on Facebook now we became friends and you know as – Oh, ok, he is a nice boy. Things didn't work out with us, you know, but I wish you all the best. And we started talk and now every time we on Facebook she would say how ya going chick, and I would say good, how you going, and I would share my experiences. You know like they engaged. So I would tell her, the other day we was talking, and I told her, and I say, you know its a very good thing and I happy for yall, but don't rush into having any children you know. Now I could do that because I have a child you know and she's like – I will take that one into consideration, you know. So we became friends on Facebook. But if we had saw one another in the road, we mightn't have talked.'

Elaborating upon this point, Vishala argues:

'And that's it – Facebook is about people knowing the real you. Even if you didn't want them to know you was in a fete, then why go out to a fete? That means you trying to be something you are not. You don't want people to know you was in Fire Fete; why would you not want them to know that? You know, so don't go in some-where that you shouldn't be. Because it could always have some-body who knows somebody. Because if you and some girl talking or dating on the outside and she on Facebook, and one day she end up telling one friend you know, I'm with Daniel Miller, she might be like – Daniel Miller but I know him, he's married, and then that's the bacchanal, you know.'

As we talk, the concept of truth that Vishala attributes to Facebook increases in complexity and depth. The first step is to understand Facebook as truth by intention. That is to say, some-body feels more secure about talking deeply about themselves in private. The second level of Vishala's philosophy of Facebook as truth is the technology's ability to reveal unintentional truths. Facebook will constantly expose things about people that they might otherwise have wanted to remain hidden. Most especially, it will reveal how men are living with several women who previously didn't know about each other, which is more or less assumed to be the condition most men aspire to and some have achieved. Given the degree to which people have become accustomed to taking pictures of others and tagging them, it seems unimaginable to Vishala that someone could any longer go out in public with a partner and this not become known.

The third step is truth by construction. That is to say, people spend a considerable amount of time crafting a profile of themselves on Facebook, with an abundance of postings, photographs and other resources. As far as most Trinidadians are concerned, the truth of a person exists in this labour they perform to create themselves. This careful self-construction is much closer to the truth of a person than what they happen to possess naturally through birth. The natural physical self, whether her legs are long or her eyes are dark, is a false guide to a person, because they didn't choose to be like that. In the same way, Vishala feels she didn't choose to be born in poverty, to be unable to get an education, or to have to do certain kinds of job. None of these are an expression of who she is; they are circumstances foisted upon her. The true person comes with her careful cultivation of who she could be, if circumstances were otherwise and allowed this imminent self to be manifest in the world. The true Vishala is not the one talking with you now, but the one who chooses to be photographed with Tobago as her background and who is found adorning Facebook. Following this logic, one can see that Facebook, so far from being a mask, is actually a technology for allowing someone to be more true than was ever possible prior to Facebook. It provides a whole series of technologies for self-cultivation that requires very little resources. You can do this with much less money than previous forms of self-production. To take this a stage further, it becomes clear that for Vishala Facebook is a means to discover who she could really be. This is why she gets irritated when people post such banal false postings wishing everyone 'peace and luv' for New Year and she instead decides to 'Go Brave'. For Vishala, this is being true to her understanding of Facebook's higher capacity for truth than the mere offline world.

The fifth stage towards the enlightenment that is Vishala's philosophy of Facebook as truth is best approached by a brief excursion into Trinidadian cosmology. Although there is plenty of formal religion in Trinidad, many Trinis seem to spend the entire year in anticipation of the one event that above all else gives a focus to their public lives, which is Carnival. One of the main themes of Carnival is the revelation of truth. Carnival starts at night with a festival called *Jouvert*, derived from the French *jour d'ouvert* or the opening of the day. People dress as creatures of the night, such as devils, or come out covered in mud. Some have placards with scandals and accusations. Gradually they move towards the centre of town where they are revealed by the dawn.

In writings elsewhere, I have contrasted Trinidadian ideas of truth with the concept of the superficial. In European philosophical traditions, the truth of a person lies deep within them, and a philosopher is a person with depth. What lies at the surface is false: the facade or the superficial. Carnival makes the opposite and in some ways rather more obvious point, that the truth of a person is what you can actually see, exposed on the surface, not what is hidden within. The other difference between these two views of truth is that European philosophy affirms a truth that lies not just in depth but in constancy and changes but slowly. For Trinidadians, the truth is not just on the surface, but is as changeable as the surface itself. So in Trinidad you may look wonderful and confident and for that moment you are. But next day there is a different you when that confidence has drained away and that has become obvious to the people around you. You are simply no longer the same person.

Who a person ultimately is does not depend just on what they think they are, or who they would like to be or wish themselves to be. It lies essentially in what others perceive you to be. If you are at a party, you know you look good by the response you get from people, not just from the effort you put into looking good. Vishala goes to a fete in the hope that some internet magazine will find her looking so enticing that they will snap a picture of her and put this up online. For her, that is objective evidence of her actual capacity to look good. It is a revelation of who she has been able to become. It is not a fake or a mask. It is a truth demonstrated by the fact that she managed to get the photographer to put up her picture as against someone else's. This may not last. She may be less successful at the next fete, but the truth of a person is always transient. A person who has power today may lose it tomorrow. More importantly, a person, such as herself who doesn't possess power today may achieve it tomorrow. So Facebook's immediacy, its transience, and the very fact that it consists of surfaces judged by others – all those aspects that make other people see it as fake or superficial – make it for Vishala, and most likely for many Trinidadians, a still more effective vehicle for truth.

The sixth and final form of Facebook as truth for Vishala is the one that is closest to the heart of an academic because it involves study. When it comes to research, Vishala is no slouch. As she says,

'A lot of these big-shot people, they make a pretence as to who they are. But you think, through Facebook you have more chance to see what they really are. It is the truth, it is about somebody. How often you could put up some lie about yourself on Facebook? You can't go up on Facebook and say you's a lawyer. Because it must have somebody who would see you and know you. People could have access to knowing who you are. Like we might be walking the streets with somebody and don't know who he is and just call him Anthony. But don't even know that he was a Sabga [an influential Trini family]. Until we go on Facebook and see him liming with a whole set of people and then you tell yourself I wonder who he is, what he doing liming with them? Because they rich, so he then hadda be something. And then, you know, you would try to figure it out. You know you might search him, look him up, put on the picture. You might see his full name, you try to add him, then you find out he related to this person . . .'

So for Vishala, precisely because Facebook is the book of truth, it is the immediate place she would turn to for carrying out research. Other people dither and worry about what status they should grant the materials they find online, and whether they correspond to what they assume is a more real person offline. But Vishala's philosophy of Facebook lies behind her ability to plunge straight in and extract the knowledge she craves about whoever it is she is interested in at the time. For Vishala, the secret is simply to recognize what it is possible to find out about the world through an involvement in Facebook and then to 'Go Brave'.

5

Cultivating *FarmVille*

The task of the anthropologist is empathy. But of all the activities on Facebook, the one that I knew I would struggle to feel any kind of empathy for was *FarmVille*. Given that currently it has more than 80 million active users worldwide and has pretty much colonized Trinidad, I knew it was something I would have to confront sooner or later. It was Arvind who finally taught me to stand in awe and acknowledgement before what may well be one of Facebook's most significant and beneficial applications: a complete reversal of everything I had felt about it up to the time when I met him.

The reason that it seemed natural to disdain *FarmVille* lay precisely in the fact that it was being played by someone like Arvind. I knew too much about the history of Trinidad. The key player in that history was Eric Williams and so much of what has gone right and gone wrong for this island is best understood as the legacy of Williams. An Oxford-trained politician-intellectual, he led the country from colonialism into independence. He did this not just by throwing off the shackles of British rule but by articulating a vision for the new nation based on his academic studies of the deeper consequences of economic, as against political, colonialism. Specifically, he was desperate that Trinidad should not become, as most post-colonial states soon would become, merely a third-world producer of raw materials, for which they would be paid a pittance while industrial states in Europe and North

America made serious money from the far more value-added secondary and tertiary forms of economic activities, such as industry and services. To this end, he insisted that Trinidad's oil and gas resources should not be merely exported as raw materials but used as the foundation for large-scale industrial enterprises based within Trinidad itself in fields such as steel production or ethanol. It was these more finished, value-added products that should be exported.

I have a huge admiration for Eric Williams[1] and feel that, given the politics and political economy of his time, this was precisely the stance that such a figure should have taken. In as much as this industrialization didn't do all that it might have in terms of developing the economy, this had much more to do with unfair protectionist policies by bullying major powers, such as the US or UK preventing imports of Trinidadian steel, than anything wrong with the ideas behind the policy itself. But good intentions don't always lead uniformly to good consequences. In at least one vital area, Williams made a mistake which continues to plague the nation he helped to found. In his zeal for industrialization, he never failed to hide his scorn for agriculture. By 1980, despite being a reasonably fertile country, agriculture had fallen to a mere 2 per cent of Trinidadian production, and most of what people actually ate was imported. But what made a mere bias in economic policy more insidious was that agriculture was by then closely associated with the East Indian population who were descended from indentured labourers brought from South Asia to replace the slaves, originally from Africa, who had largely left the plantations as soon as emancipation rendered this possible.

Partly as a result, the PNM, the political party that takes its ideology from the legacy of Williams which was in power during the time of this study, is seen as ruling on the basis of highly ethnicized political divisions which are expressed in their economic leanings, especially their lack of interest in or sympathy with agriculture.[2] This bias towards industry has still more problematic conse-

---

[1] Even if you have no interest in the history of Trinidad, I heartily recommend a wonderful recent novel that documents the rise and fall of Williams: Roffey, M. (2009), *The White Woman on the Green Bicycle*. London: Pocket Books.

[2] In the period since this work was complete, the PNM were soundly defeated in an election by a combination of opposition parties dominated by the more Indian-associated UNC led by Kamla Persad-Bissessar who on 26 May 2010 became Trinidad's first female prime minister.

quences today. It is clearly right out of kilter with the emergent environmental agenda, as compared with the embrace of these issues in nearby Guyana. This is evident in the controversy over the proposed highly problematic aluminium smelter.

Most of my time in Trinidad has been spent in the town of Chaguanas which had become informally a kind of alternative capital city for the East Indian population and which was concentrated around the old sugar cane estates of central Trinidad and the south. In these areas, there had grown over decades a palpable resentment at this neglect of agriculture. There was a feeling of disenfranchisement reflected in arguments about pensions for laid-off sugar cane workers, or those who struggled against the odds to make some kind of living from market gardening. They have responded with an equally ethnicized politics. This tearing apart of the cloak of democratic enfranchisement along the seam of ethnicity is the bane of modern Trinidadian history.

At the end of this story comes Arvind, a typical example of the landless, now living in poverty in a soulless housing estate near Trincity, one of the country's largest malls from where stretch southwards the now thoroughly uneconomic swathes of sugar cane fields. Arvind's father was one of those same cane workers who have been fighting for their pension. Before they moved here, at least they would grow a few peppers, some sorrel for the Christmas drink made from its flowers, a soursop tree, another of West Indian cherries, plus some papaya, enough to act as a reminder of agrarian labour. But this house had no real yard and grows nothing but rust from abandoned car parts. A few blades of grass as a front lawn is the only pathetic token of land left to them.

As it happens, the majority of Indo-Trinidadians were not like Arvind but had responded to this sense of rejection by developing private entrepreneurial endeavours. The more successful sent their children to foreign universities to take courses such as business studies. Chaguanas was now easily the fastest-growing urban area in Trinidad, reinforcing the new stereotype of Indian-dominated business. But that stereotype completely ignored the thousands who remained, like Arvind, the sad legacy of this particular twist of political economy. Furthermore, there was something about Arvind himself, who seemed to embody in his own personality, or lack of it, everything repressive about that historical burden. To be frank, Arvind appeared listless, hopeless and had an aura of the pathetic, bordering sometimes on the abject. He just seemed so lacking in any kind of foundational self-confidence, to be overly aware that no one considered him particularly bright or smart. Instead, in conversation he was always referred to as having a good heart, as kind, but said in a way that made these evident euphemisms rather than praise.

Arvind's house also seemed to be pared down to the bare essentials. There was almost no house so poor that it failed to contain a set of lacquered wooden shelves. Known as space savers, this is the exact opposite of what they actually are. They provide the setting for an accumulation of cheap ceramic ornaments and polystyrene stuffed animals such as a yellow teddy bear or an orange dog. There was the buffet with its plates and glasses brought out for special occasions, the grey-painted wall with its tapestry of *The Last Supper* on the other; some old greeting cards and school graduation certificates completed the decor.

Pass inside the house and here, for four, five, six hours a day, Arvind plays *FarmVille* and develops love and tender care for the labour of agriculture – but one of absolutely no consequence for the land. Not one of the people in Trinidad who were active in playing *FarmVille* suggested, when the question was put to them, that it would make an iota of difference to their concern for actual agriculture, any more than playing *Mafia Wars* made it more likely that they would go out and 'ice' someone. *FarmVille* is not just a paradox: it is a parody. While his father might at least have made something of the link between the work of his ancestors and the playing of this game, Arvind was a generation too far removed. So there was something really rather unsettling about watching Arvind play *FarmVille*, seeing his ancestors reduced to these cartoons; knowing that Arvind spent so many hours playing the game, that with the same amount of time translated into a non-virtual world, he could probably have raised a genuine crop. For all these reasons I admit, I utterly detested *FarmVille*.

The visceral side to my contempt came not only from its parody of history, but from the offence it rendered to my own sense of taste. However much I identify with and defend elements of popular culture against their dismissal by elites, *FarmVille* seemed beyond redemption. It looks like Disney-lite, mere puddles of irritating cartoon figures that plead with big cartoon eyes that I find quite nauseating. All those judgemental terms I try to avoid, like vulgarity and sentimentality and dumb – that's *FarmVille*.

So how does *FarmVille* work? Well, in essence it starts by replicating the tasks of every child's imagination of an actual farm. That is to say, one grows crops and harvests them, plants trees and picks the fruits, feeds poultry and takes their eggs and so forth. Although apparently *FarmVille* does have a selection of tropical crops, what you see on Trinidadian sites are not sugar cane, yams and callaloo, but rather bright red apples, wheat and cattle. But then living rooms in Trinidad are far more likely to be adorned with temperate scenes of conifers and deer than with depictions of the tropical, and my own living room in London has paintings of palm trees.

What *FarmVille* trades in is something that first emerged in the gaming industry through predecessors such as the early *Sims* and the *Tamagotchi* figures, a genre of toys and games that appeals to players by having its welfare depend upon constant care and attention. Essentially, the more time you spend showing concern for your gaming figures, the more they thrive, while if you ignore them they wither and die. There is a built-in form of addiction, since the more you play and the more you invest, the more you have to lose by neglect and absence. The more you accumulate and have a sense that you are doing better than your peers, the more you can see things in competitive terms and the more you are drawn to participate in something you seem to shine at. And the more the game itself seems to need you.

In *FarmVille*, each of these activities comes with its own time frame. If you plant a crop, there is a given number of hours after which you can harvest it. If you go online at that exact moment, you gain the maximum from your crop since you can then immediately plant another. It is not hard to encounter secretaries who are supposed to be working in an office but who are clearly distracted because one of their *FarmVille* crops has become ready for picking and they are losing time by being with us at that moment. The more you harvest, the more points you can gain and these can then be used to expand into some additional *FarmVille* activity. I mainly know about the game through postings which appear on my own site from time to time from friends who are players. To give a sample of those that I regularly encounter:

Arvind found a Lonely Bull on their farm. Oh no! Arvind was farming when a Lonely Bull wandered onto their farm in *FarmVille*. He escaped from the rodeo and is tired of all the bucking, jumping and kicking. He's just looking for a simpler life and could use some friends and a new home.

Arvind just completed level 2 of Peas mastery in *FarmVille*! Arvind earned a huge reward for being such a dedicated farmer and wants to share his success with you!

Arvind got a limited edition carrier pigeon for signing up for *FarmVille* emails! Arvind can now get all the latest *FarmVille* news, alerts, and extra special rewards!

Arvind found some White Mystery Eggs to share with his friends!

Arvind was collecting eggs from his Chicken Coop and found these mysterious eggs.

Arvind is such a thoughtful farmer and just fertilized Joseph's farm in *FarmVille*! Arvind just visited and fertilized Joseph's farm out of the goodness of their heart in *FarmVille*!

Arvind found a Lost Penguin on his farm. Oh no! Arvind was farming when a Lost Penguin waddled onto his farm. This little guy travelled all the way from the South Pole to see the snow in *FarmVille*! He's been separated from his sightseeing group and family. He could use a safe place to stay until he finds them.

After a few days of viewing these, I can't but develop in my mind all sorts of gothic parodies and fantasies that seem to correspond to the antacid that relieves my queasy stomach sick with the sheer cloying cuteness of it all. In my imagination, I am posting items such as:

Danny just poisoned half of London due to his overwhelming generosity to fellow farmers by gifting them surplus pesticides.

Danny has just gifted you 100 pigs' entrails and 300 loaves of stale bread to help you fill your sausage quota.

A cute brown fox with a long bushy tail has just wandered into Danny's farm and given him a friendly greeting and hence rabies.

So first *FarmVille* made me angry and then *FarmVille* made me sick. But as I started to get into anthropological gear, I could not be unaffected by my friendship with Arvind. Actually those were not just euphemisms. Arvind really did have a kind heart and a sort of helpless niceness about him that melted mine. In his presence, it was impossible to dwell on one's anger for the circumstances that made him what he was. He quickly elicited a sympathy and interest in what he himself had made of those circumstances. Gradually, this turning of my emotions came to embrace not only Arvind but that occupation in which he was so fully absorbed – *FarmVille*.

If *FarmVille* had an escapist quality to it, then Arvind had quite a lot to escape from. He had never done well at school and he had no chance of getting into one of those elite secondary schools. Instead, he went to the local junior secondary school which in those days, for lack of resources, was running a shift system so that half the day he was in school and the other half he was left to his own devices. Being shy, he didn't hang out around the shopping malls phoning girls. Instead, he was already spending far too much of his time at home watching mindless television, sitting beside his aunt through the daytime soaps. When he finished school, he worked for a while in a garage and tried a couple of correspondence courses and some labouring work.

Just as things looked pretty dire, someone spotted the one quite obvious talent that Arvind did possess: his capacity for caring and being concerned for others. Arvind started a course on caring for the elderly. At last, there was something he could feel positive about, as a kind of vocation. In this work he would, for the first time, have value as a person helping others. Almost all the other trainees were women. There was only one other man on the course. This meant that, also for the first time, Arvind was starting to get another kind of attention that was doing him no harm at all in terms of developing some self-confidence. He has now up to a hundred friends on Facebook and, since most of these are from his college, he also has a pretty decent-looking range of photographs. Many of them seem to comprise groups of women on college outings, with himself comfortably centred in their midst.

Gentle Arvind was not a natural games player. The games most of his peers played, such as *Halo*, with their violence and speed did not really attract him and he would always get beaten too easily.

This was just one of the reasons he resisted *FarmVille* at first. The other was that he associated it more with women. Like most Trini men, he is deeply concerned that other people should regard him as unambiguously masculine. But the fact was that everyone else in his class was playing *FarmVille*, and they kept talking about it in college, and he increasingly felt left out. So he gave in after a while and, pretty soon after that, he was hooked.

The attraction of *FarmVille* was partly that it drew him more closely into Facebook. It made him more likely to read about what his classmates were doing which when someone is shy works perfectly because, as he put it, 'actually at the end of the day you actually kind of communicate with them without actually talking to them.' Through sharing information about them online, he feels he has been able to grow closer to his peers than would have been the case from being together in the same classroom.

There is another additional factor here. In 2009, the murder rate in Trinidad had created a palpable sense of threat. Many of a more nervous disposition, especially women, had become fearful of going out at night, unless in a large group and in well-lit areas. Arvind was one of those who clearly felt that this was sensible advice. In addition, living in the Trincity area meant that going into town involved using the main east–west road system which was constantly blocked by traffic. Between the fear of crime and the fatigue of traffic, there was a significant part of the population that simply didn't go out very much at night. Admittedly, this being Trinidad, an equally significant part of the population would party hard, even if the disincentives were multiplied several times over. But for Arvind, and many of the women on his course, where once they might have congregated over a lime, today it was something of a godsend that one could stay at home and, instead of the isolation of television, one had the virtual socializing of Facebook, and most especially of *FarmVille*.

Arvind was quite clear about all this. 'With *FarmVille*, you could actually be in your home any hour of the day, and you don't have to study about reaching home, crime and different things.' Even then it is doubtful if a conventional game, based on an individual mastering successive levels of difficulty, would have hooked Arvind. *FarmVille* had another trick up its sleeve. While much of the activity consisted of the individual farmer collecting crops, the game favoured advancement through collaboration and reciprocal generosity. The key to *FarmVille* was the development of relation-ships with one's neighbours which could also include a keen sense of competition in scoring points or collecting ribbons

As Arvind explained it,

'Ok, like in *FarmVille* you need ribbons, the ribbons is like the achievement you do and the more ribbons you get is more points and the faster you move up in stages. So you basically, like, you could send gifts. It has one where you could send gifts and one where you actually help the neighbour. When you help your neigh-bour, the crops grow better by fertilizing it or feeding the chickens. So you want your neighbour to actually help you by sending you a gift. Like you could send, like, a cow. You could send gas things to make your work easier and when you talk about it, it's actually telling them I need this and I actually do. You feel, well, ok, more relief that you don't have to do all that extra work of . . . if you don't have gas, you have to pay for it.'

I was a little surprised and, to be honest, a little bit pleased, when it transpired that Arvind has cheated by opening up several accounts that purported to be different people but were actually all him. These allow him to be his own neighbour with accounts that reciprocally help each other. He is a bit shamefaced about this. But it started when he wanted a particular ribbon and he only had 42 *FarmVille* friends and this ribbon needed 50 friends and so he . . . But mostly such reciprocal gifting takes place between him and his classmates. This has become a significant route to developing deeper friendships with particular classmates than might have arisen just from the more anxious moments of face-to-face encounters, especially since most of them are women.

FarmVille is not entirely without skill. One may collect a bonus from a harvest but then you need to share this with five other people within a certain framework or the benefit is lost. There is a provision to use real money converted into *FarmVille* coinage but this doesn't really figure amongst Arvind's low-income milieu. Without such offline resources, it is only hard toil on the key-board that can make an individual virtually wealthy, along with consistent sharing and reciprocity, something rather less true of our offline worlds. Arvind was delighted to find an arena where poverty was not a barrier to success. Also as he put it, 'You is in control of the situation. You could put how many trees you want. You could buy houses; you could buy plots of land and is like people try to have the best-looking farm.' While once he had been near the bottom of the scale, today he is now the source of envy and admiration and can afford to be generous. Arvind today is a man with XP factor, to achieve which all he needed was his computer which his family deemed essential for his course. As Arvind explains:

> 'XP means experience. You need *FarmVille* experience and every experience you get a different crop. So you won't sell all the crops if you are level one; you only able to get like 5 crops. But at level 30 you have about say 50 different crops you could choose from. So the higher the levels you go, the more crops you could do and make more money.'

On the foundations of these virtual exchanges, he could build others. His *Farmville* neighbours tend to become his best Facebook friends, the ones who would sometimes comment on other parts of his Facebook. A next step was their giving him a call and chatting about how they were feeling, and asking how he was feeling. Now when he comes to class, the smiles are genuine and directed at him in particular. He also found there was a constant crossover between helping one another on *FarmVille* and with homework. Good neighbours can also make for good research, telling each other where to look things up. He notes he could be in the same library as a classmate, a few feet away, but they will be IMing each other online. He is telling them where to find some book in the library, for homework purposes, without actually getting up from his desk. Somehow this can feel more intimate rather than less. Rooting around Arvind's *FarmVille* activity on his Facebook site, one can also find study groups, announcements about DJs and parties, plus the usual bacchanal, like the YouTube of a Trini guy being beaten up by his girlfriend that practically everyone in Trinidad seems to have seen. A person's Facebook profile speaks volumes about how much other people integrate him or her into their lives.

So there is a pretty good case for *FarmVille*. At the heart of contemporary welfare is the need to find those instruments that can reach those who need them most, those who do least well in education, who are shy, or not favoured in looks, who live in poverty and are gauche and gawky in public. A significant quotient of any population consists of people who are regarded by others and by themselves as failures. There are charities, gestures and institutions that can help them but finding something, anything, that is not experienced as condescending, or as merely reinforcing their feeling that they are at the bottom of the pile, is actually much harder than is usually appreciated. It seems unlikely that Facebook, or the company that invented *FarmVille*, did so as some kind of charitable initiative. They presumably just wanted to make money out of it. *FarmVille* has become one of Facebook's greatest achievements despite, not because of, these intentions.

Nor is it fair to despise *FarmVille* just by associating it with a legacy of political betrayal of Trinidadian agriculture. After all, why should anyone expect Arvind, or anyone else, to work in the fields? Agricultural labour is desperately tedious. When the wind creates waves rippling down the bright green stalks of the sugar cane in the fields to the south, it can be a breathtaking site. But there are too many stories about snakes and cutlasses, let alone the history of slavery, to ever want to harvest sugar cane. And there are too many people in many developing countries who are desperate to give up such farm labour, irrespective of political support or neglect.

On an ethical count, it is surely better to judge the world by what it does for its least favoured than for its most favoured. Once I had reappraised Arvind, I could look back at the other scenes I had witnessed and realize that, yes, the people who had seemed addicted to *FarmVille* were precisely those who I had barely favoured with a glance. There were those secretaries who ignored me when I came into their office because they were on *FarmVille*. But how often do I actually notice secretaries? Knowing about *FarmVille*, being able to talk the *FarmVille* talk, was part of a politics of respect; the mutual respect of peers, rather than something coming down to them from on high. Don't get me wrong: I am fully aware of the limitations. Even the Trinidadians who play this game can't pretend it creates environmental or ecological consciousness, or is in any respect educational. If I witness some cartoon penguin wandering onto my Facebook patch, because it has lost its friends from the South Pole, I am still more inclined virtually to cut its throat and put it in a cartoon pot than return it to its supposed friends. But, thanks to Arvind, at least I can now appreciate that something that seemed so irredeemably repulsive and tasteless may at another level be noble, if never exactly beautiful.

6

Avatar

Central to Hindu cosmology is the concept of *Shakti*. It would be wrong to translate this as female energy, since it goes deeper than that. It means that energy is itself intrinsically female. The male aspect of the gods has vast potential but to be realized they need this complementary female aspect that allows them to release that power. But in its turn *Shakti* as pure energy is also undirected and itself as destructive as it is creative. It is the male aspect that suppresses and controls that destructive force, which includes the potency of sexuality, and channels it for the beneficial construction of worlds. Hindu cosmology often presents its deities in terms of a balance of gender, not simply as gendered. Listening to Ajani describing herself, a similar image emerges, one of a person who contains within herself such waves of energy that these too could become not only destructive of others but could also consume her from the inside – that is, unless she finds ways to throw off the surplus heat and remain sufficiently cool at the centre. What this produced was an extreme contrast between a calm inner core which she tries to sustain and a constant torrent of energy with which she assails the outside world.

The mechanism by which she achieves this contrast between inner calm and outer energy seems to have been derived from a personal legacy. Ajani's parents were both English teachers and the form in which her energy is most frequently and most purely expressed is through words, most purely the handwritten word but today more frequently through typed text. It was this constant need to throw out words that led to my interest in her. She had an extraordinary commitment to Facebook as a place of self-expression. She was one of the few true Facebook junkies who could be relied upon to be present pretty much whenever one went online. What emerges in this discussion is how Facebook, at least for now, has become the saviour of Ajani. It is the most common and sustained way in which she achieves this aesthetic balance upon which her life is based; between the self-sufficient inner soul and the need to expel her creative energy through words into the public domain. The corollary of this is that Ajani turns out to be simultaneously one of the most public and one of the most private people one could ever imagine encountering. Which is why understanding Ajani becomes crucial to understanding something profound about the nature of Facebook itself: the capacity that at least some people find within this technology, to help create a greater degree of privacy through simultaneously using its ability to make oneself constantly more public.

The inner calm is something one only discovers when you meet Ajani in her own home because it is only then that you realize that, despite the avalanche of posting and public material that you have been reading, you are quite mistaken in thinking that you know this person well. Actually, on reflection, there is nowhere in all that material that would enable you to say if she currently has a partner, let alone the state of their relationship. You were quite unprepared for these revelations about her private thoughts, the issues she contends with by herself, her spiritual concerns and rites. Yet this was someone who had written so much that you simply assumed she was an open book. At home by herself, it's like meeting another person entirely, much more hesitant, almost shy, not just private but almost obsessively protective of that privacy.

This deeper well within person and technology is fathomed only through an exploration of the deeper history that underlies both. Colonial Trinidad was an unusually erudite land where there were probably more people who could quote Shakespeare, proportional to the population, than in the UK. If the island was known historically to others, it was because of its export of natural pitch, used for the caulking of ships. In the 1920s, this evolved into Trinidad becoming one of the earliest exporters of oil. Part of the money that thereby accrued to the state was invested in a group of elite secondary schools that still today represents one of the world's most successful institutions of education, quite possibly in the world. A high proportion of the pupils who complete their education at these schools achieve the grades that will gain them full scholarships from foreign universities if they should choose to go. Ajani had attended one of these elite schools – Naparima Girls' High School in San Fernando, the second city of Trinidad. This had qualified her for the next stage, an undergraduate degree in Canada.

Even while still at school, Ajani had read of the role of women in the French salons of the eighteenth century. She had determined to recreate the local equivalent of these powerful predecessors who had more or less dictated the artistic revolutions of their times, women such as Mme de Staël and Mme Roland. Today, almost no artistic activity of any kind happens in San Fernando, except under the auspices of Ajani. The house she lives in is now the site of exhibitions, poetry readings, dance and performance art. This is where DJs mix with political activists. True, this is only a shadow of the much more international and cosmopolitan scene of Port of Spain, but few would have guessed that San Fernando would ever have had the kind of cultural renaissance that Ajani has succeeded in cultivating. It stands as one of the most creative results of her personal energy and aesthetic.

So Ajani paints and performs and dances, but above all she writes. This child of English schoolteachers seems to have been immersed in words with her amniotic fluid and to have been reading and writing from the time she could toddle. She wrote her way through every genre, from keeping a diary, to school competitions and essays, through childhood poetry to a ream of admittedly at first rather stunted love letters. She embraced the labour and craft of handwriting, an almost physical sense of sinuous lines that poured onto paper as though they came straight from her soul. She was in love with the pen and the paper itself. As she grew older and bolder, this writing took the form of letters to newspapers and then writing for almost any outlet that would accept her, from church newsletters to politics. Finally, she secured the job she still holds today as the editor of a newsletter for one of the main NGOs based in Trinidad.

Brought up Catholic, she drifted through religions, more with a sense of the spirituality that seemed to reside within herself than something that could be objectified as God or Gods. She recently developed an affinity with a form of Baptism far removed from the kind of Texas Baptists of US missionaries. This is with the Shouter or Shango Baptism that has its roots in Yoruba culture, a version of Baptism that has always had an ambiguous relationship to the Trinidadian state. It was associated with political opposition since the time of slavery and banned by the government between 1917 and 1951. More recently, the state has recognized and valorized it as an authentic expression of an African foundation for Trinidadian culture. Looking at Ajani's mass of locks, they seem a good match for the turban associated with the devout Baptists of Trinidad. But while she explored this faith, in truth she has become more ecumenical, as close to a kind of new age Buddhism as to Shango. She could write on spirituality or mysticism in a way that might equally appeal to church, temple, mosque and shrine. There may even be a Protestant influence in this intense concern for 'getting the Word out', that almost physical property of the Word itself and the mission to broadcast it to the universe.

The development of the internet had helped her expand her writing further. The private diary of the child could migrate into a blog, which in her case was quite sustained. She could still fire off epistles to newspaper and post poetry around her house under fridge magnets or rafters that became part of the way art permeated its spaces. Fortunately, but not surprisingly, some years previously she had come to know about one of the few old wooden colonial homes in San Fernando that would otherwise have been bulldozed. She had purchased it for relatively little and used it as the ideal frame within which to build her centre for the arts. But it was not the house which eventually provided Ajani with a means to finally fulfil this almost obsessive need to slough off her moods and feelings in words, in effect to constantly objectify or externalize herself into the public domain. Rather, it seems almost as though Facebook was invented to serve these needs of Ajani.

For all her missives and blogs, one couldn't have really understood even the public face of Ajani without being exposed to her on Facebook. This provided an essential complement to all her other forms of writing. To compose a letter or to write a blog, or to pen some literature, are all investments of time and scale. Although they can be highly satisfying, expelling that energy and cooling the soul, they are necessarily intermittent and relatively occasional. But the nature of the *Shakti* energy that possesses Ajani is that it needs more constant and consistent acts of externalization. Ajani simply can't wait to write. As she wakes in the morning, she immediately writes on paper, an act that gives her sufficient composure – in both senses of that word – to face the day, the way another person might need coffee. But in the last few years, even this proves insufficient because Ajani can no longer sleep as others sleep, through an eight-hour stretch. To do so would not provide a moment, a time, for writing to assuage this creative energy that threatens the cool interior. Typically, she is up several times a night at which times she must express herself, if not to write, then to chant, to paint, to do something that externalizes and creates the world.

The joy of Facebook is that it requires no great expenditure of thought or time; it's a kind of instant and constant relief. It doesn't matter if it's the middle of the night or the middle of the day. If you need to express something, you can turn to Facebook and, in a short burst of typing, a deed is done and the addiction is sated for an hour or two. Some of her friends are mightily relieved by this since they have become used to the constant disturbance of Ajani's nocturnal creativity. Previously, she was always putting notes up on the fridge, chanting or generally disturbing the place. As far as her friends are concerned, Ajani can be as creative as she likes during the day, but they deserve some tranquillity, some respite, so at least they can get the sleep they need through the night. Living with Ajani's energy could drive you nuts. But Facebook helped.

So Ajani doesn't just use Facebook, she populates it; there is a deluge of her that pours from her profile. Countless friends and photos and videos and postings and links and events and status updates and activity of all kinds. If you look at them closely, they are as likely to have been posted at 3.00 a.m. as at 3.00 p.m. Certain genres dominate. As mistress of her Salon, for her Facebook is ideal, since she can constantly organize and announce cultural events. These then spread instantly around her networks. With Facebook, she can ask people if they intend to be present, which gives at least some sense of how large an audience to expect at an event. Whether these are dances, music, poetry or exhibitions, Facebook can be used to post notices, images, or YouTube videos to give some enticement, to create some buzz, to promote and to expound. It creates a people's Salon that brings together those who labour for art with those who wish to participate in creative action. As such, Facebook is a kind of virtual expansion of her house, a happening place, a virtual art space, where she can have both the intimacy of her Salon but also exposure to a limitless world.

Facebook is equally an ideal medium for a certain kind of politics and activism. It allows an almost instant commentary on the world, whether this is to poke fun at Trinidadian politicians or more seriously note some exposure of corruption. It could be to lament the devastation of Haiti, or to go beneath the adulation for a more considered examination of Obama, to expose some corporate greed, to despair at some act of patriarchy, to declare a street protest or simply to express a forceful opinion; above all to organize events around issues associated with her work at her NGO. Many people were disdainful of Facebook-based political activism (at least prior to its massive and effective use by opposition groups in Iran and Thailand) because it seemed too quick, too cheap, too easy. But none of this applies to Ajani. Everyone knows she will also take the risk of other forms of public exposure, saying what she thinks on television or attending a street protest, if such should arise. For Ajani, Facebook is merely the obvious complement to other forms of political expression. After all, those people who only see politics in street demonstrations and activism might equally dismiss the politics of painting or poetry. But as a patron of such arts, she feels these represent the necessary inner values in which a true politics should recognize its wellspring.

San Fernando is not that far from La Brea, the site of one of the most contested environmental and political issues in contemporary Trinidad. This is the location for a proposed aluminium smelter. Thanks to a successful law case and subsequent injunction, there is as yet no smelter at the site. Instead, it is currently home to a bevy of Chinese workers, since the government's plan was hatched in conjunction with the demands for aluminium from China. The protestors argue that this venture is not backed by any sensible business plan, since Trinidad is a country that produces no bauxite and which has already seen one major energy supply, that of oil, extracted to exhaustion. It has also been shown that, if built, the smelter would produce a high level of environmental damage. But at the heart of the protest is also a genuine concern for the people of the area. La Brea was previously the centre for the extraction of oil and, even before that, of pitch. It is now being developed for natural gas. Time and again, a new wave of industrial development has promised riches to those who live within the region from where this wealth is extracted. Time and again, the people have been betrayed and this is now one of the most impoverished areas of Trinidad. The presence of the Chinese workers is taken as clear evidence that the cycle is about to recommence. The group that would not benefit from these riches was the local population.

So, not surprisingly, there is a groundswell of opposition and this is now the site of pretty constant political activity. While we were researching communication in Trinidad, both Mirca and myself were staying with my PhD student Simone, whose own research is concerned with the nature and clash of values that emerge from the various groups and interests involved in this case. Ajani has closely associated herself with the opposition to the smelter and galvanized San Fernando as a kind of concerned neighbour. She has been highly effective in using Facebook to gain international attention for this issue and for the work of her NGO, knowing that it is only when there is international attention that her own government will give credence to protest and criticism.

But the joy of Facebook is the way it mixes things up and Ajani is a DJ of Facebook posting. First, she spins a serious activist comment. This is followed by the problem of some tempting but fattening food left in the house she wants to avoid, or the lyrics of a song, or her opinion on the current competition in steelband, or a cryptic mystical verse. The fact that you never know what is going to come next is what keeps her audience alert and interested and expectant. If it were only the monochrome of political stance or a sealed package of arts, people would become bored quite quickly. But everything about Ajani has vibrancy and colour and her postings flash through Facebook like fish around a coral reef. One of the sources that keeps her palette fresh is that, through her work, Ajani gets to travel and to have a range of cosmopolitan experiences that she knows will be of wider interest. Facebook is also her travelogue, her observations on the quirky and the bizarre: the kindness of strangers but also their strangeness. And these often bring her to thoughtful issues such as making sense of travelling as a black woman or coming to terms with the balance between her experience of discrimination and her awareness of her own capacity for discrimination, all of which she shares through Facebook.

So the texture of her Facebook is created through this inter-leaving of an outer layer of politics and literature with a stream of personal comment, of moods, jokes, regrets, disdains. In particular, there is the way Facebook provides the co-presence of the intimate. She will post a comment directed to a friend at a given moment, such as asking why they cooked this, or borrowed that. The point is that this comment is entirely meaningless to everyone else who sees her posting. We don't know who that friend is, we don't know what the friend did that Ajani is encouraging or is offended by. We are not given any clues or further information. In its own way, this trivial aside is just as cryptic as the mystical verse she also posts. But we are thereby included in this 'presentness' of her everyday activity. We can textually overhear something she says on the side, not by accident but because she chooses to post, to communicate to that friend through this entirely public domain where a thousand other friends can simultaneously overhear. The everyday then becomes a kind of substance that is mixed into the Facebook pot, along with poets and politics. One cannot know, but there are certainly grounds to suspect, that Ajani is fully aware of what she has achieved and how. There is variety, too, within this personal expression, glimpses of her private life in text, her love for a family member or a cat, a hint of a romantic attachment or detachment, but only a faint whiff of that aroma. The mistress of her Salon, like her French predecessors, is also in some measure a tease, casting crumbs of intimacy for her devotees to peck at, but nothing that will ever fill their curious bellies.

In adherence to this tradition of the Salon, there is also a potentially erotic edge to this tease. At first, it seems there must be some contradiction in what she has been saying. She talks disdainfully about women who simply use Facebook to post sexy pictures, the skimpy swimsuit at the beach, the 'hot hot short short' pants. If you review Ajani on Facebook, it is mostly true that she is wearing unusually long dresses and modest tops. But every now and then there is something else – a picture of her at a party in a striking outfit by one of San Fernando's top designers, so short that one cannot be unaware that her statuesque figure is founded on long slender legs. Another depicts her more coyly, with her back to you, but it is on the beach and it is beguiling. After a while, it becomes apparent why these do not contradict her disdain. They have nothing in common with the almost disarming vulgarity of the Facebook landscape of Trini females, with its thousands of images of low-cut, high-cut, beach-cut, boldfaced sexuality. Ajani could never be vulgar; she simply has too much artistry and too much that defends her body from overexposure. For Ajani, it is not that she intends to look sexy; it is that eroticism has always been a quality of art. Its very ambiguity is too useful an ingredient in her humour, her play on image and appearance, not to be part of her Facebook palette. The eroticism of image for Ajani is an art that must always be literary and never literal. But it is also cold. Ajani's sexuality is intentionally forbidding rather than enticing. Here is Tolkien's Galadriel to be worshipped and feared, never touched.

In response, she has her teeming multitude of Facebook followers, a constant and visible stream of admirers who respond. She is, after all, an entertainer, a comedienne, an informer, a preacher, a friend, an intimate. She has gracefully and artfully given of herself to the select that is her network. And because she is beautiful in text and because there is artistry in her mix, with snippets of interest and imagination that make the endless browsing of her Facebook more interesting than that of her peers, her devotees are properly grateful and appreciative of this constant gifting of the outer self. The need Ajani has to cool herself constantly through exposure in writing is matched by the greed we have for the next bit of her.

At this level of performance in relation to audience, Ajani's Facebook is perfectly situated in the modern history of media itself. First in theatre and radio, then in television, there was drama: two or three hours of intense interest, always through the enactment of script. Then the media discovered the potential of soap opera which made it far more popular and part of audiences' lives than they had ever been previously. The point of soap opera is that it creates a melodrama which takes on the mantle of time. It becomes a parallel dimension so that one grows older in tandem with fictional characters who exist daily alongside their audiences. These lives thereby seem so much more real than those of drama. But soap opera nevertheless remains fictional. So the next development which enabled media to hold its audience in a still tighter embrace was reality TV. At this juncture, soap opera abandons fiction and replaces it with actual persons, celebrity neighbours exposing themselves to the public gaze so that one can voyeur-istically feast upon their foibles – but only in artificial contexts such as the *Big Brother* house. Finally, we have Facebook, where people live their lives, not in fiction, not through acting, not by placement in some artificial theatre or house. Within Facebook, people largely live their lives as they always have done, but in real time they toss forth images and items that are evidence of that co-presence in the world. They are open to reciprocity, such as the exchange of comment or at least ticking the 'like' box attached to those comments. Mostly, they are people one also knows in offline worlds, though not necessarily. But Facebook thereby achieves something compared to which all previous media now seems mere simulacra – the relationship we feel through the co-presence of another person.

Of course, this has its downside. Ajani is happy to share her abilities to make the world both more serious and much funnier than it would otherwise be, to be everyone's good friend and entertainment. But Facebook works best for her if there is an underlying sense of its netiquette where people know how to behave appropriately in reciprocity with her. This is a problem for many people who have become popular in part through Facebook itself. It's fine if her close friends comment on her asides. It's fine if others occasionally reciprocate or associate themselves with her. But there are a few people she barely knows, whom she might not recognize in the street, and whom frankly she can't remember why she accepted as friends in the first place. Just occasionally, they behave with leech-like tendencies, fastening onto her comments and exposures as if sucking her blood. They have to comment on too many postings, thereby aspiring to become a prominent part of her public profile even though she barely knows them. They fail to differentiate between an agreement to be a Facebook friend and the illusion that they are 'actual' friends. They are annoying and irritating and yet it is a harsh step to actually de-friend them from Facebook itself. You just kind of hope they will go away after a while. Actually, it's hard to blame them since there are no clear rules to this game. People are somehow just expected to know what is inappropriate or disconcerting in the same way that we practise proxemics in everyday life. Like birds on the wire, we have an innate sense of how close two bodies should or should not be when moving around our social landscape.

Put this way, one realizes that Facebook actually requires a quite subtle sensibility to work effectively. Ajani knows, and all her followers know, its voyeuristic qualities, its seductive elements. But Ajani is well aware that this only works when matched with self-discipline. On her part, she is not posting every gory detail of her life. In fact, you could spend a year on her Facebook and have no sense at all of her key relationships. Art is not mere realism. Her postings have an elliptical, sometimes abrupt, sometimes tentative nature which is what gives them craft and interest. But this discipline in their creation needs to be matched by a discipline in its reception. A Facebook friend has this intimate knowledge of you but they cannot, should not, presume a migration to another kind of friendship.

She finds it easier to deal with the men – an inappropriate remark and you can just de-friend them or disdain them. Women can be more insidious and difficult. Because these people only know her public profile, they can have no knowledge at all of the central role that Facebook plays in Ajani's inner life; that the whole point is the way it protects her interior being that must always remain unexposed and unexpelled, the cool core centre of her soul. The nature of worship is that devotees should act at a respectful distance. The whole point of throwing words out into the public is that it distances them from her; it keeps people at arm's length. It exports her to a computer and thereby to another virtual place. The very last thing Ajani wants from Facebook is that it should expose that inner self, to make her vulnerable to the outside, become an embarrassment or intrusion. All these surfaces of public exposure – Facebook, the blogs, the house, the use of art – are places that represent as much defensive armour as an outstretched hand.

The art of Facebook is a very Trini art of keeping things light and edged with humour. Ajani may have this cold intimidating look but she has absolutely no desire to be called a goddess or priestess, expressions that are far too heavy, burdensome – just not funny. Trini art has always rested on banter, humour and play at the level. It is only in this analysis, trying to understand a more profound purpose for Facebook, that we need to move through these layers to a core, to acknowledge how fundamental it is to Ajani that this relentless gifting of the outer self to her public is matched by a desperate need to be entirely on her own for long periods of time. Even her best friends are surprised by the extent Ajani has to have these periods of complete isolation from others. So much of this activity is an instrument in her quest for self-sufficiency and autonomy, to protect and preserve that inner being. So yes it is true that Ajani needs other people, if anything more, not less, than most of us. She cannot do without this vast audience. But, ultimately, she needs these people to be in her Facebook and not in her face.

This act of expulsion through writing and art is consistent with the aesthetic that Ajani cultivates through her body and appearance. Her hair, a huge mass of braids, is not the matted dreadlocks of the Rasta, yet they are one of the purest expressions of the Rasta concept of *dread*locks. The whole point of these locks is that they are dread as in the dreadful power of the holy. They are her armour and her defence and it is clear that, if she had her way, anyone who had the temerity to touch her hair would literally have their fingers burnt. These are the original dreadlocks of Medusa, petrifying in their grandeur and ability to protect and repulse. It's actually quite hard to look at her face because of the ability of this mass of hair to veil her and deflect the gaze.

Ajani's clothing is equally perfomative. If one had to give her a sartorial style, a label, then it would probably be 'ethnic', but that would be almost pejorative given the eclecticism and originality that create her combinations of textile, embroidery and accessories. The mistress of her Salon has to be the visual centre of this art world and clothing is integral to that role. She is good friends with several aspiring designers but in Trinidad to look good is often simply the right strappy T-shirt or the bright bracelet. This circle of the arts distances itself from the vulgarity of what used to be called the *cosquel*, a kind of OTT (over the top) use of shining surfaces and mismatched colour. Ajani's style is strong but can also be subtle; white with a touch of Rasta is just so Ajani.

There is a clear link between Ajani's sense of self-sufficiency and her feminism. It's very hard to imagine her in a position of deference or even conforming to the basis of most gender relations in Trinidad where traditionally men give of their labour in exchange for access to female sexuality. But this is exactly why she is also able to have deep, platonic relationships with males, something which certainly cannot be taken for granted in Trinidad. Ajani has layers; her outer armour will repulse the casual glance. But once she takes people under her wing as fast friends, then they also benefit from that sense of protective concern.

This self-sufficiency is an important component in this basic opposition between Ajani's inner and outer self. It explains why Ajani is perhaps happiest at the precise moment when something has been given out into the world, even just a Facebook posting. That *Shakti* energy is like a sloughed-off skin. Now she can rest, simply, left alone in the tranquillity of her inner being. Once she has sent some writing out into the world, that cool inner core of her soul is quiet and silent; it gives nothing away and has no desire to be interrogated or even identified with. It is just there, a yogic peace of mind, to be protected from need and from desire.

This portrait explores why and how an individual can become deeply private in a way that only such an intensely public person can be. To follow the aesthetic logic of this person is to understand also an aesthetic logic within Facebook itself. A critical lesson Ajani has taught us about Facebook is how constant exposure through restless posting can enable rather than diminish a person's privacy. Facebook has revealed an unexpected capacity to work with and on the heterogeneity and complexity of persons. As for Ajani, she has recently come to a new level of self-awareness with regard to the aesthetic that makes her who she is, not through introspection but simply by going to see the film *Avatar*. In that film, one sees an extreme contrast. Out in the public domain is this incredibly powerful, colourful and attractive being, one that knows no fear and achieves mastery and adulation and above all (however trite the storyline) a fabulous and entrancing use of colour. But it is an avatar, controlled elsewhere by another being in perfect peace and stillness, hidden from view. It's hardly surprising that Ajani felt an instant affinity with the film. In fact, she confides in me that she is desperately hoping that in this year's Carnival there will be a band called Avatar which she will lead as an embodiment of Gaia and the spirit of the earth. All she really needs now is to grow a long blue tail.

7

Time Suck

I have spent the last three hours looking over his shoulder as he does Facebook. It's not enough really. I now routinely ask people of all ages how long they spend on Facebook each day. I usually end with a pause and then the word . . . 'truthfully?', at which point many of them look a little shamefaced and acknowledge four or six hours. And they don't mean just having Facebook on in the background, because I make this distinction clear. They mean six hours a day actively doing something on Facebook. Despite the fact that I am also on Facebook and that I am studying Facebook, I realize I am still missing something vital to understanding it. I just can't work out for the life of me – what does one actually do when one spends six hours on Facebook? I can just about imagine an answer if one is devoted to a game such as *FarmVille*. But in conversation these people say that they look at what new photos have come on; then they might look at status updates; then they might post something themselves or comment on another posting. I have watched many times over the shoulders of individuals engaged in such activities for perhaps half an hour – but six hours? Friends in England often refer to Facebook as a 'time suck' – which is a pretty neat way of describing one of its most considerable powers. But what actually happens to that time; where does it go?

In Trinidad, and very likely in many other places, amongst the most committed and the heaviest users were teenagers. Aaron seemed an ideal stand in for that huge brood. Certainly there was the commitment. Admittedly, he only averaged twelve hours a week on Facebook but that was because he could only manage two days. As someone with no internet access of his own, even this was impressive. It either meant parking himself for long periods at the local library, which had seven computers, and staring down anyone who seemed to hover, implying his turn had come. Or it could mean occupying a discreet corner in the home of one of those houses in the neighbourhood that did have internet access and remaining quiet and unobtrusive while they got on with their offline lives. People in his neighbourhood were pretty generous in that way. There is not the same sense of privacy that would make this difficult in many other countries, or indeed in the more upmarket homes of Trinidad itself. It was something that had been clear to me ten years earlier when studying the internet in Trinidad. If one person had a connection, then the neighbourhood felt connected.

If Aaron was persistent in pursuit of his Facebook time, his entrepreneurship in finding ways to go online reflected the area that Aaron lived in. The name seemed apt. Enterprise was unusual as a settlement within the Chaguanas region of central Trinidad in that it was an enclave dominated by those of African descent within a region of Trinidad mainly of East Indian origin. At its heart was a squatters' encampment that had been originally made from the crates in which car parts were imported, but had gradually been regularized. When I first carried out research there, some twenty years previously, hardly any houses had electricity and water came from standpipes. Yet even in those days people used to use car batteries to power small televisions so that they wouldn't miss the then current crucial soap opera, *The Young and the Restless*. Today many of the shacks have been replaced by concrete and breeze-block, and indoor plumbing is becoming the norm. I have a great affection for the area, partly because it was the site of the best parties I have ever been to. This was where people knew how to 'get on bad', as it was called in those days, or 'party hard', which is the more contemporary expression. I supported their local steelband, Tropical Angel Harps, in competition. In Enterprise, some people get by through pickpocketing and other forms of petty crime; there were drug problems and abuse, but there was also an extraordinary positive energy about the place.

This is not something you would necessarily have gathered just from observing Aaron since, as with so many young boys in so many countries today, he seemed entirely devoted to his online life, with a commitment to Facebook that seemed to echo others' relationship to online gaming. His attitude was ideal for my research. Just as he could be unobtrusive in the living rooms of others, so he seemed almost entirely oblivious to my presence which, given that I just wanted to stare over his shoulder for several hours, seemed just fine.

He is neither as articulate nor as sociable as many of his peers. In fact, he has less than a hundred friends on Facebook. Only around five of these are relatives, mainly cousins his age. He does include pretty much everyone in his class that has computer access. He reckons that accounts for all but 12 of the 31 in the class, which is probably a good guide to the penetration of Facebook amongst his age group in low-income areas. Most of his other Facebook friends are girls from other schools in the area. So his Facebook is pretty much entirely his peer group, a simple extension of his school world. Exceptions would be the minor celebrities he has managed to friend, including an actor in the teenage vampire series, *Twilight*, and a Jamaican dance hall artist. He has six siblings, of whom two older brothers are in the US. He doesn't actually know what part of the US they live in, and next to nothing about what they are doing there. There isn't much contact between them. But the fact that they are there explains how he has his own laptop, and for that he is very grateful indeed.

Facebook provides a number of different forms of 'time suck'. Mostly though, it divides into three main activities: one is communication, the second is online gaming, while the third is cultivating one's profile. Much of the latter is a way of refining how one looks to the outside world through what you choose to be associated with. Humour is often the key to this but, as in shopping more generally, mostly it is 'off the shelf'. That means Aaron is rarely making up his own Facebook jokes. It is more that, through various channels, large quantities of jokes pass him by and from these he makes a small collection of the specific jokes he would like to be associated with by repeating them on his site. He has decided which jokes he 'looks good in' in the same way Vishala dresses in a Tobago background. The same applies to the activity 'becoming a fan of . . .' which for these kids has become more a case of which funny phrases and ideas catch their imagination. I am not going to try translating the examples that follow, a dictionary of 15-year-old Trini slang would have a shelf-life of minutes. But the fact that we can cut and paste from Facebook itself provides a means to see the wider aesthetic of Trini posting, its deliberate misspellings and play with grammar and local dialect.

The first genre of postings one can see over Aaron's shoulder are those directly associated with school life. He is a fan of:

If I could remember school work like I remember lyrics I'd be like a genius.

Teachers Who Let You: Text, Eat, Talk, and Listen To Music During Class.

FIGHT, FIGHT, FIGHT, FIGHT.........OH CRAP TEACHERS COMMING, RUNNNNNNNNNNNN.

Quite a few relate directly to Facebook itself, often with ironic comments upon these online activities, for example, becoming a fan of:

I'm not a stalker, it was on my homepage.
I hate when people add me & ask me who I am! U ADDED ME FOOL! WHO ARE U?!
Ok I couldve sworn I already became a fan of that . . . oh well *become a fan*
I HATE WHEN UGLY PPL ADD ME........UGHHH!!!!
If FaceB0ok wAs a sUbject . . . mY parENts WuddA beEn s0 proUd..........:).

But there are plenty of others which just seem like random items that have struck home with this particular individual, either jokes or feelings, as in becoming a fan of:

I Try To Finish My Dream By Trying To Sleep Again After Waking Up.
Pandas are the least racist animal, they're black, white AND asian!
Football should not be called soccer.
Become a Fan If you Had a Bestfriend, but Now you Never Talk To Them.

I DONT GIVE A FUUUUUUUUUUUUUUUUUUUCKK
I use the word "Gay" to describe everything bad.
I LOVE JESUS AND IM PROUD TO SAY IT.
When i was your age i lost a tooth, Not my virginity.

Another genre of Facebook which does much the same thing is groups. Theoretically, these are associations you can revisit again and again in order to view their activities. But these kids seem to use groups essentially in much the same way as they use becoming a fan. They tend to run together on the profile page so as to give an instant visual impression of their interests. Typical groups Aaron is a member of include:

The Hit Men, Youth Alliance Dancers, ECLECTIK, Shit Talkers {Mixing Edition}, GANGSTARS, Gaza Youths (W.S.P), Converse ®Rockers International™, I love To Skip To My Lou, Trinidad and Tobago Adventist Youth for Christ (TTAYC), ZEN Group, D SKOOL HATERZ KREW, Britney spears, Pum Pum Conquererz, Mi Seh, Fire bun FARMVILLE!!!!, PIT BULL LOVERS, Stiff Winers International!STOP EATING RABBITS!, TRINI FOR !IFE, No school days on Friday! Need 5,000,000 school students to make official, {E@T !T.........P@L@NCE.......P@RTY H@RD},Change your Facebook Skin! (ONLY FIREFOX), JanSport® Rockers International™, Fight Racism in Trinidad and Tobago

Aaron would like to have more photos up on his profile, which is the main way people 'dress' their profiles, but he doesn't have a camera. So some of what is there includes shots posted from online games, fast cars, girls and football, as well as a few shots of himself in various poses, including a couple with his family. Despite this, he spends far more time making comments on other people's photos than commenting on their news postings or other parts of their sites. On his own site, there are also some comments. For example, there is a fair bit of banter connected with football ('chelsea aite..............but BARCA FUH LIFE !!!!!!) and what amounts to an extended discussion as to whether a Chelsea player is a match for Wayne Rooney (who plays for Manchester United). Most of these comments come from boys but there are others from girls, for example, one comment on a souped-up car he posted: 'dis is my ride boy . . . lol!!!!!!!!!!!!! luvin d stylz.' Many of the comments are very personal:

Barber boy movado go bull yuh yea in ur asssssss hole lol.

yes brethresn cutting edge style. that is what i talk bout . . . different and real dashing!!!!best dress.

dats my further alyuh chatin bout day eh..........so watch it i does get very defencsive 4 wat is mines

u gay fuck

WATCH MEH NAH BOI, I STUNTIN

BIG BOIZ, WATCH D GYAL IN RED DEY,SHE SWEET EH,SHE SEXY

lol!!!I feel like takin a pic . . . problem??
Shontel....i eh go tell yuh nuttin . . . ah like yuh daz y :P
Clem ask she yuhself u actin like u doh hav a number fuh she.
Jen ah was bored. . . .
Who nah like it me nah business, i find it was a normal pic

Most of the photos that people post of themselves are on the tame side. Some represent when they think they look particularly good, others when they were caught doing something silly, but not too silly. In fact, Aaron was quite shocked when one of the girls he knew posted a picture of herself in a bikini.

The only other primary activity for 'dressing' one's profile for general public display is what happens on one's 'wall'. Aaron's is dominated not by his comments or replies but by a mass of Facebook gifting. This is pretty much a constant but becomes a crescendo of activity around Valentine's Day or his birthday. They usually consist of little graphics of virtual gifts, or often 'blessings' that are the equivalent of choosing a card with a particular motif. Examples might be 'I just hit you with delicious In-N-Out Double Cheeseburger!' or 'I just hit you with the Comfy Pillow. You have 2 days to hit back or you lose!' As the latter implies, there is a clear desire for reciprocity, since what makes a personal profile look good is more often what other people have posted, how many other people visit, and how many postings there are, than anything a profiler might do for themselves.

The wall is also used for personal postings, to and fro. In his case, though, and this seems typical of boys, his own postings are rather briefer than those of girls who post to him. A selection of his include:

i now remember hw boring home could be.........stupezz

Who's afraid of the big bad wolf?

computer messing up bad dred . . . stupezzz

kandice go home plzzzzzzzzzz . . . u like 2 bother me!!!!!!!:(

gotta go our church dinner 4 7:00 but i'm still home . . . lol . . . small ting the dinner will not start until i reach . . . lol

as the great quagmire once said........*giggty giggty goo*

i fed up
A moment of silence 4 haiti...*sigh*

By comparison, postings on sites of girls he knows include:

if u hate me remember it bcuz of ppl like u i wake up and smile cuz i prove all of u wrong every day and bcuz u keep me popular wen talk bout me so keep on hatin and watch me progress

wel 2 day was real hectic an sum how fun at d same time i real whine up my self an ting so it was real nice and once again 2 my A.... i luv u much >mwah<

wel d dance was nice in skool it ova kinda rly but i real dance and wel...................... PALANCE!!!!!!!!!!!!!!!! IT WAS NICE!!!!!!!!!!!!! 4 REAL NJOY MY SELF.

At that time, there was also clearly something going on with one particular girl who posted some sense of her frustrations with him in two postings:

HI HI! 2 MY AARON JUS KEEPIN U UPDATED U NEVA DISSAPOINT U KEEP ON TALIKIN BEHIND MY BAK AND JUS KEEP ON LAUGHING AT UR RIDICULUSLY FUNNI STUPIDITY HAV U NUTTIN BETA 2 DO? WEL I GUESS NOT SO

KEEP IT UP WEN IM OUT OF JOKES I THINK OF U STINKAZ
AND JUS LMAO YEP ITS DAT FUNNI !!!!!!!!!!!!!!!!!!!!!!

WELL 2 MY AARON AS USUAL IM KEEPIN U POSTED AND
SO FAR WELL.......... U STILL DONT BOTHER ME AND U
STILL HAV ME ON TOP OF MY GAME SO 2 ALL U AARON
TAKE A BOW U JUS DID ME PROUD LOL >MWAH<

What is helpful about these wall postings is that they provide
examples within the public domain that give something of the
flavour of another major activity, one that I am spending much of
my time observing but have no means of reproducing here. These
are Aaron's private chats that are going on within Facebook.
Unlike others whom I have watched and who may have many of
these going on simultaneously, he tends to do one chat at a time.
These in turn reflect the two main bodies of friends on his site.
Either chat is an example of simply hanging out after school with
kids from the same class, making comments about girls, music and
games, or it is a means of communicating with girls from nearby
schools. Both have developed particular genres. With these girls,
Aaron didn't really say anything too explicit, or too personal.
What he was trying to do was to demonstrate that he could be
quite funny, had a light touch, and was reasonably interesting and
attractive. The banter would be on topics such as whose school
was better, what girls in general from her school were like, or what
all girls were like. There were hints about dances and parties that
might crop up in the future.

So without saying anything directly, he and the girl would
know where they might 'bounce up', that is, meet at some stage
in the future. None of this demanded that anyone actually ask
anyone out on a date which would have carried the dread possibility of refusal. But they simply got to know each other a little
better, found an angle into the other's personality that gave them
an inkling of whether they might want to make more of this
contact. It was also possible that Aaron could conclude that this
was a girl who was fun to hang out with online, even if her looks
suggested there was no way he wanted to turn this into anything
serious offline. For those who didn't consider themselves that great
looking or cool, Facebook was particularly valuable as a place to
socialize. Without anything being said, everyone was nonetheless

aware why some people, who had become good friends online and would remain so, didn't really acknowledge each other much face to face. In the public domain, you tended to try and associate with the better looking, the cooler kids, even if you didn't actually like them that much. You just couldn't afford to do otherwise.

Sometimes these chats become more personal, with people talking about their feelings in relation to a sibling, their parents or a teacher, or just teenage perceptions about how life sucks at that particular moment. Aaron freely admits to me that he finds it more difficult to talk about feelings when actually with a person than on Facebook. He sees this ability to express oneself in public as something girls have less of a problem with, though, from what I can see, even on Facebook girls are much readier to be personal and emotional than boys. But in as much as this is something he ever does, Facebook is where it happens. The key to understanding Aaron's Facebook is not to dismiss too quickly these apparently much lighter postings, conversations and associations as inconsequential or shallow. Make no mistake: these teenagers are scrutinizing and carefully judging each other via banter and humour. Facebook is now a critical site where they learn and practise the arts of being articulate and savvy, becoming masters of innuendo. These abilities will be judged by their peers just as seriously as visual cues, such as what people wear or with what jokes and groups they associate.

The third element to 'time suck' is online games. Currently, Aaron passes the time flitting between three of these. He has reached level 53 in *Yakuza Lords*. Several kids a couple of years older than him are serious devotees of Japanese *anime* cartoons. He will also play *Mafia Wars*, perhaps the most common game in contemporary Trinidad after *FarmVille*. He is also into something called *Café World*, which, as his mother quickly notes, is no indication of any offline interest in cooking.

So the hours pass, and time gets sucked. There is the endless browsing, chats and banter, a bit of gaming and then some chatting – then more of the same. To the outside observer, this just seems mind-numbingly tedious; it is quite hard to concentrate on after the first hour or two. But for Aaron, this attention to detail and constant updating is not a distraction, or an entertainment that takes him away from things that matter. He manages his interactions with his friends adroitly, the incredibly complex weave between being sufficiently funny, sufficiently interesting, sufficiently concerned with other people, quick in banter, and learning how to hint just the right amount so that he doesn't lose face when the other fails to respond. These were the skills that would lead him to be confident and successful with other people, or despondent and unattractive, key social skills that could make the difference between a happy life and an unhappy one. It wasn't hard to see why this mattered to Aaron and how he saw the hours on Facebook as a pretty good use of his time.

8

Getting the Word Out

It is perhaps not surprising that the church that emerged as of particular interest during this fieldwork was the very same church I discussed in *The Internet: An Ethnographic Approach*,[1] written with Don Slater ten years earlier. The Elijah Ministries was founded by an ex-university lecturer from UWI (University of the West Indies) and recruited heavily from students and academics. From its beginnings, this church had been in thrall to new technologies, though the encounters in 2010 produced rather more sober reflections than the exuberance for new media that I encountered in 1999.

If one goes to Pentecostal services, which is hard not to do when working in the Caribbean with any serious ethnographic commitment, you soon become used to one of the key motifs of this branch of Christianity. This is the desire to 'get the Word out'. These churches are intensely proselytizing and with a marked degree of success. Pentecostalism has had a vast impact, not just in the Caribbean but throughout Africa, the Pacific, Latin America and the US. It is one of the most radical and significant transformations of the twentieth century. Yet, at least in the UK, apart from those who are actually involved, there is a remarkable degree of ignorance about such churches. If people are aware of them at

[1] Miller, D. and Slater, D. (2000), *The Internet: An Ethnographic Approach*. Oxford: Berg.

all, they may be regarded as some kind of weird cult, part of an equally incomprehensible adherence to extreme religion within the US in contrast to a largely secularized Europe.

Attendance at a service would probably reinforce these views about Pentecostalism, with its laying on of hands and talking in tongues, not to mention the conscientious giving of tithes. To the secular, Pentecostalism comes across more as a state of being possessed than simply a faith. But this is not something its adherents would find in the least problematic. This born-again evangelical Christianity is intended to be a state of possession, entirely given over to the quest to be among the saved. One of my closest Trinidadian friends is a Pentecostal preacher. I have been to services of up to 9,000 people in Jamaica and the UK, as well as in Trinidad.

The Elijah Centre, however, is not a Pentecostal church. It claims to have taken one step further and become an Apostolic church. Apart from theological differences, the most important distinction is the way it has distanced itself from more US-inflected Pentecostals, being more grounded in Trinidadian, though largely Afro-Trinidadian, communities. Several Indo-Trinidadians admitted that they found themselves uncomfortable in the church on these grounds.

The members interviewed in 1999 had given theological explanations for the very existence of the internet. As they saw it, nothing happens in this world except that it should be interpreted as a sign from God as to the divine purpose. From this perspective, we did not invent the internet. The proper question is why God has given us the internet at this time. If the internet creates unprecedented possibilities for transnational communication, it must be because God is telling us that the time has come for the church to realize its mission and become manifest globally. It is a sign of the coming of global salvation. In short, we are given the internet as a far more effective way to get the Word out. Taking this to its logical conclusion, which is something an Apostolic church is generally pretty good at, everything in the church should migrate to the internet and fully embrace it as God's chosen instrument. There was a movement in 1999 to abolish all non-internet based aspects of the church, including face-to-face services, in order to manifest fully the church as an instrument of God's chosen technology.

By 2010, this fervour had somewhat abated and the church had in fact retained regular, more conventional services at its base near the university. But this remained the most technologically orientated of the Trinidadian churches. In keeping with these ideals of 1999, the Elijah Ministries has used the internet to become a global movement. In the intervening ten years, the church, now called The World Breakthrough Kingdom, had grown from its original base in Trinidad and established 'embassies' in twelve countries. These formed what the church calls 'A Global Borderless Kingdom Community'. They ranged from sites within the Caribbean, such as Belize and St Lucia, through to the US, Wales, South Africa and New Zealand. In its other guise as the Congress World Breakthrough Network, the church website gives *Global Communication and Technology* as one of the eight primary sectors of the church. To quote from the website:

> This Sector represents a major part of the glue that holds the entire sectoral structure of the Congress together. Its mission is to design and activate communication protocols and systems that allow the Congress leadership to bring maximum sight, coherence and productivity to the advance of the Congress.
>
> The objective is the total facilitation of what we call "frictionless" Congress advance and this is achieved through strategic communications management, the construction of appropriate Congress mentalities and perspectives that align themselves with the principles of the Kingdom of God, the maximizing of information flow across all Sectors of the Congress and the development and maintenance of effective external and internal interfaces.[2]

Michael, a keen member of this church, was as articulate about new media as those interviewed ten years previously. Communication technology is not simply a means to an end. Probably the most important term within this church is that of continual 'reformation'. As Michael noted, the first reformation of the church was closely based upon the relationship between Martin Luther and the printing press. The latest communication technology is a sign then that 'God is moving' and propelling the people forward. Michael is God's geek. Quite apart from his church activities,

[2] www.congresswbn.org/cwbn/Sectors/GCT/tabid/189/Default.aspx (accessed 28 July 2010).

he is taking a degree through long-distance communication. His supervisions take place on Skype with webcam. This is a man with seven separate email accounts. As he puts it, 'if you understand the Apostolic, everything is scripture. So the whole thing about raising the valleys and lowering the hills. That is the word of God talking about globalization, the effect of the internet, the potential for some degree of equalization through the technology.'

Michael is part of the church's communication group and helped set up its unique international format. Today all the embassies are linked by live streaming video which transmits the main Sunday service. The single exception is New Zealand where the 16-hour time difference makes this impracticable. Another screen allows the speaker in Trinidad to project a PowerPoint commentary on the text to the embassies. According to Michael, below that there will be a sort of IM chat room 'so anytime you log on so you could actually see who is logged on'. This particular facility was not in evidence at the London embassy Sunday service but the integration of new technology was impressive. The service contained many direct references to these technologies, for example, 'you don't have people writing in their blogs about that'; 'just rely on Google Maps'; 'thank you for the emails'; 'right now I am not clickable'; 'I don't know whether our deeds are kept in computer files to be played back on the day of judgement'; 'you don't have people issuing a CD on righteousness'; 'have everything in one file – put some basic systems in place'.

The centrality of communication is equally reflected in the way the congregation themselves take notes. Around a third of the congregation had laptops. More surprising was the number taking abundant notes via one-finger typing on an iPhone. The service is very different from a typical Pentecostal church. There is nothing like laying on of hands; there is not even a collection. Although the needs of one member are mentioned, the issue of money is discreet in stark contrast to most Pentecostal services. The main sermon is delivered through commentary within a PowerPoint presentation which includes abundant scriptural references. The preacher appears in a box at the top right of the PowerPoint screen. The genre is like an academic lecture, and the standard of argument, reasoning and textual evidence is that of a highly professional university lecture. The ideal of reformation is to strip away presumption and get back to basic meanings and messages in the text.

Although the church has a clear vision of new technology aligned with both the message and the medium of the church, it is rather less clear how Facebook will fit within this vision. Facebook made an appearance at the very commencement of the service. It was projected to the congregation so they could see pictures posted of a new baby born that week to two of its members. But, for a Trinidadian, there are evident problems in associating the church with *Macobook*. A technology so readily associated with gossip and scandal doesn't look like an unalloyed blessing granted from heaven. But then neither did the internet. As Michael put it,

> 'If you are twisted on the inside, you will use it for whatever you want; it has been very useful to us, but you have to be wise. What happens depends on who we are. Don't go on the internet and be looking for porn; don't do this because you are breaching other things inside of the word of God. Don't use the internet to attack people, because you are breaching other things.'

It is fine to use the technology to help people create relationships. But this has to be done the right way. If one embassy has more men and another more women and this communication can bring them together in church-blessed marriage, then it is working in the service of the Lord.

Michael wasn't in any personal need for this particular facility. He was about to get married to someone he had first met on the internet. She had been in Canada doing a PhD but they were both members of a Christian internet site that pre-dated his involvement in this particular church. It was a site Michael had helped to establish when he was still at school. He found many of his fellow students rather introverted and reluctant to come forward with ideas and opinions. When he re-established this site on Facebook as a place for religious discussion, at first it seemed very successful. The students seemed much happier exchanging ideas and getting involved. But being online also led to recurring spam and finding postings from more extreme or cranky groups that made things more difficult.

This was the site where he met his betrothed. At first, they talked about theological issues and debates, originally intermittently and then every day, mainly through Facebook, but then as things became more personal, communication migrated to MSN. They had got to know each other pretty well before finally meeting face to face. The irony was that once she came back to Trinidad, he in turn had to go abroad for a year's study. As is the way with Facebook, making a connection with her had led naturally to friending much of her family, including a few cousins he found he got on with pretty well. He started interacting with them more and more, nothing especially serious 'just like leaving messages on their wall' and 'stuff like that'. He discovered her family to be a very close-knit group, different from anything he had known. They would have group discussions with all her brothers and sisters and cousins joining in. This was very different from anything he associated with his own family and he rather enjoyed it. Soon he found himself accepted as an intimate in their constant family posting and discussion. In particular, she had some younger cousins who looked up to him as someone who had travelled abroad. They would consult him on various matters. Facebook wasn't all that significant for his relationship with her most immediate family. He tended to see quite a bit of them anyway. Rather, Facebook helped facilitate a different kind of family. He had become part of a cousinhood. Being more peer-based and less judgemental, it could be fun and friendly in the way as a child he had imagined a big family picnic of the kind his own family never actually had.

So, quite some time before he actually proposed to his fiancée, he had felt fully accepted and integrated into her Facebook family. Facebook was also the means to learn a great deal about her old college friends and the kinds of photos they posted about themselves. He wasn't as drawn into this circle but it gave him considerable insight into her personal history, who she had been before he had met her. When a person came up in the family or her conversation, he could put a picture to the name. It helped because, while he felt comfortable with the technical side of media, his own childhood had been more isolated and previously he was not as naturally at ease in this world of broader relationships that he associated more with females. As in other areas of his life, Facebook, and the computer more generally, was there to support him.

These were also the motivations for the initial contact with and then increasing involvement in the Elijah Ministries. This church seemed to understand the seriousness with which he took communication technologies. It granted him a singular role and purpose within the church, and perhaps legitimated and gave higher purpose to the inner geek. But also it consolidated the pleasure he found in the virtual company of his wife's cousinhood. It provided a strong sense of community which counterbalanced the more isolationist aspect of his geekish devotion to technology.

Michael was characteristic of the many men who found the technical side of Facebook, and communications more generally, a comforting point of entry and an even more comforting place of retreat. Such men often found it more difficult to fully engage in the incessant relationship maintenance and development they associated with females. Typically, it was his fiancée's female relatives that seemed to do most of the work in creating the buzz and chatter that brought him into their Facebook world. He enjoyed this, but could never have created it for himself. His natural medium was either more abstract in the discussion of theology or more concrete in the practical tasks of technology.

It is therefore worth complementing Michael's story, which was similar to that of many men who managed to find some way to foreground the technology itself, with that of another church member, Camille, who seemed more typical of the women involved in the church. For them, the technology itself remained in the background. They also had much less of a problem with whether Facebook was theologically appropriate. What dominated their discussion was content: topics such as photographs, clothing and weddings. For Camille, Facebook is a constant in her life. Since she has arranged things so that messages come not only through Facebook itself but are repeated onto her BlackBerry and her email. As a result, she is practically bombarded by Facebook updates throughout the day. She somewhat guiltily admits to spending around three hours a day on Facebook.

In one respect, Camille's usage is pretty typical of Trinis in general. The textual content is largely based on the visual. She spends much of her Facebook time responding to comments made by other people on the photos she posts. She sees people because they are tagged on photos and follows them through. Often it is seeing someone in a photo that prompts a question about a friend's brother and whether he actually got that scholarship. So she can see the benign side of gossip as simply expressing a proper interest in others which is exactly what makes this a community of concern. She has joined many groups, fan pages and other interests. This often seems natural to people who have been students and in effect trained in the means and the need to keep up to date with information as it becomes available. Most such training in educational techniques is quickly assimilated as a means also to knowing about the latest in music and clothes as well as the latest in research. In her case, it is photography which particularly interests her and Facebook is a means of actively participating in an international group in which she is about the only Trinidadian. Having young children, travel is now restricted, so Facebook has become the natural extension and mode of maintaining a taken-for-granted cosmopolitanism.

Unlike Michael, she doesn't bring up pornography as the symptom of Facebook's problematic side but she is worried about the way people post other kinds of images. 'I see some people putting up what I consider to be inappropriate photos. Like some of my friends they have had babies. We don't need to see into the delivery room and your stomach all out. I am, maybe, I am a bit conservative. So some photos are inappropriate, but again, I guess they feel very free.' She has clear ideas of her own netiquette, for example, only adding as friends those people she actually knows or has known. Within the church she notes that some of her friends 'are like very paranoid, so they would email me directly'. By contrast, there are people so unconcerned with what they post they make absurd mistakes.

Through her work, Camille is part of a much wider network than just the church itself and is thereby exposed to all sorts of Facebook usage. 'If you are skipping off from work, don't go on Facebook to say that you are on the beach, or take a mobile photo and upload it straight to Facebook. That's just not wise.' For example, she took aside one friend 'and I told her I saw you drunk on Facebook. It was Carnival time she was drinking, and you saw whoever was with her or around her. You saw the full progression, the full degeneration, from sobriety to drunkenness.' The important point that emerged from this case was that it was a friend of hers who was not on Facebook and had been clear that she didn't want to be on Facebook. But as Camille pointed out to her, 'You know, maybe being on Facebook is safer than not being on Facebook. At least that way she would be aware that such postings have taken place and could take steps to untag such photos, or impose appropriate privacy settings.' As Camille sees it, given that there is nothing to stop other people putting you on

Facebook, the idea that you retain privacy by keeping away from it is an illusion – at least in a place as public and as fixated with Facebook as Trinidad. For her, it is better to simply be present and use it sensibly. She prefers to see it primarily as a technology of efficiency:

> 'What Facebook has allowed me to do is keep in touch with my friends in a faster way. It takes up less time, because everybody is all consolidated in one group. I can just click on your name and like "Oh, I haven't heard from Sandra in a while I wonder what she is up to." I go to her page. I see that she is away now or she is at some conference, something like that.'

There are, however, some irritations with the consequences of Facebook that affect her personally. However positive she feels about Facebook's ability to update her on relationships, she would like to keep this under her own control. The problem is that she already spends as much time as she can on Facebook, given the demands of her work, parenting and the church. Her mother, by contrast, recently retired and has far more time on her hands than Camille – perhaps too much. Her mother was always one to feel that a ten-minute phone call was a kind of personal insult; it had to be the full hour. Once she had taken to Facebook, she saw no limits to its apparent propensity to proliferate networks. It seemed quite natural to her mother to friend Camille. Then she started to see the postings of Camille's friends. She then friended Camille's friends and started to get involved in messages and comments on their sites. Camille's mother thought this was a positive thing to do. But . . . for her daughter . . . it *wasn't*. These were Camille's friends, who could sometimes find it more than a bit weird that Camille's mother has interpolated herself in precisely the networking where previously her daughter had been. That now, when they met, it was more likely to be Camille's mother telling her daughter what her daughter's friends were up to than the other way around. Even if Camille was busier and less able to know of some interesting connection, still this didn't make it right for a mother to thereby usurp the communications of her daughter.

Another problem was the impact of Facebook on clothing. It has tended to be a tradition in Trinidad, one for which surprisingly there are references even back to the time of slavery, for women to be concerned to wear new clothes for all special occasions. Until recently, it was possible to at least get some wear from an outfit. But with Facebook:

> 'And I was like Oh My God ... now I am feeling bad to wear this dress again. It's like "Oh, didn't you wear that to so and so's wedding 6 months ago?" What I used to do is juggle the different events. For example, a schoolfriend getting married, as opposed to a cousin getting married. Two different crowds, maybe there's a bit of an overlap, but by and large two separate crowds. I'll wear the same clothes. Now I am on Facebook, even if I don't put up photos of the wedding, other people are putting up photos of me at the wedding. So I don't want everybody seeing what I wore, and making comments, and sending me personal messages – where did I buy my clothes?'

If you look through the Facebook pages of members of the church, you find that weddings really can dominate the visual side of an individual's online presence. This is a reflection of the community itself. If there is one event for which Camille will try and find the resources to actually fly to London to attend in person, it is a wedding. After all, these are people she shares services with every Sunday, and often there is strong encouragement to marry within the church. So weddings are central to the self-representation of the church as a community. There may be endless comment on who wore what at a wedding, but this is testimony to the larger role of such photos as a means of catching up with the news about the individuals who make up the church community. Following the weddings, Facebook updates you with who becomes pregnant, how the birth went, how the kids are getting on at school. When there is a new photo posting, it prompts comments on how they have grown up, how they look just like their father, the same comments that are made when you actually see people at a wedding, at one level banal and predictable, but at another the glue of communities. And if this includes the odd negative comment on what people are wearing, one has only to read English novels of the eighteenth and nineteenth centuries to appreciate that this was even then as integral to attendance at church as singing hymns. Indeed, Camille suggests that conversation when people actually meet is more likely to be of deeper intent and interest precisely because a lot of this 'oohing and aahing' about babies and children and clothing is now done through comments on Facebook photographs.

Camille, in common with Michael and pretty much all the members of this church, is very conscious that they have a closer relationship to media than most churches and that they explicitly discuss the theological aspect of this usage. As she puts it:

'We do believe that the introduction of the internet does facilitate a great dimension of the purposes of God, in terms of achieving connectivity. I mean, the benefits of the internet are basically limitless. That's how we feel, and I was speaking very emphatically in terms of the opinion of my church organization. We feel that it has been an instrument that has been introduced into the reality of human life that can be used as a basis for connecting people all across the globe. Because if it wasn't for the internet, we wouldn't have embassies, we wouldn't be able to be aware of things outside again. Everything that is introduced is obviously used for, dare I say it, good and bad. For me, I feel that it is a very strategic tool and we honour the "strategicness" of that tool, if you wanna call it that, by actually representing one of our sectors as global communications technology. We are not a normal church.'

In several respects, the different relationship to Facebook of Michael and Camille reflects wider gender distinctions in Trinidad. Michael identified closely with the more geeky aspects of technology but didn't feel as comfortable with the gossipy social trivia of Facebook. Camille, by contrast, happily embraced Facebook as an ideal site for collating wedding pictures and engaging in family and community chit-chat, with all its drawbacks. But as members of an Apostolic church, both felt the need to contend explicitly with the bigger relationship which was between the technology and the church itself. Facebook, along with all new technologies, is first and foremost an instrument given at this time and place to humanity by God. And they must never forget their responsibility to interpret that gift and understand its bigger import which could be to serve their community, but ultimately the internet in general and Facebook in particular would help them become the vanguard of the greatest social network of all: the Global Borderless Kingdom Community whose centre is their church.

9

It Was Just Sex

It might not be intuitively obvious that one of the best ways of trying to convey an understanding of Trinidad is through writing a paper about an imported US soap opera called *The Young and the Restless*. Yet this had unexpectedly become by far the most popular of the many imported soap operas and it seemed important to try and find out why. If one asked a Trinidadian to summarize their country in one word, the most common response was the term 'bacchanal'. The word evokes the values celebrated in Carnival; that is, the general heightening of excitement, disorder and expressive sexuality. But, as noted in Alana's portrait, perhaps the most significant moment in Carnival comes in the ritual of *Jouvert*. This is not the much more celebrated *pretty mas,* when Trinidadians parade for hours in their costumes, dancing through the streets. Alana's point was that it is the devils and placards of *Jouvert,* exposed by the dawn, that illustrate the Trinidadian concept of revelation. The ritual expresses the idea that people reveal themselves in the first light as the 'truth' by their satirical exposure of the pretensions of established order.

The first synonym for bacchanal is clearly 'scandal', with calypso lyrics such as 'Bacchanal Woman, sweet scandal where she walks', or 'We people like scandal. We people like Bacchanal.' Scandal again implies the bringing into light of that which others want to remain hidden. Bacchanal also connotes confusion, disorder and wildness. The two ideas are linked by the term *commess,* which is a local word for the confusion and disorder created by scandal. In my first experience of Carnival in 1988, a key masquerade figure was that of Bacchanal Woman who illustrated a calypso with that title, composed by David Rudder. This was a woman with exaggerated breasts and buttocks, but above her, in fan-like arrays, rather like a peacock, were rows and rows of open eyes. These are the prying eyes that create scandal and hence 'bacchanal'. Her figure represents the wanton ways of the kind of woman who succeeds in this mission by flaunting her sexuality.

The popularity of the *The Young and the Restless* made sense in this context. Trinidad is an extraordinarily dynamic society. The 1970s oil boom gave a tremendous impetus to the growth of the middle class, to the extent that they emerged at its peak dominant both numerically and culturally. With the recession, however, many of the more fragile pretensions of the nouveau element within this class were becoming exposed. There is a continual discourse about the financial plight that exists behind the closed doors of the home, only brought to light by events such as the disconnection of the phone because of unpaid bills. Even in the suburban community which formed part of my fieldwork, there were frequent rumours about how many properties were back in the hands of the banks or deserted by migrants to Canada. It was a period of revelation. But in the Trinidadian conception of bacchanal, its most important and common manifestation is sex, as when a prim and proper but unmarried schoolteacher is suddenly found to be pregnant.

Although the people who made *The Young and the Restless* may never have heard of Trinidad, the most common theme in their programme were stories based on individuals whose particular ambitions were devastated because they couldn't help themselves when it came to the temptations of sex.

In Trinidad, this has still deeper roots. In older times, the word 'sex' was also often synonymous with that of nature and the natural, following the presumption that sex represents the truth of human nature, what we really are. The assumption is that people try and build their reputations in life and also their facades but this is disrupted by sex as human nature which brings us back to our own biological selves. So Carnival represents a highly ambivalent attitude to bacchanal. In many respects, it celebrates this disorder and destruction as positive. It is a force that reflects the basically egalitarian ideal of Trinidadian society, that in the end we are all just human beings who will eventually be brought down to the same level of truth and nature. Bacchanal, from the viewers' perspective, is almost always fun. Attitudes to a large degree correlate with class. People in the very impoverished districts included in the research who had no right to own land tended to see the positive side of bacchanal and were usually hoping for more of it. By contrast, the middle class was more fearful of its powers of destruction and the way bacchanal disrupted serious and moral endeavours, including the political and economic development of Trinidad itself.

I will explore this further in the final, more academic, section at the end of this volume. But the concept of bacchanal is also closely linked to the Trinidadian conception of Facebook itself as *Fasbook* or *Macobook*. These are two terms that imply an insatiable nosiness about what other people are 'really' doing. Like *The Young and the Restless*, Facebook may have been invented in the US by people who were unfamiliar with Trinidad but they have inadvertently created something that goes to the heart of what it means to be Trini. So it is critical to the representation of Facebook in Trinidad that, whatever else it does, it must also manifest its capacity to create bacchanal and confusion. Ideally, this should be through the public exposure of something related to sexual activity.

Fortunately for this aspect of Trinidadian cosmology, but unfortunately for the hapless victim herself, by the end of 2010 everyone had to hand an ideal example of Facebook's relationship to bacchanal. This was the release onto the internet of the private sex video of Josanne. Josanne was not just anyone. She had, up to that moment, represented another ideal, the pure unsullied beauty which Trinidad also prides itself on. Josanne was the lead singer for a major band and it wasn't just her voice. Josanne was *hot*; she was known as Miss Pepper Sauce to an island that considered it had some of the spiciest women in the world. Trinidadian culture often revolves around wit and innuendo, but also works through clothes and the body to achieve an ideal of not merely looking good but, specifically, sexy. These aspirations were enshrined in the culture of Carnival itself, in which almost everyone who doesn't directly participate at least cheers from the sidelines when someone this good looking saunters or dances past.

This level of support is very evident on Facebook itself. Mostly, the discussion is of her music, but one of the photo albums on her

Facebook site includes the following comments: 'Josanne!!! you really showing the world the Trini beauty . . . you stand out so much in these photos it isnt even funny!!!!'; 'Josanne . . . your skin is amazing . . . that Caribbean bronze . . .!'

But at the end of 2009 this unequivocal celebration had turned into a quintessential case of bacchanal. Josanne had made a private sex tape involving two other members of her band. There are various stories circulating as to how this was released into the public domain. Most common is the report that she had taken her laptop in for repair and one of the technicians at the repair shop had spotted it and released the video. Less common was the suggestion that the man on the tape wanted the world to see him having sex with two beautiful women. The tape itself didn't appear on Facebook, but knowledge about it did, and it was soon downloadable from many internet sites.

Facebook was not the only medium by which news of this tape was disseminated. In fact, the role of Facebook varied considerably. Some of the people from older or more established social circles could not recall anyone mentioning it at all in their Facebook circles. More typical was the memory 'Oh, that is how it spread. It's like I was just getting all these messages and I was totally clueless, but not messages directed at me but the general post. It went out to everyone.' Facebook proved an extremely effective way of rapidly sharing and commenting upon the release. For young men, the clever/funny response was immediately to sign up as a fan of Josanne's Facebook site. The tape itself was most commonly obtained from YouTube.

Something several people noted was that the new media, such as Facebook, seemed to capture the moment of its release. By comparison, the old media, such as the newspapers, took some days to enter into this fray and actually pay attention. This is ironic since many of the weekly papers have names such as *The Heat*, *The Blast*, *The Bomb* and *The Punch* and are dedicated followers of bacchanal. Mostly, they have to cultivate or exaggerate it, but when something so fully redolent of bacchanal actually came onto the scene, they almost didn't know how to cope, leaving the field clear for new media: YouTube, mobile phones, emails and Facebook.

Trinidadians, as many peoples in the world, make a firm distinction between implying sex and its actual presence. So much of

Trinidadian culture consists of double entendre that it is almost impossible to talk about anything without people assuming there is another layer to what is being said. That other layer will always be sex. Yet the official line is very much against pornography itself. As in Brazil and elsewhere, you can turn up at Carnival in a costume that is essentially a thong and tassels, but you can't sunbathe topless on the beach. This makes it very unclear as to how to respond to a videotape that is not about sex, or hinting at sex, but consists entirely of the act of having sex.

The recording itself is pretty much exactly what might be expected of a privately made sex tape in that it includes oral, anal, and lesbian sex and a few positions which demonstrate that Josanne is pretty lithe. This is quite obviously a sex tape, and as such it parodies and copies several elements of what would be called hardcore pornography. And yet it is also very different from the commercial versions. It's not as if they are taking their sex overly seriously, or fully acting out their roles. They are having various kinds of sex, but the general atmosphere is more one of young people enjoying themselves, not just playing to the camera, but just simply playing. They are having some fun with sex partly through the presence of the camera. If anything, the tape reminds me a bit of those animal programmes when the young offspring start playing at having sex. It's not that sex isn't potentially serious; mostly it is. Sex can be the climax of high passion, the reason people in some regions get stoned to death, and is the essential ingredient for procreation. But in this case there seems to be nothing much at stake. The man is wearing a condom, they are not going to get sexually transmitted diseases, or pregnant. They are not having an affair. They are not serious even about how good the sex is or over-simulating the sounds of passion and orgasm that would be found in actual pornography. Actually they are simply fooling around. If sex could ever be described as a harmful bit of fun, then this is it. This isn't going to convince anyone of their depth or their maturity but then this is not philosophy, just sex.

The very first academic paper I ever published about Trinidad[1] was on the topic of the dance *wining* and the role of sex and exchange in Trinidadian society. The aim was not to highlight

---

[1] Miller, D. (1991), 'Absolute Freedom in Trinidad'. *Man*: 26: 323–41.

sex but simply to include it within ethnographic reportage to the extent that it seems significant in this context. Sex needs a far more prominent place in writing about Trinidad rather than, say, Britain, simply because it is far more important to all other aspects of Trinidadian life. Some years ago, I was researching a book about business in Trinidad. I was trying to understand why one company's products occupied more shelf space than those of other companies. The woman in the store looked at me as though as I was an idiot because I didn't presume that the explanation lay in what she assumed was the sexual relationship between the suppliers and the stockists.

So a primary example of bacchanal, based on the unintended exposure of a sexual event, is central to understanding the nature of Facebook in Trinidad. As my research on Facebook progressed, it became clear that this was by no means an isolated incident. Many informants could give examples, at a lesser celebrity level, of such inadvertent exposures of sexually explicit material. There were interviews about a girls' school in the south, and material passed via mobile phones. But several people also discussed such episodes with respect to someone they actually knew, a brother's ex-girlfriend and such like.

In terms of how people responded to this exposure, it was also noticeable that, for many of the younger or less educated informants, the issue of morality was not mentioned at all. In keeping with these generalizations about Trinidad, all many of them seemed concerned about was assessing the quality of the sex itself. 'That gyal real gud, she real know she stuff' was one of the more positive comments. More negative was 'Just her performance, it wasn't good, it wasn't all that great, the guy must have been really lucky because there were 2 chicks.' 'I think any Trinidadian – the main comment would be was she any good?' There was also a smattering of 'bitchy' comments, such as 'She showed she was going for the best singer in Trinidad. She have a better career being a porn star.' So, for many Trinidadians, the public embarrassment was based on the idea that a tape might exist in the public domain in which the sex wasn't very impressive. Younger people are rarely that bothered about the mere existence of online sexually explicit material. As far as they are concerned, a key point about the internet is that porn is free. So only a fool would fail to capitalize on that 'freeness'. From that point of view, Josanne's tape is merely integrated into a growing body of sexually explicit material which is primarily viewed as entertainment and a resource.

Others focused on the link between the two public personas that Josanne now possessed. They implied that things were rather different in her case than for any other individual. As a singer who was known for wearing raunchy costumes on stage, so much of Josanne's body was already in the public domain as a singer that a sex tape which included her fully naked was much less of a stretch than would be the case for another person. But this was a rare view. As soon as discussion moved from the sex itself to the wider morality and issues involved, the dominant popular view was both more liberal and more sympathetic. One man commented that

'I was feeling frustrated because a lot of people I thought were being hypocritical about things, and they were trashing her, and I was like "you need to shut up." My mom was deeply distressed about it, the embarrassment. I disagreed – I thought it was embarrassing but I wasn't pointing fingers. Like it was a mixture of awe and distaste . . . when I saw it, the more I realized among my age we don't really care that much because when I spoke to friends they were like "what? Everybody makes videos. It's just that not everybody has them leaked all over the internet." '

This echoes a much more general concern with the impact of the tape that arose simply because, in social terms, Trinidad is such a small place. If they didn't know Josanne herself, they knew her family or her schoolteacher or close friend or some person that was connected with her. In general, they felt for her, and felt that this was an injury that would never entirely heal: 'people were saying she might have to go and live abroad as a result of it and so on.' On the other hand, the bacchanal was also linked to her celebrity status. After all, one could equally have said that Josanne will always be known as one of the top singers from one of the top bands in Trinidad. Her achievements brand her for life as much as the catastrophe of the tape.

This ambivalence remains clear on Facebook itself. If one looks at Josanne's Facebook page, one of the key ambiguities becomes immediately obvious. Although she clearly had no desire to be the subject of a sex tape, the portrait photo remains that of a raunchy singer. In her tight black hotpants, there is no doubt at all that the picture is intended to have an erotic edge. The idea and ideal of looking raunchy is integral to that of being a lead singer in this kind of band. The comments on the photos are revealing; mostly, they are expression of support such as 'You look beautiful!!! Great to see you're back!!! I'm sure what you're dealing with has to be tough . . . , but keep your head up sweetie – this too shall pass!!! Stay positive!!!'; or 'We're all so very proud of you Josanne!!! Yaaay'; or 'Good pic girl we know how life can be keep ur head up and be that star we all know'; or 'This is one hot chick. All who want to talk cant do better.' While one comment says 'People stil talkin bout that video? hmmm they bored', it is followed by another that says 'But what happen to you Joel boy? You really had to mention that. Oh gorsh, you so yesterday.' In fact, an earlier comment noted that they hoped her children never see the videos. 'Something private gone wrong. Very wrong. We all have our "secret things" that we do. Lets just wish Josanne the best :).'

This site shows the quite extraordinary nature of Facebook. For all this bacchanal around the private being exposed to the public, it is on Facebook itself, that most public of domains, that we still find open debate about this same topic. Directed largely at trying to overcome and transcend the very same issue that this public conversation simultaneously represents, I am caught in the same paradox. I never did interview Josanne but she is a person I could well have met on any number of occasions. She is a friend of several of my friends. In an entirely different context, I heard about the death of her cousin. She therefore encapsulates a key problem that is also central to Facebook in Trinidad. People most certainly desire bacchanal and hugely enjoy it. But Trinidad is such a small place that the victims of scandal are commonly people one either knows directly or could know.

So, in considering the consequences of Facebook in its capacity to generate bacchanal, we perhaps need to start from another position entirely, that is, our own sense of empathy. For that purpose, you need to read this, take a deep breath and imagine that your parents or, if you are of a different generation, your children made for themselves a private sex tape. Your family may be, as people say of Josanne's, very private so that, far from courting bacchanal, they loathe the idea of being snared in its web. Depending on your beliefs, you may or may not blame your parent/child. You may think there is nothing wrong with using video as part of enjoying sex, and this disaster has struck your family arbitrarily, rather like a plague. Or you may feel your parent/child has done something that is immoral and regrettable in their personal behaviour. No one was hurt in making this tape; many people were greatly hurt by its exposure. So, at least for a liberal ethics based on avoidance of harm, the problem is its dissemination, not its production.

We have established the way such an event encapsulates an understanding of certain core Trinidadian ideas about truth and revelation and sex as human nature. But what we have not yet done is put the person herself back into context, to help bring her away from this moment of objectification as a figure having sex to an appreciation that she could have been our parent or our child who, at this moment in time, needs most of all to push this incident into the background and regain her self-respect and the respect of others for everything else that she is.

So we need to start again with Josanne to find some other point of articulation between her and Facebook that can shock us out of this too singular focus. Sadly, this is only too easily done. On Facebook there remains evidence of quite another tragic relationship between the person and the medium. This is the Facebook site devoted to the memory of her cousin Darren who died in a car crash a few months before the sex tape debacle. As it happened on this research trip, I came to know the partner of one of the other victims who was driving the car Darren crashed into. The site has 1,255 members, 119 photos and two videos.

Mostly this is a site created by friends of these friends. Typical of the postings would be 'Darren . . . my main man lol back in the dayz . . . grade 9 wow . . . it seems like yesterday i remember we took this one picture one day we skipped class and of course u were smiling in it i wish i can find . . .'. Or:

'Darren boy . . . yesterday was so weird in class without ya, but we all reminised on u. We thought that the type of classes we had yesterday were definetly what u wud have liked an we all hoped u were there with is enjoying it. Alot of people shed tears 4 u boy! Is hard boy, rell hard, but you kno, my mom pointed this out. U, Brent an JST were able to be together till the end. When you look at it like that, it makes things a little easier knowing that u were with ur friends an u enjoyed ur time here :) Missin u lots boy an cum to class today!:P Take care of ur family . . . im sure they need you now, C u one day Darren . . . take it easy! Xoxox'

After hundreds of personal postings, the site itself takes on its own significance, as another posting shows:

> 'WOW the support on FACebook . . . ius CRAZY good dred . . . its soo overwealming how one accident can affect soo much ppl . . . wow . . . for all those showing the support for ALL the families... Darren...i want to send out my utmost thank you . . . it means soo much! . . . and i only pray that you shower us with yer bles . . .'

> 'i spoke to my gramps today and he told me how he had seen the group and it was really amazing and that he really appreciated it. he wants to thank every1 for their support. Missing you boys RIP♥'

Facebook here bears witness to grief, to the catharsis of being able to express that grief to a public, but also to share it. It seems testimony to the way death, as a moment of loss, can also bring people together in an expression of common humanity, a form of repair and restoration that social scientists would immediately associate with the writings of Emile Durkheim. And Facebook does this not merely by repeating earlier modes of grieving in an act of 'remediation'. The ad hoc spelling of these postings, their lack of grammar, their mixture of grief and informality, give the site an authenticity in a way that makes the act of grief feel very immediate. The very lack of organization on the site contrasts with more established and conservative forms of ritualized grieving and somehow makes this whole process feel once again more authentic and sincere. It shows a quite different potential to Facebook than that associated with everyday trivial exchanges.

We do not, however, find Josanne herself on this site. As was found in the portrait 'Avatar' (see chapter 6), the degree to which people are exposed in the public domain tells you little about their relationship to the sense of being private. As it happens, Josanne's family, like many families, clearly care about and protect their own privacy and their desire for a more modest, self-contained world of intimacy that is not shared. They have quite different reputations, for example, for their involvement in charity. While they may have fully appreciated and felt consoled by this public outpouring of grief, it was not their natural mode for expressing what must have been their most innermost suffering at the loss of someone so loved. It is only through this event that one comes to realize how the public side of Josanne is essentially what we think of as a 'stage persona', something required by the expectations people have of a band, and no reflection at all on Josanne as a person. Once again, Facebook was not an instrument for Josanne's self-expression but rather a structure of public exposure and debate based on what for her personally can only have been the most awful and tragic blow of fate.

This concern for privacy was central to Josanne's response to the revelations of her own most private life. Up to now, she has refused every request for an interview or public statement on what happened. Her friends confirm that this is because she feels this would only give ammunition to what she took to be a cynical exploitation of herself for the purpose of bacchanal – this would surely be correct. The downside of this response, however, is that by the time of my encounter with her story, her persona could be so completely reduced to the single instance of that bacchanal.

Yet it is more than just coincidence that Josanne confronts these two entirely different facets of Facebook. Bacchanal is central to the meaning of being a Trinidadian, but it is certainly not the whole thing. There is just as much within the island devoted to that which bacchanal brings down, the patient construction of serious concerns and reputations. There is a huge desire to build a country which respects the lessons of its own history and looks to the future. There is a constant tension between the orientation to the present represented by Carnival and the desire to look to time in terms of past and future that dominates the rest of the year; the concern to lay down the kind of long-term inscription that is represented in this act of memorialization. These are the two sides of the coin of Trinidad, and one cannot understand this island without appreciating the importance of both. So the response to the death of Josanne's cousin says just as much about character-istically Trinidadian uses of Facebook as does the response to her sex tape.

Josanne still also maintains a personal site on Facebook. The site was started in June 2008 and is clearly part of the band's com-mercial profile. She posts several thanks to the band's promoters. There is also a disclaimer: 'This Facebook page is dedicated to the FANS of Josanne. This Wall is not a discussion board. Admins of this page reserve the right to remove any posts, including those that are profane or defamatory in nature.' It has 1,268 friends. The two most recent postings are 'is sending love and prayer to haiti' and, before that, a posting for New Year: 'Thanks everyone for their love and support in 2009 and wishes you and your family all the best in 2010! Happy New Year.'

But even this site doesn't really give a sense of Josanne as a person. It is clearly a campaign site controlled by others. There is evidence that it was developed by those responsible for marketing her band. The one place where Josanne does not appear simply as the face of Trinidad or the victim of tragedy, the one place where she seems present as the agent of her own creativity and intent, is the site devoted entirely to the music itself. This introduces another person entirely: 'Josanne is the newest singer to hit the Caribbean scene. Her album, *Darren*, was launched in June 2009 in Trinidad and Tobago where it received rave reviews and has been making waves throughout the region ever since.' She has a versatile background as a singer, pianist and composer. Clearly, her album is named after her late cousin. The MP3s on her site introduce us to what, to this untrained ear, looks like a blend of ragga and pop, a cross between one of my favourite Trini bands, 3canal, and one of my favourite singers, Ataklan. Given the way Facebook is developing in Trinidad today, it is likely to be quite central to the commercial success of her music. Rumour has it that the Facebook site has already played a major part in helping to sell the album.

A friend suggested that maybe the best thing Josanne could have done would have been to take to the streets at Carnival, that festival of sex, wearing a T-shirt with the slogan, 'Hey it was just sex', because it was – just sex. That would have been a classic Trini response but, to be honest, much easier said than done. There is no doubt that Josanne is marked for life in that she will always be the person who appeared in that sex tape, just as she will always be known for having been the lead singer in her band. What we cannot say is whether, as time passes, the former will fully heal or remain as something more like a scar or disfigurement. There is a decent chance that in the longer term it is her own creativity, expressed through her music, which will become the more signifi-cant expression of her abilities, very possibly through Facebook-led success.

10

It's Who You Know

Mirca and I are sitting in a modern office, in a modern office block, in a modern area of the capital Port of Spain. The office is all white walls, the block is all glass and concrete and the district is all rectangles bisected by endless traffic. We were late, Burton was even later. But, as Burton noted, if people in England talk endlessly about the weather, in Trinidad the supplier of infinite conversation is traffic. Should you come into Port of Spain via the highway and risk a log jam? Should you come in over the Lady Young Road, a much pleasanter view but a rather circuitous route to the centre? Then, if you get into Port of Spain, will you ever get out again? Rush hour starts at around 3.30 p.m. after which time you are 'bound' to be delayed by a good three hours. So take a book, a packed meal, a friend, or a pillow. Then there is the unresolved question of how to get away from Port of Spain late at night. The highway passes the notorious Beetham Estate, which is said to have regular lookouts who will pilfer any car that breaks down at that point and possibly murder the occupants. On the other hand, the Lady Young is only one lane, and your keen murderer might prefer to place a block in that road at night.

I didn't take all this stuff about being stuck endlessly in traffic too seriously, at least until I got to watch my student Simone, while we were still very much in motion, take both hands off the wheel, shift the rear-view mirror relative to her face and then take out some tweezers for plucking her eyebrows. Clearly, this came more from habit than simply a desire to terrify her passengers, Mirca and myself. But then it was Simone's savoir-faire that saved us on that same night. Mirca and I were driving back after midnight from the south. I had actually noticed a little thing on the dashboard light up and vaguely wondered what a watering can was doing there. Had I remembered to water the plants in Simone's apartment that morning? She was convinced a mere day's drought would be the end of them. Anyway, apparently being out of oil is a big deal. The car ground to a noisy halt and I just about directed it to the edge of the highway. The one thing you were never supposed to do in a country with over 500 murders in the last year, amongst the highest per capita in the world,[1] was to break down on the highway. We tried to remember how one was expected to respond to such a crisis. Should we put the hazard lights on? That might attract attention. Should we rock the car gently to make it seem like we were making out? That would probably attract a lot more attention. Later, we were told we should have left the car altogether and hidden in the bushes, since at least then, if someone had come, they would have got the car but not us. What we did was ring Simone.

Delighted at being woken up so late, Simone quickly informed us that, from our description, we had broken down next to the Caroni Swamp which, she pointed out, is the favourite stop on the whole island for the dumping of bodies. She was impressed at the consideration we had thereby shown for our soon-to-be-apparent murderers. She did, however, get dressed and employ her amazing speed as a driver to find us as fast as she possibly could. Once she had safely brought us home, she phoned up the garage to pick up the car. Even though it was the early hours of the morning, it was essential to recover the vehicle before it was found and wrecked. Then Simone, who hails from Guyana, taught me more about the eloquence of Caribbean cussing in the next hour and a half than I had learnt in the previous twenty years. I was left wondering what more abuse I could possibly have suffered if Simone hadn't, as she noted, felt constrained by virtue of her being my PhD student. Actually it could have been worse. A few days later, the garage informed Simone that they would no longer rent

---

[1] Hopefully a temporary aberration, for most of the time I have worked in Trinidad the island had been exceptionally safe.

her any car at all since she had allowed it to be driven by an imbecile. I kept out of her way for quite a while. Otherwise, the torrent of abuse might have matched one of the most poetic phrases I ever heard in Trinidad. A few days earler, I had been listening to a conversation between a friend and a market trader who had been declaiming on a conflict that had taken place in the market. At one point, she remarked about a rival, 'I washed his arse with cuss.'

Still, we had lived to interview another day, and here in front of us was our current participant, Burton. After the various pleasantries about traffic and being late, we got down to business. Burton looked like someone who would drive safely and sensibly and accept traffic delays with good grace. In his late thirties, the child of parents who also worked in business, he was almost bound to take his tertiary education in North America, where he stayed for over a decade. But, unlike most of his peers, he then decided to return to Trinidad, marry, settle down and accept a lower salary than he could have commanded abroad. This was the reason we had regaled him with our tales of highway breakdowns. It wasn't just because we wanted advice on the best road to take home. We were also interested to know why, given all these issues with traffic and violence, he had bucked the trend and come back home. Burton clearly felt, as did we, that there had been too much dwelling on the negatives and that local people were forgetting the extraordinarily positive side to Trinidadian life that was obvious to us as visitors. Above all, he valued in compensation something we couldn't share, a feeling that he was thereby contributing to a place he could personally identify with, the place where he had had a happy childhood, that he hoped would provide the same for his own family.

You felt Burton was a better businessman because he was first and foremost a family man and a Trini. He had in fact achieved a high management position, most likely because he seemed to be the sort of person who would quickly slough off any constricting models learnt at business school and replace these with an affable personal style that was trusted by clients. He had that ability to gain wisdom from experience when it came to the balance between risk and opportunity. He was the sort of person I would have wanted to do business with in the unlikely event that I should ever have any business to do.

Burton had a long digital history, given that he was playing with an Apple II when he was 10 years old. Although he is still young, you are not surprised that he has certain old-fashioned values which turn out to extend to the orthography of internet communication. He will still check grammar and correct spellings, even on Facebook, and would rather emails were more like letters. But this slightly pedantic streak does not detract from his sense of the human side to Facebook. First and foremost, he wants Facebook simply as an instrument of friendship and concern for others. He finds people interesting and wants to keep close to them. So Facebook starts as 'a portal into friends' lives'. He looks with genuine interest at the photos of his cousin's children. His office is lined with photos of his own children. He is of an age where most of his friends and cousins are having children or their children are growing up. As a devoted parent himself, he is fascinated by the minutiae that would quickly bore others. He appreciates that he is thereby also gaining tips on how other parents treat and relate to their children and how they represent their children to the world. Rather than having to bother people, he can just catch up on their news and development by scanning their Facebook sites. He doesn't feel pressured to comment, or to resist commenting. If he has something to say about a photo or posting, he will just say it. He reckons he spends between half an hour to an hour a day on Facebook, which strikes him as reasonable and sensible. It remains something he uses rather than it using him. His ideal Facebook is matter of fact.

In practice, this is never quite the case, mainly because his usage is under constant scrutiny from his wife. She disapproves of him retaining friends on his site that he doesn't really know. She thinks Facebook is something that should be constantly pruned like a rose. She knows that he is rather vague about people on the periphery of his social life. To be honest, quite often he can't remember whether he has met such people or not or what he is supposed to know about them. Facebook is an absolute blessing in such cases. He can do some quick research when he is going out on some social occasion and appear to be well informed about someone he would otherwise have completely forgotten having met. These days, quite a few people act as though their true brain – in the sense of remembering what they are supposed to do and when – exists only on hard disc. But his wife thinks there are things a person should remember for themselves without this digital crutch to lean on.

About 70% of his Facebook friends are friends and 25% are relatives. That leaves 5% colleagues, and it's those 5% that trouble him. The more difficult side to Facebook use is the business aspect. He originally joined the site when invited to do so by a particularly important client whom he felt he couldn't really refuse. Given the choice, he would prefer to keep Facebook separate from his work. But Trinidad is the kind of place where such boundaries are completely blurred. His personal style turns many colleagues into friends and a lot of business is done over meals and in people's homes. But there is more to it. The problem starts with the way Facebook appears as an entirely apt instrument for the way business operates in this country, which, long before Facebook was invented, was in essence already a form of networking.

This seems evident in the typical behaviour of his colleagues. He suggests that whenever they meet someone new, they have two main questions in their minds: where are they from and, given their last name, who are they connected to? A Trinidadian never meets another Trini as an individual; they always see them as a node within this larger network. Whether you take them seriously or not is going to depend much more on what you know about their family or the group you think they might be part of, than anything about them as an individual personality. He gives an example. Yesterday he went to a meeting and was talking to a banker. The banker confessed that there was no way he would have come to that meeting based on the quality of the investment proposal itself, which he didn't take too seriously. Still, he had dressed nicely and come along, since he recognized the names of three people who were listed as likely to be present. He simply knew that these were not names that would be associated with anything that was rubbish. So he was intrigued – were they slipping or what was it he didn't know? As it happens, it was simply that this proposal was in its infancy and they perceived a potential that had a long way to go, but might amount to something.

But that's how things are. If a person has connections with one of the more powerful families, such as Elias or Sabga, or if they are connected to a minister in the government, then it may not matter too much if they are not overly effective as individuals. They could still be a vital link to someone who has the power to make or break a proposal. These networks are often deeply ingrained in Trinidadian society. They are inseparable from class and ethnicity. There are so many groups in Trinidad – Chinese, French Creole, Portuguese, Syrian – each with certain core families, influential for generations. If you look at the board of directors of a Trinidadian company, you will already know some of the names that are going to be there: Fernandez, De Verteuil, Aboud. The safest form of capital is not an asset, such as stocks or cash flow: it is a name.

And this was one of the problems of Facebook. The first thing a Trini looks at when they see an invitation to be a friend is not the information about that person, but the list of that potential friend's friends. How many and which significant people are they associated with? But what Burton knows well, but so many others seem not to, is that Facebook is a pretty spurious way of getting a sense of who someone actually is. In many ways, this social network is not in the least effective when it comes to business social networking because it is so easy to add someone, and many Trinidadians remain fairly relaxed about accepting several hundred friend requests. If you want to amass a reasonable looking portfolio of Facebook friends, it's not hard to do so. He has watched individuals who had the knack of managing the kind of viral spread that Facebook allows. 'This guy was friends with a friend of mine. Next thing is he becomes my friend. Next thing I find he is in conversation with someone he finds out about through their being my friend and then becomes that person's friend, and I can see I am just a stepping post to other things. Who knows where he ended up?'

Generally, once people see you have common friends, they can be quite relaxed about friending you, especially since Facebook allows you to comment on the site of a friend of a friend. Then they feel they sort of know you already. Similarly, Burton knows full well that if a man wants to impress other people, even in terms of business, then being associated with a whole lot of good-looking women gives them a kind of aura of success and confidence not so far removed from being associated with a whole lot of money. But if another person tries to interpret your Facebook site in a more traditional manner, they would probably draw quite the wrong conclusions. Facebook friending is like over-inflated money: its quantity has suppressed its value as quality.

Burton had had a good sense of this even before Facebook.

Returning home from his ten years in Canada, he was half shocked and half charmed at people in Trinidad who would come up to him and state that their name was so and so and that, although they don't know him, a third person had told them he was a good person to know. So they would like to propose . . . This guileless approach to business networking seemed quite refreshing. Burton has even less of a problem with Facebook being used in what he would consider a straightforwardly utilitarian manner. Facebook as simply a tool of business was something else that was obviously spreading fast in Trinidad. There was the example of his own nephew setting up a music studio. His nephew's Facebook profile has in essence become his work profile, a place where people can see all the details of his studio and what it has to offer. The site is constantly being updated with videos and music clips and photographs that in effect advertise his work. He has 2,000 friends but almost all are actually work related. He connects to one group that links various sound engineers and has another group associated with his own studio. Burton is impressed that his nephew has already made real money from Facebook in attracting new clients who are impressed by what they have seen there. In Trinidad, it is Facebook (rather than MySpace) where his nephew finds all the underground and independent music he might be interested in. His nephew has his own version of this overlap between his work and his personal life. There is his video of a protest song about something he deeply cares about, which has garnered many comments. Even more powerful was the song he recorded by a friend in memory of the friend's three-year-old child. Both these songs appear on his Facebook site.

For Burton himself, as for most Trinidadians, there was no problem when Facebook first started to juxtapose various previously differentiated social networks. Most commonly, the first example of this was the mixing of cousins and old school friends. But in Trinidad cousins generally provide a core to an individual's friendship circles. So there seemed a natural mix in the way both these networks stretch across various countries and diasporas. But these were actual relationships and he preferred to see them as other than instrumental. As we have seen, he also doesn't much mind when people have said to his face that they were using him as a business link. But he rather bridles at those other attempts to friend him on Facebook which claim friendship as the grounds but which he quickly surmised were only attempts to cultivate business interests. For all the overlap of dinner parties and cocktail parties with business discussions, he was used to presenting himself in a somewhat different manner at work and at home. He still liked to retain a certain professionalism in his work profile. The proliferation of business and professionally linked clients on his Facebook had led to a certain self-consciousness and self-censorship when it came to his using this site, which was a pity. His natural inclination was to see Facebook as a time to relax and just keep up to date with nephews or nieces, a more playful and bantering engagement. He doesn't like the idea that he now has to worry about some colleague peering over his digital shoulder while he is doing this.

In this context, he was able to turn his slightly pedantic streak to an advantage and, at the same time, meet with the concerns of his wife. His Facebook site is unusually organized. Privacy settings are carefully set and changed to keep things under control. He has albums of his daughter posted, but only accessible to family and perhaps two or three friends. His wife is much more guarded than him. For everyone involved in business in Trinidad, there is a palpable fear of kidnapping. But even apart from such dangers, his wife had always been a rather private person. She really couldn't understand the whole logic of Facebook as a site where one put essentially private and personal information in a place where pretty much anyone could see it. That stuck her as completely contradictory. She clearly disapproved of her husband's tendency to relax into this generous and incautious dispersal of their lives.

The one privacy she did not respect was that of his use of Facebook. She was often present, hovering and concerned when he was online. She would be asking 'Who is that person, how do you know them?' What really annoyed her was when he didn't really know who the person in question was. He had just found something they had said online interesting and was responding out of that interest. As far as she was concerned, to be in conversation with someone one didn't, as she would put it, 'actually' know was just wrong. She too has plenty of friend requests, but almost invariably she ignores them. As Burton notes, 'You are lucky to get on her friends list.' His wife's response might have been a problem, but typically Burton finds a positive side to all this. He feels he knows quite a bit about his wife's past before they met, but he was never as good as her at systematically relating his own stories. Much of her interference is genuine curiosity, a desire to know his friends in order to share his friendships, to not be left out of any aspect of his life because she loves him and feels that anything about him that isn't shared is a kind of lost opportunity for coming closer together. She searches his Facebook as a way of knowing him still better, a means to perfect their relationship rather than spoil it which he in turn recognizes and appreciates.

Burton may feel that Facebook has limited potential as social networking for business but he likes the way it gives rise to knowledge and even a more general sense of truth. He is one of those who feels Facebook has made it more difficult for people to have affairs, since it is so easy to find out about where a person is and who they are with. He can't understand why people present a fake or doctored image of themselves on the one place where everyone who would know it is fake is able to see it. For example, he has a friend who is an actor in the UK but who claims online that he is ten years younger than he actually is. Sure, he may look as young as he claims, but even if this is helping him within his profession, he must be aware that this site is full of his old Trini friends who would know otherwise. And there would always be one or two who would seize the opportunity to out him in public and embarrass him which, of course, is exactly what happened.

It's not just the extent of its reach, but also the rapidity by which news travels via Facebook, that appeals to Burton. Working as he does in business, it helps him feel up to speed on that kind of grey news that isn't quite gossip but tells you what people are thinking about, or what it is believed might be happening, often several days before the newspapers actually confirm it. Facebook has that ability to spread a story through comments within a few minutes. It doesn't really matter whether it is true or not. What it means is that you are up with the 'town talk' that people in business expect you to know about. At the same time, it helped Burton to keep abreast of other information, from sports to more conventional news, which Facebook effectively aggregated as a generic internet portal. Some of his friends who saw themselves as too busy to read newspapers had come to rely on Facebook as a direct source of news. Basically, if something was important enough to be circulating on Facebook, then you knew you needed to check it out in more formal media. If it didn't appear, then it probably wasn't worth your while reading about it anyway. That wasn't Burton's view. He still liked what was now sometimes dismissed as 'old media' but he could see a trend. In fact, in some cases, such as when it came to the antics of Trinidadian politicians, he too was as likely to believe the Facebook line as that of the newspapers.

The advantage of Facebook for Burton was that in the one place you could catch up with this kind of news, as well as all the more personal comings and goings of family and friends. Facebook was starting to become more comprehensive in a manner that rather interested Burton. He was wondering aloud if Facebook wasn't undergoing some sort of shift at this time. Until recently, one of the problems was that Facebook was much better at informing you about good news than bad news. You could be pretty certain that anything like a birthday or a wedding was going to make a real splash on Facebook, with loads of postings and comments. But there was no really established netiquette for dealing with bad news, with death or illness, the exception being relationship breakup, which in Trinidad was like bleeding in front of sharks: within minutes they would be circling, waiting to feast on this new prey. But what about an illness – should you or shouldn't you post?

Burton's sense was that things were changing and that 2009 had been the year for that. Before then, he could barely remember Facebook ever being a site for informing people of bad news. But two instances had occurred over the last year. He had a friend whose father had cancer. It had pretty much been downhill all the way until eventually he died, but throughout the whole ordeal, from diagnosis to death/funeral/wake, every single detail was posted: from doctor's prognosis to personal comments about dealing with grief. All of these appeared simply as status updates: day after day, week after week, month after month. Another friend gave birth to a premature baby, and there had been many complications and trials and tribulations throughout the delivery and over the following year. Again, nearly every day there was an update on the baby, how he had vomited, how he had fever and had to be rushed to the hospital during the night. At first, Burton had wondered why and how people could share these extremely personal and generally not very pleasant stories. But then he noticed that they received constant feedback and comment from other people, sometimes sharing their own experiences and offering advice and condolences. He would have thought that their close friends would have found out about such things anyway, but perhaps in such situations even the comfort of relative strangers was some measure of support. Or perhaps just the posting, as a kind of witnessing, was cathartic in its own right. The point was that, having now observed this a couple of times, he suspected it was going to become much more acceptable and common in the future.

He had never done anything so overt but he had been part of a more subtle version of the same thing. When his mother had been ill, he had told just a few close friends. Yet somehow this news had spread quickly, especially to relatives and friends in the diaspora. He was pretty sure Facebook had played an important role in serving his need to spread the news. It was testimony to the way people knew people who knew people. It had certainly helped him because the problem of netiquette was also a problem of etiquette. Trinis offline were not great when it came to telling people bad news. What they excelled at was making jokes about even quite serious issues, not taking things to heart. So Facebook in a way helped complement offline communication by spreading news that was a little difficult or embarrassing to deal with otherwise.

Adding bad news to good brought Facebook into closer alignment with what Burton saw as the natural propensity of networking as a form of social communication. Facebook had proved itself good at reflecting some prior networks, poor at others. People who thought it was going to be a useful means of business advancement would quickly learn that it was anything but. What Facebook did very well, however, is to aggregate networks such as friendship and kinship. It also helped in some ways to fill in the gaps or bridge the gulf around the cultural norms of networking that pre-dated the site. Ultimately, Burton had, in his own way, come to a realization about Facebook in Trinidad that was the most important finding of all. It wasn't that Facebook was a social network site; it was that people were a social network site.

11

Picking BlackBerrys

For many Trinidadians, most of the year feels like holdings one's breath because life itself is really only given breathing space at one time, that of Carnival, when, to use a local popular expression, a person is exhorted to *play yourself*. Consistent with Vishala's concept of truth, this means that one can become the person you really are only through masquerade. But it is not just the two days of Carnival that people eagerly await all year. When they talk of Carnival, they allude to the entire period from New Year through to Carnival itself. The rising tide of parties, new music and competitions brings such freshness and enjoyment that in some ways the final two days matter much less than the previous two months.

There are three interrelated supporting structures upon which the Carnival edifice is raised: soca, steelband and mas. Each of them includes a competition in its own right. The gradual reduction of competitors en route to the final winner helps to deliver this driving rush towards the exhilaration of Carnival itself. The mas camps provide the costumes for the bands, which can be thousands strong. They are judged as they stream past the specially constructed platforms on the Savannah grounds at the heart of Port of Spain. But the masqueraders are swinging their hips to the sounds of soca, the calypso music of Trinidad. For soca, there are two competitions: the first for 'Road March', which is the most popular and danceable soca tune chosen by most bands to accompany them as they pass the judging point. Then there is also the more serious competition between that year's crop of calypso songs, which are expected to have some political or social comment and are judged at Dimanche Gras, along with the Kings and Queens of Carnival costume. Finally, those who compose arrangements for steelbands will select one of the new soca songs which are launched from New Year. The bands then have until Carnival to train for the Panorama competition. In turn, the steelbands accompany the masqueraders as they dance through the streets during Carnival.

Individual Trinidadians graft their particular attachments to these different roots of Carnival. Some (actually most) are looking for the best and wildest parties with their accompanying soca music. Others are searching for hard-hitting political critique in the calypso. But for Joseph, his time, the time that grips him emotionally and gives him the kind of pleasure that could make him weep, comes unusually early in the season. It is when the pan (steelbands) start their practice. With almost any other kind of music, hearing it on CD or download gives at least some sense of how it sounds. This is entirely untrue of steelband. Joseph insists that hearing pan played on speakers does nothing at all to convey the music. You simply must see pan played by a live steelband, ideally in the place designated for practice called the panyard, to experience the sheer volume of sound, created when up to 120 players build crescendo after crescendo. These towering waves of music flow through and over your body. You don't so much listen as 'surf'. But it is not just the impact on the body of the listener. A Trinidadian steelband player almost invariably dances as he or she plays. The rhythm is not just in the hands that move across and around the pan. It flows down to the players' feet and upwards to the swish of their dreads around their head. This combination of sound and movement in the best bands is exquisite and entrancing.

Yet for Joseph, as for many aficionados of pan, his pleasure does not just come from the final product, the revelation of extraordinary cohesion and transcendence, when all the players seem to fuse into one organic band that plays before judges. This is one of the most intensely fought of all the Carnival competitions, when you feel the players would promise their soul in trade for winning. Joseph is equally entranced six weeks beforehand when the arranger has selected one of the soca tunes of the year and transformed it into pan music. From that point, on practically any night

you choose, you can go down to the panyard and there spend
several hours. All you may see, at least at first, is a segment or two
of the band practising because at that point it is mostly a section
of the whole, the base or rhythm or tenor pans, learning its contribution, rehearsing some part again and again. Only then do you
gain an understanding of the architecture of the music, the way
each part builds towards the whole by playing with and against
the other sections. Even at this stage, this is powerful stuff. At the
heart of the pan lies what the calypsonian David Rudder called
'the Engine Room'; traditionally an old car brake hub (today it
is made for the purpose and tuned) that is beaten with a piece of
metal to hold the underlying rhythm. In the meticulous scholarship of historian Kim Johnson, one can read how once upon a
time pan was an integral part of territorial disputes between what
were in effect gangs resident in these same areas. The competition
could itself give rise to fighting. Most of the yards represent the
most deprived sections of the towns and their supporters really
could bring violence to bear. Today, part of the sweetness of pan is
actually almost the opposite: its very cosmopolitanism. Typically,
the players may include people from the age of sixteen to sixty,
women as well as men, devotees from Japan or the US who are
staying in Trinidad just for this purpose, playing alongside those
born within a few feet of the panyard.

Joseph will come regularly and lime in the yard, which these
days may often have a booth for selling alcohol or perhaps corn
soup. To help people while away the hours. This year, he started
turning up at one of the panyards that has the most historical reso-
nance. Desperados belongs to Laventille, for long the most notori-
ously territorial and toughened district of Port of Spain. Later he
turned his attention to Pan Two Phase Groove which he thought
might win this year's competition – it actually came second. The
result may not have caused violence but, as is so often the case, it
was hugely contentious.

It was no surprise that the high point of Joseph's Carnival was
not that of going out and having a good time at fetes, but rather
the respect he felt for the art of pan. Most of the appellations for
Trini men have derogatory overtones. You might think it was
quite a good thing calling a man 'smart' or 'sweet'. But a smart
man implies someone who uses his intelligence to outsmart a
woman, while a sweet man is a man who has the gift of the gab

and can 'sweet talk' a woman not only into sleeping with him but even into giving him money to live on. Most of the handy descriptions of Trini men refer to the ways they make fools out of women. And there is no shortage of derogatory terms for women implying symmetry with this gender exploitation. Yet Joseph is a sweet man and a smart man, in the most positive of ways. He has a combination of intelligence and shyness, with a hint of naivety, not to mention a very well-toned body. Women have, in his case, very good reason to find him immensely attractive.

As is often the case with men, this positive bearing in his character derives from an inner confidence, the fruit of consistent success, but in circumstances where he has had to acknowledge both his good fortune and how easily things could have been otherwise. His family was never well off; they always struggled. He could never take things for granted, not even a basic livelihood, a quality found in many men where there was once a more dominant older sibling. He was relatively quiet as a child but built up a reserve of determination, so that as he grew up he surprised everyone in his family by doing much better in his exams than was expected. First, he made it to a very good school, then to university. But only just, so that he was never tainted by pride or overweening ambition. He has also been fortunate in his work. He has to spend long periods abroad but his earnings are sufficient. He attained his job through a chance meeting at the airport, and kept it during the recent recession. Again, he was lucky; he happened to have a technical skill they couldn't make redundant, when so many friends were losing what they had taken to be safe and secure positions. So Joseph counted his blessings and was neither complacent with regard to himself, nor condescending to others.

Joseph wasn't just nice; at heart he was thoroughly romantic. What he craved was passion based on love. He was the kind of man about whom, after an hour in his company, you could think of a dozen women who really needed to meet this guy and how he would make such a good father. Joseph was positive about certain aspects of Facebook. His sister had gone to the States while he was still quite young, becoming besotted with the place and only twice returning home to visit. She was more a memory than a current companion in his life. He was sad that, although she was his only sibling, he had never really felt part of her life course, missing her marriage and then the birth and development of her children. He was amazed, but also delighted, at the degree to which this changed as a result of Facebook. In the last two years, it had entirely transformed their relationship. It brought back that feeling of everyday co-presence. Facebook delivered a naturalistic feel, providing just the right amount of updating on each other's lives that should occur between grown-up siblings who are no longer living together. Information was being posted just once or twice a week, enough to learn how things were with each other. Thanks to Facebook, he had been able finally to banish some ambiguous memories of the once domineering sister and appreciate this mature, interesting and vivacious woman whom he simply hadn't known before. He could also become a real uncle which was perhaps even more attractive to him.

That was the good side of Facebook. The downside was that, while he was innately private and cautious, his now ex-wife Nneka had a bad temper, something he found appalling, the single greatest barrier to love. A temper seemed to him like a complete abnegation of the self, transforming her into Miss Jekyll and Mrs Hyde. There was the reasonable, sweet woman he had grown to love, and then this completely irrational body that seemed possessed by some demonic force. The weird thing was that they both agreed on this. Once her temper had subsided, she too loathed the harridan she had recently been and was utterly remorseful. All of this could be coped with when the foaming wave broke in private and the broken china it left in its wake could be repaired or dispensed with at leisure. But Facebook changed all that. Now, during one of his stints working abroad, he would turn on his machine to find a storm of emails: accusatory, bewildered, defensive and outraged.

He had been supposed to contact Nneka and wish her well prior to an operation but the network had gone down and neither his nor any phone he borrowed had worked. He was upset but, being in another country, there was simply not much he could do about it. The problem was that Nneka had lost her temper and, being unable to phone him to vent her spleen, had turned to Facebook. She had cussed his mother, accusing her online of legendary promiscuity, and told the entire world what a worthless, insensitive, selfish, bastard of an apology for a husband she had had the cataclysmic misfortune to end up with. Not surprisingly, a quotient of friends on both sides felt the need to respond. Mostly his friends did so through private emails, while her friends posted directly on Facebook itself. Of course, things had blown over almost as soon as she had done the deed. He had thoughtfully ordered a huge bunch of flowers as a surprise for her when she arrived in hospital. But she was not able to go online again until after the operation and by that time several days' worth of public bacchanal left an indelible mark. What might have lasted a day or two was now something his friends reminded him of far too frequently, although nearly a year had now passed.

Joseph increasingly had the feeling that Facebook had certain analogies with Nneka's temper. It was one more of these other-worldly places where all sorts of unexpected things happened that then had to be dealt with. Almost as disconcerting had been his recent experience of death on Facebook. He had been working abroad and was filling time by browsing the Facebook pages of old friends. Suddenly, he encountered the profile of a friend with whom he had been at school and was confronted by a flood of messages that were responses to his death after falling from a roof. Joseph felt as though he had been walking and suddenly stumbled across a cemetery just at the time of a burial. There was the immediate family, barely able to come to terms with the snuffing out of a life in its prime, juxtaposed with messages, half apologetic, from people who scarcely knew the deceased but wished to add some sense of shared memory or condolence. Some were written as though to the dead man, saying things to him that people wished desperately he had known before he died. Others were addressed to the mourners and seemed in a different time zone to the latter, some clearly feeling that only dark seriousness was appropriate, others that a humorous anecdote could still be an act of respect. Photos were still being posted, not just of the deceased but also of the wake.

It was this mix of postings that made Joseph feel he had inadvertently overheard a cacophony of voices. It was evident that, after a while, the close family must have taken some decision to take over the site more formally, in effect to become the curators of this memorial to their loved one. Arrangements for the wake had been noted. A kind of short, formal obituary added. Yet in addition it was clear that there were many, like Joseph, who were only now hearing about the death. They had found out about it only through Facebook and were adding their own thoughts and comments out of synch with this ordering and consolidation of mourning. But for Joseph, the problem was that, because all this was happening on Facebook, he couldn't quite accept that the actual person was dead. There seemed to be some difficulty in bringing these two planets into alignment. There was the one where his friend was being mourned online and the other where Joseph still half expected to meet him when he returned to Trinidad.

Joseph began to develop a new concern to explore, understand and appreciate this landscape that was being colonized by Facebook. As he travelled across it, he could see that on the one hand it was a shrine to trivia, lives turned into Post-it notes and fridge magnets, snippets of intimate life ranging from the TV someone watched to the colour of their underwear, the games they were playing, the bits of banal philosophy or pop lyrics that had appealed to them. There was something genuine and appealing about this modest bric-a-brac that was being shared: what has been termed 'ambient intimacy'.[1] He could relate to this relaxed willingness to be present in text and photos. On the other hand, beneath all this flotsam and jetsam, he could see harder sedimentary layers being laid down to form a different kind of geomorphology; things that were intended to stand for the long term as key moments in a life, whose transience as events was being overturned by this digital inscription on Facebook. It had started with a birth announcement, an engagement, the opening of an exhibition. Now there was the devastation of Haiti or, increasingly, death and mourning.

There seemed a new mood on Facebook. Wedding and baby albums seemed to stay put. It would have been sacrilege to wipe clean these memorial sites for the dead. Facebook was gradually coming closer to a genuine reflection of our own oscillation between the trite and the crucial in our offline lives. The trouble was that people like Nneka with her temper prevented this maturing of Facebook into a more cultured netiquette. She had turned the site instead into an ugly disfiguration of his most important relationship. Thanks to his wife, Facebook had become the purveyor of scars that remained when the underlying wound had long since healed, a different and much less welcome memorialization.

When he reflected upon it, he realized that Facebook had also exacerbated differences between him and Nneka that he had pre-

---

[1] See Kirkpatrick (2010), pp. 203–4 for the origins of this term.

viously viewed as the natural divergence of gender itself. Initially, Joseph simply didn't care about Facebook much. He had no special inclination to share his private thoughts. He had come to appreciate Facebook's value in relation to his sister, and the schoolfriends whose contact he might otherwise have lost. Social networking seemed to have an obvious value. But it was the value of a utility, in the same way that he saw value in his phone or his television. It was obvious what it was good for but that was the end of it. Most of what he put up about himself was casual and jokey. On his profile, it states that he is a ninety-year-old woman. He had become reticent about friending any new women he met since Nneka automatically assumed the worst. These days he mostly couldn't be bothered. He recognized that he was one of those who particularly benefited from Facebook since he spent so much of his working time abroad and had more reason than most to favour an instrument that kept him in touch. There was less of a sense of dissonance or gap to be bridged when he returned home. That was all to the good but it wasn't vital. Things would otherwise have been a bit more awkward but he would have managed. He was happy to use Facebook but it wasn't such a big deal.

By contrast, Nneka treated Facebook like a fetish. For her, it wasn't an instrument for relationships with other people. Rather, other people were the legitimacy for what had become her single most important relationship, her relationship to Facebook itself. This was where she found solace when she was depressed, companionship when she was lonely, a means to express herself when she was angry, a constant demand upon her time and attention. It was as if not one friend could post one new picture without Nneka having to see it and note it. Joseph had sometimes felt tempted to take off his wedding ring and hand it over to her true consort, Facebook. It wasn't even as though he was the kind of man who took marriage for granted. He went often to the gym, had a well-toned body, the whole six-pack thing. And he sometimes thought he was the only man in Trinidad who actually did this largely in order to appeal to his wife. But clearly nothing he could do would make him as seductive as Facebook. By comparison, he was starting to feel boring, superfluous. For the first time in his life, he found that he was beginning to doubt his self-worth.

There had been times past when, sure, she wanted to finish watching a TV programme, or a long, long, phone call to a girlfriend, when he was just shushed into a corner to bide his time until she was ready for him. But such events paled beside this addiction to Facebook. If in the past he had had to wait for hours while she redid her makeup, or decided she couldn't possibly go out in the clothes she had chosen and went back to the wardrobe for what she promised would be one last change, at least he could feel that her concern with her appearance came from her desire to look good for him, thereby conforming to what he regarded as quintessentially female in these and many other matters. She might try his patience, but this remained part of her appeal.

By contrast, it had become increasingly clear that whatever it was that Facebook was about, it was not about him, except as a figure to moan about with her friends. When she finally came off the wretched site and deigned to have dinner with him (increasingly a dinner he was cooking for both of them), the conversation was almost entirely about Facebook: what she had seen, who had been with whom, the comments she had made on some photos, the news, the clothes, the relationships. Because he had not been on those same sites, and mostly didn't even know these people, he felt not just boring but bored. After the first few years of marriage, what most Trinidadian couples worried about is 'being horned', one of the most common terms in the Trini language. A man feels those two protuberances emerge from his forehead at the mere whisper that his wife's car has been recognized by its number plate once too often outside the house of so and so. He might think there was probably nothing untoward going on, but in truth he does not absolutely know, hence the desire to run his hands over his head and just check for bumps. Horning is the basis of half the jokes ever told on the island. A friend had just posted on Facebook about how she was horning her Mac with a new netbook that was red hot, 10.5 inches long and could last seven hours. Joseph was beginning to wish that his wife had actually horned him, at least with a living human being. Instead, he was seeing a truth in his friend's posting. He was being horned by a very personal computer that did indeed seem to last seven hours every blessed day.

There was a real irony behind all this. He could never have predicted it but the same over-reliance on Facebook which was now breaking up their relationship had once helped forge it. Some years ago, Joseph himself had used Facebook rather more than he does today, when he was studying for his MA at Nottingham University in the UK. It was a time when university students assumed Facebook existed solely for them and would remain exclusively theirs. They used it to organize pretty much everything: their parties, going out to the cinema or ice skating. Unlike his peers, Joseph had seen Facebook above all as a means to share his foreign experience with Nneka. Even in those days, Nneka loved pictures. She didn't just want to hear about what he was doing; she wanted to see for herself. And Facebook was ideal for that purpose. For some people, one picture paints a thousand words, but for Nneka you needed a thousand pictures, literally. Quite apart from what Joseph posted, Nneka had gigabytes of pictures of everything she ever did.

For Joseph, posting so many pictures was at first unnatural and rather an effort. But after a while he too came to feel that he was only having an experience if he also took a picture and posted it on Facebook for her. He can't imagine how many ducks in how many Nottingham parks flew to Trinidad that year via his Facebook pages. At least, with trees and flowers and landscapes, it seemed somehow natural. He went to Devon on a special photographic tour so that he could share this with her. He remembers one particular sequence in which he wanted to convey to Nneka the importance of picking blackberries as a kind of English ritual: the threat of the thorns, the way they dyed your hands, the treat of blackberries and cream in front of an open fire. He used a macro lens to blow up one thorn to bring out the menace and ended with about a dozen pictures of the way the white cream topped the black and purple fruit in his bowl. He was really quite proud of himself. On reflection, maybe taking pictures of the meals he was eating was a little weird. Still, it wasn't just photos. Joseph also used Facebook to banter and tease and thereby to help him and his wife come closer together when they were so far apart.

While most people seem to never revisit pictures taken at some earlier time, Nneka didn't just catalogue these hard-drive records of his time abroad and bury them in some digital graveyard. Quite often, when they were married, she would refer to an event from that period. She had that facility of quickly finding the relevant illustrations and it enhanced the memory to look once again at a picture of his halls of residence or his graduation. In retrospect, it was quite an achievement. A year apart came to feel like a year shared. It had become a key time that helped bring them closer as a couple.

In those days, she never commented on the other women he was with. She was too proud to draw attention to them, and maybe he should have spent more time explaining who they were. After all, there were some quite gorgeous women in his class but then that would have seemed defensive, as though he had something to account for. There was only one person that mattered a bit, a Trinidadian girl whom he talked about at some length to Nneka. But it seemed Nneka understood. It was really important, in that cold climate, to have one friend who could cook the occasional Trini food and reminisce about things that still lay under the sun. Eventually, Nneka came to visit and could see for herself there had been nothing to worry about.

This way of experiencing the world continued when he returned, though, instead of pictures of swans and lakes, there were photo albums for every time they went to Maracas beach. Sometimes it was just the two of them, sometimes they were with friends and family. Joseph came to appreciate the aide-memoire benefits of photographs generally and Facebook in particular. He liked the way Nneka already knew everything she needed to know about his relatives and would use this sensitively to ask the right questions and avoid asking the wrong ones. So while he had retreated back to his sense of Facebook as mere utility, she had become ever more dependent upon it.

This then was the real tragedy of Facebook for Joseph. It was only now, with hindsight, that he had come to rue his own role in feeding this reliance and this desire that had been so benign for so long. What could be wrong with sharing an appreciation of how Facebook and its photos could help build a good life together? He really didn't know at what point desire had become fetishism, when exactly reliance had become addiction and the means had become so destructive to the ends. He couldn't have guessed that it would be this same Facebook which one day would displace him, and destroy the very love that it had helped to cultivate; when that woman, too proud to even think of jealousy, had become just one more of those Trini females stalking their way through Facebook. But now it was over, and his relationship with Nneka was finished, he realized that he too needed to develop a new relationship to Facebook. And it would need to be something quite different from Nneka's. Partly, Joseph had retreated to that typically male strategic defence against emotional involvement, treating the whole thing as fun. He used cartoons instead of photos, and pretended in his Facebook profile that he was old and decrepit. But then another strategy emerged which effectively released him from this bitter and tragic relationship to Facebook, that transformed it into a rather cold and effective instrument for a different part of his life.

It all began with a rather different story about picking BlackBerrys, something that seemed to have happened to Trinidad as a whole. It was pretty hard to find an iPhone in Trinidad even though almost anything that was high fashion in London or New York tended to achieve a very visible presence in Port of Spain. The cause was simply that Trinidad had picked the BlackBerry instead. Or at least that BlackBerry had marketed a very effective campaign and had pretty much won the field. It was BlackBerry that was most effectively bringing GPS to Trinidad. Given that this is a country in which it is almost impossible to understand or give directions and that published maps are almost entirely useless, this is going to be an unalloyed blessing. It was BlackBerry rather than iPhone that spread the kind of payment plan where almost every-thing, including internet access and unlimited calls and messages, seemed free within the plan. For someone like Joseph, for whom so much communication was international, this was especially attractive, as was the concept of a smartphone as a mini-laptop where you could view an Excel spreadsheet and store it in your pocket.

Yet there was no doubt which particular facility of these new Swiss army knife-like phones, which seemed to have a tool for every purpose, had actually been the deciding factor for the company in securing Trinidad: everyone knew it was the ease with which one could use a BlackBerry for Facebook. For Trinis, if you were serious about staying in touch with Facebook, and you had a good income, you pretty much had to have a BlackBerry. It helped that, with the right deal, you could pick a BlackBerry for around TT$500. Facebook had one quite problematic limita-tion for those who couldn't last five minutes without checking for updates. Previously, you had to first find a computer and then log on, which meant Facebook lacked the one quality that would make it as truly Trinidadian as liming. That quality was sponta-neity. Thanks to the BlackBerry, there were now no restrictions, no planning, no pause. Facebook was finally as close temporally as it was physically and mentally. Facebook, stuffed down your jeans pocket, now occupied that intimate and personal realm that reflected its place in your life. Within the last few months, Joseph had seen people about to go on Facebook, while sitting with him at a restaurant, and react to the discovery that they had forgotten to bring their BlackBerry with an expression of horror more commensurate with having lost a child.

Yet this was a rather curious juxtaposition, since the other major selling point for the BlackBerry was its marketing as the ideal business phone. It was regarded as the phone with which to organize meetings, advertising and promotion, in order not only to be efficient, but to be seen by all other Trinidadians as efficient. This had become the self-fulfilling prophecy desired by the company, as these days there was a real danger of not being taken seriously in business if you did not communicate by BlackBerry. We may not think of business as a fashion display, but so much of it rests on confidence, on how to decide who or what is worth investing in so that mere appearances become more important in business than almost anywhere else in life. It might not seem obvious that you would need the very same device for promoting both business and Facebook but, with regard to the relationship between appearance and reality, it seems they have quite a bit in common.

Joseph found that, of all the things he could put forward in order to gain attention and respect, it was the creation of a marketing plan based on Facebook that had become the key to his continued success. The buzz was around social marketing as the future of business. Remember Marvin marketing his cocoa plantation. Even there, it all had to be Facebook. The smart money was on doing something quite novel. Joseph saw it couldn't simply be putting the old forms of advertising and marketing into this new format. Instead, you needed to be very subtle, to keep the social side of Facebook, all its banter and 'macotiousness' and word-of-mouth qualities. You could use all this to spread a 'feeling' about your product, to promote it via peer-to-peer connections. There were rumours about a company in Brazil that had worked out the formula, how to leverage the speed and effectiveness of social networking for business promotions. They had carefully traced how people discussed products naturally with each other through Orkut (the Brazilian equivalent of Facebook) and were ready to test out their ideas using their own products.

So it was just fine that Joseph's profile revealed schoolboy humour and male playfulness. Even with his boss, communication had become more relaxed, Trini in a different way, with far less concern for spelling, grammar and form. In phone messaging, playful shortcuts were seen as skill, the thing that told everyone that Joseph was where it is now at. They could see that all his messages about and through Facebook came with a little tag, the sign that told you he had typed it all on his BlackBerry. This is one of the reasons why the increasingly popular messaging service in Trinidad was BBM, BlackBerry's own proprietary service.

Once his BlackBerry mediated between him and Facebook, it managed to achieve the thing he most needed at that point in time. It turned Facebook from an instrument of tragedy, with cruel memories of love and loss that had marked its role in his relationship with Nneka, and replaced it with a completely different vision of what Facebook could be in his future, an effective instrument for his becoming even more successful in his business operations, to thereby regain the self-confidence that had been his backbone – all achieved simply by picking BlackBerrys.

12

The History Woman

It seems crazy to think of Facebook as some dusty archive from history. Last time most of us blinked, it wasn't even there. Yet for Nicole that's exactly what Facebook is. She talks wistfully, in a spirit of pure nostalgia, about Mark. After a while, you realize that (a) Mark is actually Mark Zuckerberg, the inventor of Facebook; and (b) Nicole has, of course, never actually met him. But no matter: Nicole still speaks with heartfelt nostalgia for the time of Mark, her Mark, not other people's Mark Zuckerberg. In 2004, Nicole was studying at a college in the US, one of the first colleges where Facebook became popular after it was released from its initial base at Harvard. Rather than being an opening onto the world, initially it was something that reinforced the experience of this small college as a rather personable place where everyone knew each other. Facebook was used to organize parties, meet for dinner and exchange news. She associates it with the enjoyment of her student days and their sociable nature. This created almost immediately an intense conservatism with respect to Facebook. She desperately hoped that Mark would not release his invention beyond the college environment and would not make changes to the original format. Facebook was something she felt she owned, and that Mark in turn owed something to her and her fellow pioneers. She clearly relishes the time when, in Trinidad, she could look down on the MySpace brigades who simply didn't know what she was talking about. She returned as John the Baptist, denounced such false prophets and gave hints that the social networking messiah had come down to earth and would eventually be revealed (though only to university students).

She still retains a level of scorn for the newbies of social networking. People today don't use Facebook, they defile it. She can't bear to hear mention of games such as *Mafia Wars*. Her original Facebook friends all wanted to fly off when their fledgling swan turned into such an ugly duck. But as she put it, by that time, 'we were so frigging addicted to Facebook, we were not going to get off it, so that's that.' Far from it, she reckons that, until her child was born, she was on Facebook for possibly half her waking hours. It could have been more. It is still very rare that, on getting up in the morning, she will get as far as cleaning her teeth before feeling the need to reach for her keyboard.

The problem is that Facebook is just too close to friendship. The more you put up, the more friends will comment. The more they comment, the more you feel you have to comment on them. You can't withdraw without causing slight and offence. Over the years, they have given you so much comment and concern that you can't just fold your cards when they are still up for the game.

Recently though, she has started to become uncomfortable with this ratcheting up of Facebook's place in people's lives to the extent that you haven't been to a restaurant unless you have posted that you have been there. The Twitter effect, as she calls it. For example, her friend Nafeisha was over the other day and had pulled some songs from a mutual friend's iTunes over the wireless connection. And then an hour later she notes that Nafeisha has posted that she was 'cooking up some tunes from the razorshop'. And Nicole was thinking, cooking up what tunes? All she did was download some songs from a friend's hard drive. But then for other people this was 'cooking up some tunes in the razorshop'. Today on Facebook, an individual seems to have to present themselves as a kind of cool-sounding, popular person to whom other people will respond. The temptation is to dismiss all this as some kind of mask or artifice that makes us more superficial. But Nicole knows both Facebook and people too well to be dismissive. She knows that Nafeisha would be doing much the same thing with or without Facebook. When did you ever see Nafeisha not doing everything in her power to look cool and sexy? Not only that but you could spend all day crafting these postings intended to make yourself seductive and powerful, and still end up being seen by your peers as a pretentious fool. Given how easy it is to get things wrong, it was perhaps not such a bad way of being judged, cheaper than a new pair of shoes and more authentic as a reflection of a person's labour and ability. Nicole sees all this but still she can't help feeling that all these games and performances seem to have diminished Facebook itself, a kind of inflation effect that has reduced the Facebook currency to a coinage of little worth, where you need triple the exchanges to achieve the same value. She still stalks her putative boyfriends' ex-girlfriends on Facebook but even this feels wrong, not because it's stalking but because in the 'old days' people put up really interesting stuff about their likes and dislikes on the information page and now it's, like, they can't be bothered. So when finally she did reduce her commitment to Facebook, it's not certain that the birth of her son was entirely to blame.

Nor is it as if Facebook just had two phases: the pioneer phase and the present. It continually changes, producing a succession of these betrayals of her commitment. Earlier on, 'We clamoured and shook our fists at Mark for cheapening our elitist little circle.' More recently, Nicole had got into groups. She liked the way these might be scattered across the world. They brought all sorts of people together in a small virtual community. She would check out her groups every day. Her favourite was a group called 'I stay up late and I don't do anything productive.' She thought much of it was hilarious. But then someone hacked into it and started posting racist and anti-Semitic stuff. And then gradually people seemed to lose their commitment to groups in general, just when she felt they had become more worthwhile, not less. In this case, she couldn't blame Mark: it was the users who were fickle.

Although she spends so much time complaining about these changes, Nicole can still be an 'early adopter' for developments she actually quite likes. She quickly took to window-shopping, if not actual shopping, on Facebook. Her favourite clothing store is a Facebook site that only advertises its stock online. She browses it regularly and if she had the money she would buy from there. But with an infant to look after, this is out of the question. Still, whenever you see her, she can tell you what items she would buy if she could. Currently, it's a white corset top.

Nicole knew that she could easily become a Facebook history

bore. No one was too interested in the old days, in black-and-white snapshots of Facebook's time as a toddler network way back in 2004. But Nicole's historical relationship to Facebook took a perhaps even less expected turn. She really did turn it into a dusty archive. A couple of years ago, there was a difficult personal issue when she met a guy she had had a 'thing' with some time before and who had come back into her life. If she was going to re-enter his orbit, she had to decide for herself what there was to learn from the earlier encounter. How much of it had been his, and how much her, fault. She knew she was a different person today but that is what made it so hard to determine. So she turned to Facebook. She patiently trawled backwards, turned the pages one by one, retracing every conversation and posting that documented this relationship all those years ago so that she could at once reappraise what had been and determine whether it was sensible to re-engage with him today. Facebook is not built to be archived and this had been a pretty laborious procedure, even when she isolated wall-to-wall postings. On the other hand, there was an unexpected dividend. What she unearthed was actually extremely funny. She felt she had been hilarious in those days, as was he. In response, she carefully copied all the best bits, 'all those insane stupid things', from 2004 onwards and put them into a paper 'novelty book' she could keep as a memory of who she had once been and what she had been capable of in those times.

Nicole found other ways to deepen Facebook's relationship to the past well beyond its own relative youth. Like just about every other Trini on Facebook, one of her main uses was to get back in touch with people with whom she had been at school. This even included her primary school, where she had spent what she now regarded as some of her most formative years, a time of sharp memories. As it happens, her parents had always been into recording and photographing and making films, so she has many pictures of those years. From these, she had created an album, posted it on Facebook and tagged pretty much everyone that she remembered from school. There was a huge reaction. Everyone was pleasantly shocked: 'they were all "Oh My God, where did you get those pictures", blah blah blah.' After that, they really started to re-establish contact in a more intimate, serious kind of way. It was essentially a new set of friendships, based not on common experiences today, but on a common past. It has produced a broader range of friendships than her contemporary circle in Trinidad. Nor have these just remained online. There were invites to weddings she otherwise would definitely not have received.

Facebook transformed itself for her, one more time, when she fell in love. Indeed, it made her realize just how closely intertwined the very experience of love itself can be with Facebook. Ever since college days, Facebook had played a role in her various relationships. Students had seen it almost instantly as a helpful buffer against awkward or embarrassing situations. You didn't really know whether you wanted to go out for a drink with this guy but in those days adding someone to Facebook felt natural, a non-committal mutual agreement to check each other out.

'I know someone for a while. So I speak to them. I saw them. I hadn't seen them in a while. I saw them at the gym. They said "Oh, add me to Facebook". We were talking about this charity thing. "So no problem. I will add you" And so "oh your pics are amazing, do you want to go out for a drink" and this is on Facebook.'

She wasn't one of those who approved of couples quarrelling publicly online: that was kind of horrible. Instead, she would put up a posting consisting of a song lyric about how she was feeling but indirectly so that no one else would be able to interpret it. For example, she posted the lyrics from a band called Paramore, 'I put my faith in you. So much faith in you. But you just threw it away.' At the time, she was annoyed with her boyfriend because she wanted him to go to a party but not drink too much. But he drank just as much anyway. He recognized the import of the lyric but no one else did. Why she needed the public domain of Facebook to do this was less clear. She concludes that it must have been cathartic, like writing a little poem but not using her own words. But then cathartic is the term she uses to explain Facebook postings more generally, none of which prepared her for the role that Facebook would eventually play in her falling deeply in love.

She had known this guy for ever. He was friends with her friends and moved on the periphery of her circles. There had been plenty of face-to-face encounters, but always shallow ones, since she had come to a very early conclusion that this guy was pompous. And that was the problem. Once you decide, even as a teenager, to label a guy, then everything about him gets sort of filtered through these categories, and you never have a reason to go beyond that. He almost certainly would have just stayed on the periphery. But when she expanded her Facebook friends, he naturally became a presence there, and, equally naturally, when she is bored she tends to *maco* even the more distant Facebook friends.

> 'And then I realized this guy had a lot of stuff in common with me. So just one day I think I asked him if he went to see *Ironman* and we started to talk about comic books and stuff. From there on and after that we started chatting all the time. [What other things did you find you had in common with him?] Um, taste in movies, um type of music uh, I think that was probably it. The movies and . . . oh and video games.'

Typically, in Trinidad people don't use Facebook as a key medium for more intimate courting. Things tend to migrate to a combination of texting and speaking by phone, as happened in this instance. But that doesn't mean that once it has shown people how much their tastes and opinions are aligned, and has brought them together, Facebook then fades out of the picture. Facebook has also become one of the most important expressions of her boyfriend's love for her. Nicole had never considered herself pretty and for that reason tended to hate it when people took photos of her and posted them. But he has now taken some 400 photos of her and tagged every one of them across Facebook. At first, as someone who almost entirely avoided public photographs, she was completely horrified. But she recognized this as an act of love, a love that is proud of itself and proud of this wonderful creature that is its object. An act brimming with confidence that the whole world should see who it is he loves. Nicole also knows that this requires her to believe that he really does think she is pretty. And this confirmation that someone can see such beauty in her has started to change her own idea of what she looks like. Of course, her mother had said things like that, about how pretty she was, but that was just what mothers do. But her boyfriend has done this so systematically, so publicly, through Facebook itself, that she is almost beaten down by his truth which is now starting to become her truth. Perhaps she is, at least, sort of pretty.

While this is by any standard rather an extreme case, she has noted something parallel in the way some of her friends have become prominent online. She sort of expected that it would be the extraverts who would colonize Facebook, that the friends who were always in your face would be in your Facebook. But she also has a circle of friends from central Trinidad's East Indian community. Several of them were very shy, completely immersed within conservative family life, traditional and demure. Their parents tended to send them to the Presbyterian or convent schools, even though they were Hindus or Muslims, schools that maintained traditional values with respect to deportment and how women should behave in public. What Nicole finds curious is that, although several of these friends remain shy and retiring when you meet them, not just in front of men but even with girlfriends such as Nicole, some of these same women have been extremely active on Facebook, constantly putting up material, nothing brazen or shocking, not acts of rebellion, but still extensive personal information, opinion and comment that give vastly more insight into what they are thinking, often quite surprising thoughts, than you would have ever encountered otherwise. On Facebook, they are not extravert in the sense of performance, or being silly. But they easily outweigh the extraverts as a dominant presence in the Facebook of their friends.

If those friends were posting more, then Nicole was posting a whole lot less than had ever been the case since that memorable year when her peer group had played midwife to the newly born Facebook. The problem was her own newly born baby. It wasn't just that she had less time to post; it was that she had less to post about. She knew that others had the diametrically opposite experience. She had friends who had barely posted in their Facebook lives, but, once they had a child, it was as though the entire world needed to know every single thing that baby did. If they could have broadcast the baby burping on Facebook, they probably would have. She had honestly not known whether she would become that kind of Facebook mother but rather hoped she wouldn't. She knew that this wouldn't be under her control, that you never can tell what kind of mother you will turn out to be. If anything, things had gone in the other direction. At first, she thought she had some version of postnatal depression. As time passed, she rationalized her response to childbirth rather differently. She had always thought that babies were extremely boring. You just put stuff into them and cleared up the stuff that came out of them. It took a year or two before they had much personality. She had always felt this, but assumed that, as a mother, she would inevitably react differently to her own infant – but she hadn't. The fact that she found this stage pretty tedious didn't mean she was less likely to bond fully with the personality this baby would no doubt develop over time. Instead, she was quite happy that being a mother didn't leave her bereft of the powers of reason and observation that had always made her a top-notch student. She didn't feel she would be any less emotional or less in love with her children in the long term. It was just that she wasn't particularly attached to changing nappies and being woken up several times a night.

If she was bored by what babies did in their first few months, there seemed no reason to bore the rest of the world with intimate details of babyhood. But there was a wider problem. It wasn't just that mothering was boring. Life in general was inevitably less interesting. A year earlier, when she was out partying, liming and going to the beach, she would post constantly because there was lots to post about. She had become one of those 'I just did this'/'I am home now' on Facebook, keeping everyone updated on every detail. Life had been fun and worth sharing, so if she wasn't posting now, it was largely because it no longer was.

But that had complicated consequences she hadn't really thought through in advance; Facebook was so much part of her previous life, and remained so much part of the life of her friends who didn't have babies. What was the impact of Facebook on this divergence between her and her friends? Did it compound the problem? Not only unable to participate in their offline life, she was now unable to participate in the equally vibrant and important online life. Where Facebook might have compensated, was it now just too-evident testimony to what she no longer was? Although she had far fewer postings of her own, she had more time than ever to spend looking at all her friends' postings.

There is a bitter-sweet tinge to this activity. Facebook keeps her up to date with her friends. They remain part of her everyday life, as before. This was a huge part of what Facebook could do for you. On the other hand, it constantly reminded her of what she wasn't doing, couldn't be doing, and would have just loved to have been doing with them, the limes she is not taking part in, the parties she can't go to. This has become a critical test of her relationship to Facebook. While her friends' style of posting has remained the same, these take on a completely new significance for her because of her changed circumstances. She has turned into a mother, and she can't entirely fathom what is happening. She didn't have a child in the pre-Facebook era, so she is unable to compare the two experiences. Overall she thinks that, for all the pangs of missing out, Facebook has the benign effect of making her feel she hasn't completely lost touch. When the time comes, it will be much easier to rejoin that world, though that might not be true for others. She recognizes that she is probably more self-conscious about this than her peers. She remains hugely interested in Facebook and not just its impact on her life. She also sees her life as a kind of documentary about Facebook, what it is and what it is constantly becoming.

Nicole is Facebook's history woman. For each phase of her life, she has had a completely different Facebook. There was the original identification with the Mark Zuckerberg enterprise. Then came the Facebook that found her love and changed her image of herself. Later, there were the compromises with Facebook as she became a mother. But if each phase has seen Facebook expressing a different woman with different concerns and needs, then Nicole's experiences have also revealed the degree to which, within a few years of its invention, Facebook itself has a significant history.

Lagniappe
The Philosophy of Doubles

I first met Doubles over twenty years ago but their reputation certainly preceded them. I don't now recall, but it would be no surprise, if someone had told me about them the very first day I arrived in Trinidad. Even then, it was never simply someone telling me that we should meet soon. The advice was very particular about exactly where and when would be the ideal time and place to get acquainted. There was this street corner near Curepe junction, and if I went there at lunchtime, I would not regret it. Sadly, I can't now actually remember the first occasion we met; it may well have been Curepe. This wasn't far from where I lived at the time on St John's Road, near UWI. Once we had met, I fully understood the appeal; this would be a relationship for life. Of course, we met again on this more recent trip. I know nostalgic regret is one of the most boring of conversational tropes, but on this occasion I have to indulge it. Unless I am much mistaken, Doubles are not what they were twenty years ago. There was that tautness – that particular flick of the wrist – that seems to be missing today. We had many encounters on this latest visit to Trinidad but whenever I approached with the same traditional greeting I have always used – 'slight pepper' – I knew there would also be just a little disappointment in the encounter compared to what it had once been . . . but life is like that.

The one thing I had never guessed, although I suppose I am not the least bit surprised, is that Doubles seem to have more friends on Facebook in Trinidad than any rival. At the last count this was 13,401. Mind you, that's not a patch on the offline friendships, which must be at least a million. I am trying to think if I know a Trini who isn't fond of Doubles. There must be some but I can't think of a name right now. Anyway, I have teased you enough, and it is time that you too should get acquainted. Doubles is simply *the* street corner food of Trinidad. Although it clearly derives from South Asian cuisine, I have lived several years in India and have never come across Doubles there. So there is every reason for thinking it is an Indo-Trinidadian invention. As we shall see, it may also be as good a testament as any to the continued power of Trinidadian creativity and invention as applied to Facebook.

Trinidadian food is often eloquent and subtle as an expression of Trinidadian ethnic identity. If you look carefully, there is some mix of affinity and difference in cuisine that mirrors the way people think about and understand each other. So the main ingredient in the filling of Doubles, *chana* (chick peas), is unequivocally Indian, as is the use of curry powder and *jeera* (cumin) as its main flavouring. But this is then encased in a certain amount of ambiguity. The *chana* and its surrounding sauce is spooned as a filling between two *barra*. These are basically yeast-risen dough circles that are then fried. Most of the origin myths (and there are many) suggest that the South Asian origin consisted of the chick pea mixture spooned onto a *barra*, but Trinis, wanting a more sustaining street food, kept asking for a second *barra* to be placed on top, leading to the expression 'I want a Doubles'. Placing it on greaseproof paper, the vendor then wraps the whole into a parcel by holding the two ends and, with a deft turn of the wrist, makes knots at both sides of the paper parcel to hold the Doubles firm, though some Trinis will still take this apart and eat it as *chana* on *barra*.

Meanwhile, at the other end of the cuisine spectrum, the foundation of everyday Creole (i.e. of African origin) food is the bake. A bake is much more firm than any South Asian bread and, as the name suggests, is baked. It is typically between a centimetre and an inch thick. The meeting point of the two traditions may have come with another form of street food, best known from the most popular beach in Trinidad at Maracas. Anyone who goes there to swim simply has to indulge in a Shark and Bake, which is a slice of shark between two circles of yeast-risen dough. But the bake that is served with a Shark and Bake is fried and it has the more chewy consistency that comes close to a *barra*, which should also be flexible, very unlike the firm traditional bake. This food syncretism goes further. Whether you order Doubles or a Shark and Bake, or pretty much any street food, there is the optional accompaniment of pepper sauce and in most cases a further possibility of half a dozen other sauces such as tamarind. So Doubles is definitely understood as Indian, but in the sense of East Indian, i.e. Indo-Trinidadian rather than South Asian Indian. It is Indian with a Creole twist.

The mix is also tailored to the customer. When I go up to a Doubles vendor and ask for 'slight pepper', I strongly suspect they appraise me quickly as a foreigner and I end up with even less pepper sauce than a Trinidadian who makes the same request. What to me has deteriorated in Doubles is not so much its flavour but the distinctive way it is presented. The best Doubles contains a filling that is not too liquid and the whole forms a proper parcel within knotted greaseproof paper. This makes it possible to eat a Doubles without too much spillage. More recently, though, I have found the filling does not have quite the right consistency: it is too loose. Or, horror of horrors, the vendor doesn't even try to parcel the whole thing up but just hands you the mixture spread over two adjacent *barra*. Will someone please tell these people, 'boi – dat is not Doubles'?

Doubles is an experience I associate with Trinidad but, just so you know, it can be found elsewhere. For many years I used to go to soca fetes in London. And when one came out of these, typically at three in the morning – on one memorable occasion copiously dripping sweat onto the snow – it was often the case that there would be a little van outside selling this sweet savour for a modest fee. For a daytime indulgence, Roti Joupa in Clapham is my personal favourite London site. If you visit them, you will find that Doubles is not alone in terms of East Indian street food. *Roti* for Trinidadians is much more than the roti of an Indian restaurant. It is effectively a *dhalpuri* skin with a filling such as curried goat, or (for me) pumpkin *aloo* (potato). You might also try some *phoulourie*. Strangely, there is also something special about Trini macaroni pie which has managed to become a national dish without any claims to either Indian or African origins. Now, not to neglect my Trini friends, I should also pronounce my personal verdict on street food – the single most useful observation you will find in this volume is that there is a van parked between the NP station and Church Chicken in main street Chaguanas that serves the best *sahina* and *aloo pie* imaginable ... no, correction ... unimaginable.

I don't know who first had the idea that Doubles was fully deserving of its own place on Facebook as a virtual shrine, where people could worship, celebrate, and with deep respect make fun of their good friend and each other. I could try and discuss the phenomenon and pontificate on it but I think the Doubles site largely speaks for itself. So, as I can't (sadly) give you a taste of the food, I will content myself with giving you a taste of the site, presenting a few selections. But, before I do, just one more aside. Everyone on Facebook has a profile picture to the fore, and on the day I am writing this there is some controversy in progress on the Doubles Facebook site. Doubles has just been given a new profile pic. It consists of that iconic moment when Kanye West was supposed to be presenting an MTV award to Taylor Swift, but instead decided to 'big up' the video by her competitor Beyoncé. This caused a national incident such that even Barack Obama had to comment (he called Kanye a jackass). In the profile pic, we have Kanye West with a speech bubble saying 'You wah sum Doubles owa?' (You want some Doubles or what?) with a bemused Taylor Swift replying 'Ehh?'

As it happens, this recalls the moment when I first became aware of the power of Trini Facebook. I was sort of minding my own business – well, this was Facebook; I was sort of minding everyone else's business – when suddenly a flood of comments about the Kanye West–Taylor Swift incident erupted on the screen, drowning out all the other normal stuff about whose baby looks cute and who is fed up with the rain. But every single one of these postings was coming from Trinidad – nothing from the US or the UK. And this seemed, even then, so quintessentially Trinidadian, an island people who would take Facebook to places more quickly than anyone or anywhere else could. This was the first moment I considered undertaking a serious study of Facebook in Trinidad. As it happens, not everyone is happy with Doubles' new profile pic. There are plenty of comments such as: 'Not this again plz I begging' or 'ah tellin yuh ... dis and palance was total overkill for d month ... steups.'

This seems a good point of entry to the rest of the site. So, welcome friends to *The Philosophy of Doubles*:

Not surprisingly, on Valentine's Day the topic was – could you have Doubles as a romantic meal?

I jus sayin, I not askin a girl if she want doubles to Valentine day dinner, I don't want to get slap LOL Maybe a wife cud b understanding n hav a Doubles dinner or out of kix . . . but as for a date with a girl nah nah nah Daz REAL trouble right there . . . Allyuh Agree???

It depends . . . a laid back kinda girl, on de beach somewhere or something cool like dat (doubles and a movie, or even a picnic under de coconut tree self) wouldn't mind. Now if you into dem high maintenance kinda gimme-tiffany's-and-the-world-on-a-silver-platter kinda girl, then you go be in trouble. It all depends.

I love doubles . . . so as a wife i don't mind if my husband take me out for doubles . . . as long as we hanging out together, it's all good

If dat man could make a doubles and bring hot in bed . . . he cud be my valentine!

Watch meh we making de doubles hotter dan bed and yes dats ah reasonable dinner date!! cuz when she ah bite de bara she biting de other bara and yuh knw wha going on deh homiess!!! dawg roti stronger than ah bara caus de bara hot like pepper pepper pepper!! booow!!! If ah gyul doh like yuh for doubles den she not from trinidad she's no trini!!! yuh don knw!!!

Check this out, i LOVE doubles so much i wanna move to trinidad & marry a doubles man~~~is there any available doubles men out there???? am dead serious ♥ ♥ ♥

Accept your destiny . . . you are there to be loved . . . not used . . .

yr jus d love of my life theres nothing can keep me away from u . . . doubles i love as i i love u. . . .

If love and friendship weren't a part of the experience of life, then life would be 'dark' gloomy, not worth it! 'The thread of life darker still if not the intertwining of bara and channa . . . with pepper.'

I went for doubles with my gf a time, and she didn't want to stand up to eat the doubles, but wanted to eat it home, i should of see this as a sign, bc she is now my ex . . . Could be worse, she could have asked to use knife and fork

This leads to the question of 'horning' (adultery):

A man or woman will leave yuh, but doubles will always be there . . . At least doubles wont horn yuh!!!

Yea u always have a doubles to munch on

I feeling to hug up a double

Believe this i carry my girl out for doubles and she eat 3 triples and drink a apple j now check this after she done eat she done with me . . .girls aint easy.

Gf:Let We Go Out Tomorrow, Bf:I Was Going For Doubles, Gf:You Choosing Doubles Over Me?, Bf:Yes, Gf:Well I Hope You And Your Doubles Are Happy Together, Bye!!!.... First Things First, Doubles Is Hotter, More Satisfying, And Cheaper... Did I Mention Wet And Hot, With Plenty Sauce? Lol

This gives way to the topic of violence:

I gonna by a hot doubles, with plenty pepper . . . and throw it in the eye on the fella who tracking meh gurl . . .

Lol . . . make sure he cah see, because they shooting

People eat doubles its FOOD you know . . . why use it as a weapon??? I am from the original Ali's who created the doubles so I KNOW . . .

Yea y waste de doubles soo

Just give him ah double . . . then he go fall in love with that and start tracking doubles and u go come out looking good still . . .

Politics always seems to creep in somewhere:

Pnm Screwed Trinidad And Tobago Citizens Totally, Unc Cant Get There Ack Together And A Buch A Thief. C.O.P A Bunch Of

Disgrunted Old People ... Doubles Raised Over 5 Times Since There 12 Year Rule. If I Could A Cuss On This Fb Page I Would. Change? Yes I Want Change When I Buy That $3tt, Doubles To Small! I Voting Who Reduce The Price Of Doubles To Save All That Trouble Who To Vote For. Talk Done Yes!!! People Hungry!

Crimes? get rid of crimes??? just as we sow, so shall we reap!! a bitter pill 2 swallow but this is the reality of our crime issues, and btw, I feelin 4 a double right now.

Allyuh feel dem politicians eating doubles? ... dem politicians eating free doubles ... preach the word brudda

Man! we better watch our back!! they may start TAXING our DOUBLES ...

Rather more surprising was the Doubles' take on religion:

I Almost Went Crazy Today, Going Home, And My Mind Was On Some Hot Doubles, And Then Thinking, Praying, I Hope It Have A Doubles Man At The Corner Where I Usually Buy ... My Prayers Was Answered ...The Doubles Man Was There ... Thank You Lord!!!

So trust in the lord always and he will always provide doubles blessing

Amen my bro., i had the same thing this morning, and damn i enjoy every moment of it.

The lord had 5 doubles and 7 pullorie and called his deciples they prayed over it and fed 5000 men and women and still they had enough to carry home

My face lights up when i see that big umbrella around that corner. if u believe, the doubles man will manifest. .... I know what u mean D, it's like when we see that umbrella, we see God.

Of course, the big fixation was where to go for the best Doubles:

CENTRAL!!!!!!! Sauce is d boss

South has de best bara!!!!

I like south doubles . . . but central ha d best . . .especially by chag market

It have this Doubles vendor in San Juan who does be by Luck Bakery does taste bestest best. yeah Doubles yummy yum yum

Well M i wouldnt say curepe double gone through its just that other people making better doubles now hahahahaha lol times change ppl hehehehe...

Sally in town on d 4 corners of d universe on mondays an fridays!!!!!!!!!!!!!!dats d stuff!!!!

Debe doubles is d frickin besttttt!!!!!!!!!!!

Curepe doubles just doh cut it anymore...i say by Kelvin in Valsayn in the night have the best.

Best doubles is the old man in Mayaro with the coconut chutney. second is curepe.

The best double by SAUCE in chaguanas, caroni savannah road, the best

These arguments go on for pages, as do those about the best things to add to your Doubles:

I getting vex . . . Rel vex . . . I ent want sweet sauce, I ent want pepper sauce, I ent want cucumber . . . I want Kuchela, Sour tamarand sauce, and roast pepper . . . ok . . . Grrrr!!!!

I want shadow benny . . . mango, kuchela, tamarand sauce, sweet sauce, slight peppa!!!!

I ♥ extra cucumbers

Coconut chutney, cucumber, roast pepper, chandon beni . . . nothing sweet pls

bandanya. pepper sauce . . . cucumber . . . an som tambran sauce if it have . . . diz wha we takin bout . . .

Every Damm Thing!!

Of course, there is bound to be sex:

I Like Them Big And Chunky . . . Doubles That Is.

And i like my channa like my women....saucy and savory....lol

I only need one . . .just one . . .lol . . . plz . . . .what does a girl have to do just to get one . . . lololol

Its tasty and delicious and when i eat doubles and i kiss my babes it sends chills up her spine lolzzz

Why Do You Love Me? Why Do You Constantly Want Me Hot All The Time, Why Do You Want To Lick My Sauce? Why Do You Demand Two, Three, Maybe More Of Me . . Why??? Why??? Why Do You Want Me Night And Day . . . I Feel So Used!!!

Judge Me Not By The Size Of The Bara, But Taste.

. . . fuh real eh . . . some ah the smallest bara i ever put in meh mout . . . have the SWEETEST taste! o gorm. i does just be lickin meh lips and fingers!

Sometimes the conversation meanders into mini-debates, such as whether you would want to have a face like Doubles:

Hells no that mean that yuh have a chew up face!! 0.o

Dah mean it bumpy an stink lmao!!, acne evrywhere lolzzz

It depends on if iz a doubles wit slight or if it is wit heavy pepper!!? lol

Is either d person hv an greasy face or a wrinkly one . . . or maybe it's both . . . could a person have a saucy face?

Or a debate as to whether men or women could eat more Doubles:

Daaaaaaahhhhhhh men hands down me and my sis went to eat doubles and she eat 4 and I eat 12 no Woman could beat a man when it comes to eating double

Men. I know a guy who ate 43 doubles!

Allyuh eh kno some ah my female friends nah . . . doh get between dem & dey doubles . . . lol.

Finally coming up to Carnival, people just want to celebrate:

Come on, wave your grease paper in the air . . . Carnival around the corner, palance wit a doubles in yuh mouth . . . Bodow!!!

And sing:

First I was afraid, I was petrified. Kept tinking how can i eat Dis alloo pie. But I spent so many nights, Eating sahena & cachurie, I grew strong, I added channa all along. & so you're back, from Debe. I jus walked in to find u here, Wit dat tamarand sauce in yor face. I should hav told u buy more doubles, I should hav made go back 4 more. If I had known for jus 1 second, Dat u would eat all d Doubles, I can sure do wit 1 more!!!

There are dozens of pages like these. Clearly, unlike the rest of my evidence, this is not a personal page but a 'fan' page. But it demonstrates the way Facebook facilitates a public arena in which people, having taken the trouble to craft their wit and innuendo, are able to use the results, not just in banter with a couple of friends, but digitally to inscribe them for an audience of thousands, as in this case, or hundreds when they post on personal pages. I therefore wish to extend my thanks to all you original writers of these excerpts, may you never run short of Doubles when you need them. Meanwhile I now have a desperate urge to take the London underground to Clapham North and pay a call to Roti Joupa. See you there ☺

Part II

The Anthropology of Facebook

Introduction

The three final essays of this book will provide a more analytical and more anthropological consideration of Facebook. The first reflects the methodology of anthropology, based on an ethnographic examination of a particular population, rather than a study of Facebook more generally. This essay considers Facebook as though it were a specifically Trinidadian construction, asking how Facebook impacts on Trinidad, but even more how Trinidad impacts upon Facebook.

The second essay moves from the local ethnography, broadened by this comparative analogy, to consider some general issues about Facebook. Despite the extraordinarily short time that Facebook has been with us, we can at least tentatively enquire what we have learnt from it, not so much what Facebook is but rather what its consequences might be for society, community and social relationships more generally.

The final essay starts from the other end of the anthropological endeavour. It seeks to balance the parochialism of ethnography with a comparative perspective, in this case, taking an exemplary anthropological study of a small island off the coast of New Guinea with only around 500 people, and composing an extended analogy between a theory created to comprehend that population as culture with the findings of this research on Facebook. The intention is to construct a theory of Facebook.

A

The Invention of *Fasbook*

The starting point for an anthropologist researching Facebook is that there is no such thing. The word Facebook stands for the social networking facility developed in the US. But what any given population actually uses, based on that facility, quickly develops its own local cultural genre and expectations, which will differ from others. One of the more extraordinary findings is the degree to which we may discuss specifically Trinidadian netiquette in the use of Facebook after only, in most cases, less than two years of usage. The portraits are replete with arguments and evidence as of the particularities of Trinidadian usage. So this essay provides only a brief résumé of the main points of localization, implicated within the portraits themselves.

While this chapter will generalize about Facebook in Trinidad, and the next offer tentative theses about Facebook in general, it is not easy to determine the extent to which Trinidad Facebook corresponds to any global Facebook. The situation will become clearer when comparative studies are published. On the one hand, statistics (see the Preface) show that Trinidad has a smaller population of users (26 per cent) than countries such as the UK and the US, but a higher one relative to the possession of internet connections. Currently, the fastest increase in usage is the 65-plus age group and there is a general correlation between the increasing spread of Facebook and increasing age. During the conduct of the ethnography, my impression was of a still higher access to

Facebook than that given in these statistics and also of comparatively high usage per person in terms of hours of the day spent on Facebook. Both the statistics and my own observations suggest higher female than male use, both in numbers of accounts and hours spent on Facebook.

In Trinidad, the idea that Facebook is Trinidadian, rather than merely an imported facility, is captured by the terms *Fasbook* or *Macobook*. To be *fas* is to try and get to know another person rather too quickly, as compared to the accepted etiquette. To be *maco* is to be nosy, constantly trying to pry into other people's private business. Since both of these terms are seen as particularly characteristic of Trinidadian behaviour, there seems to be a natural affinity between the propensity within the infrastructure of Facebook itself and the cultural inclination of Trinidadians. A leading historian of Trinidad told me a story about how, when the Caribbean islands were considering coming together in a united political entity in the late 1950s, they decided against making Port of Spain their capital for fear of the disruptive effect of the Trinidadian love of rumour and gossip.

The portrait of Josanne (chapter 9) includes a detailed discussion of the centrality of bacchanal to the very idea of being Trinidadian, how, when working on an imported US soap opera, *The Young and the Restless*, this appeared as the one-word shorthand people used to describe Trini character. It is the term that helps us understand the role of Carnival, the festival of bacchanal at the centre of Trinidadian life. Bacchanal in turn relies upon the central role of sex in Trinidad as an expression of the truth about what human beings in the end really are, and what they will inevitably end up doing despite themselves. It used to be said that the absence of sex leads inevitably to madness. The basis of gender relations was exchange, where men are granted access to women's sexuality only to the degree that they labour on their behalf. Still today many women are sceptical of formal marriage since their male partners may then take sex for granted, rather than it being dependent on men continuing to work on behalf of the wider family.[1]

This would have been a better description of Trinidadians fifty years ago rather than today: since then, migration and

---

[1] Miller, D. (1994), *Modernity: An Ethnographic Approach*. Oxford: Berg, pp. 168–201.

cosmopolitan experience have exposed people to many other values. It was always truer of Afro-Trinidadian cosmology than that of the Indo-Trinidadian. There are other co-existing value systems, such as those based on religious belief, which abhor such ideas about sex and nature. In a previous book on modernity, which represents my most detailed exposition of Trinidadian society and cosmology, this culture of bacchanal appears as only one part of Trinidadian cosmology. The other explores the desire in Trinidad to build long-lasting reputations and structures that take from history and create a future. If the values of bacchanal that include the tearing down of facades in the interest of egalitarianism are celebrated at Carnival, then the values of family and respectability and the past are celebrated at Christmas, an equally important moment within the annual cycle of Trinidadian life. In this earlier book, I had suggested that modern life in Trinidad, indeed modernity more generally, is based on the structured opposition between these two forms of time, one orientated entirely to the moment, the other to the longer term. This explains why, in Josanne's portrait, the description of a sex scandal is juxtaposed with the example of a memorial website after the death of her cousin. Nevertheless, the concept of bacchanal and its enshrinement in Carnival remains pervasive and the portraits themselves demonstrate how appropriate the terms *Fasbook* and *Macobook* have become to the experience of Facebook. All those participants who live in more traditional communities regard Facebook bacchanal as slight and tame compared to offline bacchanal. For those now detached from such communities, it is probable that Facebook restores to them at least some measure of nosiness, gossip and scandal.

So when Facebook washed up on the shores of Trinidad, it felt as though someone in the US, who had never heard of the place, had unwittingly invented an instrument that is the purest expression of Trinidadian culture. Equally, *The Young and the Restless* was seen as a soap opera predestined for Trinidad because its storylines so often resorted to the disruption caused by sexual scandal. As noted in the Preface, I would make similar argument even about commodities such as[2] *Coca-Cola*, insisting that we cannot just assume that to drink *Coca-Cola* is to import the symbolic meanings of

---

[2] Miller, D. (1997), '*Coca-Cola*: A Black Sweet Drink from Trinidad', in D. Miller (ed.), *Material Cultures*. London: UCL Press/University of Chicago Press.

this drink as created in the US, rather foregrounding the primacy of local constructions of meaning – based on the opposition between what are locally called *black sweet drinks* and *red sweet drinks.*

These arguments are crucial to contemporary anthropology. If the globalization of drinks such as Coca-Cola, or of digital instruments such as Facebook, indicate only global homogenization, then this implies a decline in cultural diversity and specificity. These are the core subjects of anthropological investigation. However, if these imported products then become subject to processes of localization that make their regional appropriation distinctive, then they can become the source of new forms of cultural diversity. So anthropology is showing some self-interest here. It becomes a more relevant and necessary discipline to the degree that Facebook is transformed into *Fasbook.*

The point is made evident in the detail, as well as in generality. When Marvin's marriage breaks up, it is not because he thinks there is some more universal or psychological generalization to be made about what people tend to do with Facebook. It is because he has a very local and specific expectation of what his partner can't help but do, as a 'macotious' Trini, constantly looking into the private world of every single woman he has any contact with on Facebook. It is less clear whether the evidence that in Trinidad 'to friend' traditionally meant 'to have sex with' has a bearing on such cases. Alana is not comparing Facebook with some general definition of community derived from social science but with her own hamlet. When Vishala says that the truth of another person is more likely to be found in their Facebook profile than through meeting them face to face, this implies a very Trinidadian concept of truth and authenticity. Similarly, the businessman Burton's argument that, in order to understand Facebook, you need first to appreciate how people are themselves social networking sites, is framed by what he regards as the particular way Trinis engage in business as opposed to the behaviours he witnessed working abroad.

The starting gun that launched this research was the way the debacle between Kanye West and Taylor Swift spread virally through my Trinidadian Facebook, rather than my US or UK Facebook friends. When this was mentioned to a woman in Trinidad, she argued as follows:

'I found this out 5 seconds after it happened on Facebook and I was in London and I had absolutely no clue. And everybody's status was, "Oh My God, I can't believe Kanye did that." And then other people also said, "I don't know what the hell we have to get so excited about. Who the hell is Taylor Swift and Kanye to us?" Because they're obsessed. There's a complete obsessiveness about our preoccupation with what each other are doing. And I think it has to do with the smallness of people's minds in terms of their social interactions or the allowed social interactions. I'm not saying that people are small-minded. I think it has to do with their sense of themselves and how their sense of the world is shrunk.'

We don't have to agree. It could instead be evidence of how much their world has expanded. As seen in the portrait of Dr Karamath, there is an upside to this gossip about an event in the US. Trinis in general seem far more knowledgeable about world events and far less parochial than, for example, citizens of the US, quite possibly for the reasons she has just given. Global gossip is also research and knowledge, and a facility for gathering information that also reflects the unusually high levels of education, and respect for education, in Trinidad. Apart from anthropologists, academics may not like the idea that they train people to be good at gossip. But this is research. The comment just cited was negative but Trinidadians engage in this kind of self-critical examination from a position of generally possessing far higher degrees of personal self-confidence than one usually encounters elsewhere. As a highly educated middle class, Trinidadians who migrate to work abroad are, in the main, very successful in their careers.

Given that so many of these participants had spent time abroad, mainly in Canada, the UK and the US, it was often possible to ask them directly about what they saw as the differences between using Facebook in Trinidad and elsewhere. The most common response, apart from references to *Macobook*, was not about what people actually do on Facebook. It concerned the number of times they hear people discussing Facebook in offline situations, such as on a maxi-taxi or in a shop. One of the final stories recounted during this fieldwork was from a woman who plays a game with her boyfriend, involving which of them can be the first to say the word 'Facebook' out loud when they overhear such a reference in a conversation. This is a striking distinction. Facebook is not such a constant motif of offline chat in the UK that would make it possible to play such a game. This corresponds well with the Trinidadian focus on bacchanal, since ultimately the impact of Facebook as gossip will come to depend at least as much on the degree to which it permeates the rest of offline life as anything that happens on Facebook itself.

For an anthropologist, this wider context is of particular significance. Facebook does not exist in isolation. No one lives just on Facebook. When people talk about Facebook in Trinidad, they don't suggest it is a community in its own right. It is just one of the structures of social networking. They compare it more often to liming. A lime is not the same as a community, but without liming Trinidad would not have this specific kind of community. To lime, with its spontaneity and unpredictability, is the most characteristic form of Trinidadian socializing. The lime is the ingredient that gives Trinidad its flavour, which then extends to Trinidadian Facebook.

It is these arguments that confirm the initial point: that there is no such thing as Facebook from the perspective of cultural relativity. Facebook is only the aggregate of its regional and particular usage. This essay aggregates at the level of the island. It thereby emphasizes heterogeneity of usage as compared to the world, but overly homogenizes usage within the island itself. But the twelve portraits in turn bear witness to this internal diversity. On the other hand, while we need to acknowledge diversity, if this whole volume was an exercise in tracing localized cultural appropriation, then it would leave us cast adrift on the isolated rocks of regionalism and parochialism, unable to say anything about Facebook more generally. So the anthropological complement to this first chapter is the last chapter which presents a general theory of Facebook based on an extended analytical comparison with an anthropological theory of culture. Between them lies the world of partial generalization which is often where most of the significant consequences will be found, and to which we now turn.

B

Fifteen Theses on What Facebook Might Be

So far, Facebook has been discussed as *Fasbook*, its local manifestation in Trinidadian culture. Without this injection of cultural relativism, we could easily be drawn into making vast generalizations about what Facebook is and its social consequences, based on assumptions about the functions of technology or some general model of human psychology. With the protective caveat of cultural relativism, we have reached the point where it should be safe to engage tentatively with some of the more general consequences of Facebook. These remain tentative since the sources for generalization are not yet robust. The main evidence will still be the research in Trinidad, together with my wider experience of Facebook as a user with friends in the UK and other countries. In addition, this is the point of engagement with the burgeoning literature that is currently emerging about Facebook through various academic books and papers, though I tend to make only very slight use of journalism and anecdote since, with a base of four hundred million users, almost anything that can happen today will also happen on Facebook, but an instance is not of itself a sign of anything consequential. These fifteen theses will commence with issues of personal relationships, proceed to the idea of Facebook as community and conclude by considering other transformations, such as those of time and space.

Facebook and the individual

How Facebook helps to make relationships

As noted in the portrait of the businessman Burton, the anthropological starting point in understanding Facebook is to appreciate that each and every individual was quite literally a social networking site long before Facebook existed. Anthropologists tend to focus upon kinship in which we see not individuals but always persons relative to other persons. Even in urban situations such as London, perhaps the most common way to forge new relationships has always been via the relationships we already have, the friends of friends or relatives. Sometimes this is explicit, as when you ask your best friend to help you find a date, or when Burton's business friends ask him to help them find a new profitable connection. At other times, this is less explicit, just hanging around with friends of friends. Facebook doesn't invent social networking but it certainly facilitates and expands it.

Most people feel awkward in the company of people they barely know, self-conscious about the possible effect of their words and actions. Facebook provides an attractive buffer in this regard. It helps us to find out a considerable amount about potential friends, without requiring any awkward face-to-face interaction. As they develop, more serious relationships are even more fraught with issues of potential embarrassment and misunderstanding. This is partly because relationships often assume equivalence, that at any given time both partners are approximately equal in their commitment. Fiction is full of the problems of one person wanting to commit before the other is ready, or one person misinterpreting signals as to how much someone else really wants them to spend time together. Facebook enables people to research others before they decide whether to invest themselves in a new relationship. This is most often done anonymously without that person knowing they are being researched. In Aaron's and Alana's portraits, Facebook is a place for banter and chat, especially between young men and women. They can thereby get to know about each other without the dread embarrassment of actually asking for a date and possibly being refused. Many people also research long-term friends, whom they are about to meet again, in order to save themselves from the embarrassment of having forgotten some important life event or more trivial details about what they have been doing for the last few days so that, when they do meet, they can seem up-to-speed on the friendship itself.

Prior to Facebook, the internet had already developed as a vast dating agency. Some of the most significant social networking sites, such as Friendster, were initially developed largely with this function in mind.[1] In Trinidad, the knowledge that men and women certainly check each other out is one of the key reasons for looking fit and sexy online. In the first portrait, Marvin puts this at its crudest when he claims that, whatever relationships people are in, they also always fantasize about 'trading up'.

Much of the most tedious literature on Facebook concerns the question of whether a *friend* on Facebook is a real friend. This blithely ignores the vast spectrum of people we may choose to call friends in offline worlds.[2] There is no one so stupid as to presume that all their 700 friends on Facebook are suddenly equivalent to close offline friends. One rather neat academic paper showed college students being impressed by peers whose Facebook friends numbered up to 302, but over this number the esteem in which they are held falls again.[3] We recognize that there is a huge spectrum of actual interest or concern among Facebook friends. Best friends, who are barely out of each other's company, may also post incessantly on each other's walls. They will commonly be best Facebook friends. Equally, there are people who are friended for the sole purpose of adding to the total number of friends, so that the act of Facebook friending can be inconsequential. More importantly, people have quickly come to recognize the new genre of purely Facebook *friends*, people you come to know much better because you see their postings every day. You may occasionally comment on them but you are never likely to meet them in any other capacity than on Facebook. When I first went onto Facebook, I agreed to be friended by ex-students, though after a short while I stopped this. But some of those early Facebook friends are people I feel I have now come to know quite well,

[1]   boyd, d. and Ellison, N. (2007), 'Social Networking Sites: Definition, History and Scholarship', *Journal of Computer-Mediated Communication* 13(1), article 11. http://jcmc.indiana.edu/vol13/issue1/boyd.ellison.html.

[2]   Pahl, R. (2000), *On Friendship*. Cambridge: Polity.

[3]   Tong, S., Van Der Heide, B. and Langwell, L. (2008), 'Too Much of a Good Thing? The Relationship Between Number of Friends and Interpersonal Impressions on Facebook', *Journal of Computer-Mediated Communication* 13: 531–49.

which was not the case when they were students, yet I still never expect to see them again. I don't think any of us care whether or not we are properly called a friend.

The reason for the prevalence of such debates may be more than just pedantic semantics. In conversations about Facebook, there is a common theme that pertains to a fear of the modern. This is the fear that we are all becoming more superficial, that Facebook *friends* represent a kind of inflation that diminishes the value of prior or true friendship. I see no evidence that this is the case: close friends are even more intensely in touch. We can also theorize about how Facebook can proliferate friendship without diminishing it by observing that Facebook clearly provides greater efficiencies in friendship. Thanks to Facebook, one can maintain a friendship with less expenditure of time or dependency upon transport. It is possible to argue that driving two hours to see someone is a sign of deep friendship. But it is equally possible to argue that using those two hours in direct IM communication, discussing, for example, the breakup of someone else's relationship or reciprocally viewing our activities, makes for a deeper friendship than sitting in traffic just so we can meet face to face.

Ethnographic fieldwork over several projects provides evidence that communicative technologies can have a significant effect on sexual relationships. Working on the impact of mobile phones in Jamaica,[4] it seemed very likely that the increase in the ease with which people can have private personal conversations had, in and of itself, made illicit or multiple sexual liaisons more common and easier to get away with. This may be one of the most significant consequences of the spread of mobile phones. By contrast, while Facebook can also be used for secret assignations, the evidence from Trinidad suggests that in the main it has the opposite effect. No one ever knows who might be taking a picture of them and posting it on Facebook. Almost everyone had stories about friends who had had photos posted with people they were not supposed to have been with. My guess would be that Trinis are having less illicit or multiple sexual relationships simply because it has become that much harder to keep these from the public gaze, in

---

[4] Horst, H. and Miller, D. (2006), *The Cell Phone: Anthropology of Communication.* Oxford: Berg.

which case, Facebook and mobile phones work in direct opposition to each other.

This exposure can also devastate established relationships, as in the case of Marvin, mainly through making partners much more aware of other friendships. Facebook also facilitates the stalking of partner's friends. As one woman put it,

> 'You check their page religiously. OK did they add someone new because that number was 147 yesterday and now it's 148 today. You can get obsessive about it. I'm trying not to, but it's just hard when you see it. I think some of them do it on purpose. Because I think Trinis in general just like that bacchanal and confusion and the fact that I could break up someone's relationship, even though I don't want them myself. I think so, it's very spiteful.'

She is not suggesting Facebook creates such activity, but it helps to make it more effective in destroying established relationships – see Munn on witchcraft below, p. 214.

Finally, there is the role of Facebook in the breakup of relationships. Here we possess an ideal point of reference in one of the most extensive anthropological studies of the consequences of Facebook, Ilana Gershon's[5] recent book about relationship breakup amongst US students. She is able to provide much more detail about three important aspects of Facebook: firstly, the way it is employed and the consequences of this new public arena within which breakup may occur; secondly, the way people respond to the actual choice of Facebook as opposed to face-to-face or phone or other media as the mode for actually breaking up; and thirdly, she documents the degree to which the recent advent of Facebook means that people are still very uncertain as to how to interpret other people's selection of these specific media, creating considerable scope for misunderstanding in what is an already highly sensitive situation.

How Facebook helps those who struggle with relationships

There are two portraits here that speak most clearly to the way Facebook assists those who have problems in either making or

---

[5] Gershon, I. (2010), *Breakup 2.0: Disconnecting Over New Media*. Ithaca: Cornell University Press.

retaining relationships: those of Arvind and Dr Karamath. Arvind stands for many others, both male and female, who could be described as shy, introverted or lacking in confidence. Quite often, as in his case, this can be because they have been relatively unsuccessful so far in life. They haven't had the education, the work and, so far, the partner they would have wanted. For Arvind it is possible that *FarmVille* represents a turnaround in his fortunes in all three regards. He is working to educate himself towards a job, and, thanks to *FarmVille*, towards more and perhaps deeper friendships. Time will tell. It is doubtful that Facebook is a panacea or can make all those who find relationships difficult suddenly more secure in this task. But, in the case of Arvind, it clearly helps, and it is unlikely that his case is unusual. Facebook may also reflect rather than resolve such basic inequalities. Another shy male who spends a great deal of time on Facebook looking at the activities of others almost never has the confidence to post about himself. He stands in contrast to confident extraverts who constantly make postings themselves but may not spend much time looking at those of others.

A previously noted more general example is that of the Indian women of central and south Trinidad, a society in which the individual woman was traditionally held responsible for upholding the reputation and honour of her family. When they proved to be far more forthcoming and adventurous on Facebook than anyone had expected, some saw this as demonstrating that they were growing more extravert, while others saw it as merely external evidence of a shift that had already occurred. Either way, it is clear that Facebook provides an additional space for personal expression, especially a more creative or extravert public presence, which may previously have been much restricted.

Facebook seems to be capable not just of making relationships, but also of compensating for factors that may have ended them. One of the key findings of my fieldwork in Trinidad is the rapidity with which Facebook is moving from being a site largely dominated by student use, and youth in general, to becoming an instrument available to people of all ages. Although conservatism and reluctance to embrace new technology is still associated with being older, the company's own statistics show that the most rapid increases in Facebook usage in Trinidad correlate with increasing age. Dr Karamath is not that old but he stands for all those facing increasing disability that affects their capacity to socialize. The individual in this case is the very opposite of shy and introvert: Dr Karamath was used to being the life and soul of the most cosmopolitan of parties. For him, Facebook has ridden to the rescue when physical disability seemed destined to end that sociable life.

These are just two examples of the importance of Facebook for those whose social life has become restricted. As the demographic profile of Facebook has changed, more and more groups become potentially enabled. It is entirely possible that in the longer term Facebook will be dominated by three groups: the elderly; mothers who find they have to stay at home with young children; and those who feel shy, or less attractive, or less confident, in face-to-face situations. In some measure, then, Facebook may substitute for face-to-face relationships but there is also plenty of evidence from Arvind and others that it enables people to gain more experience and confidence, which in turn facilitate offline relationships. This would then become Facebook's most positive achievement with regard to individual welfare.

Facebook as a meta-friend

What if, instead of seeing Facebook as a means of facilitating friendships between people, many of us used friendships between people to facilitate a relationship to Facebook itself? What if someone puts, under the title of relationship status, 'Married to Facebook LOL'? A common trope in modern discourse is that we feel we live in an era of materialism or fetishism, such that proper relationships between people are being replaced by relationships to things instead. This is a rather simplistic rendition of our world. In the final essay in this book, we shall see that anthropologists do not see culture as a medium constructed to facilitate friendships between persons. On the contrary, relationships and exchange between persons, for example kin relations around marriage, are usually seen as a means to develop culture, for example through exchange. So a relationship to Facebook as a thing is not axiomatically inferior to a relationship with a person.

Given that it is a social network, perhaps the simplest idiom for conceiving of this relationship to Facebook itself is to think of it as a sort of meta-best friend. In the popular culture of TV, in programmes such as *Sex and the City*, a best friend is the person we turn to when we are feeling lonely, depressed or bored, when life seems to have less purpose than usual. Our best friend is the one who is least likely to mind being disturbed when having a meal, or wanting to go to sleep, because they sense our deep need to engage in long, gossipy discussions about ourselves or others, just to make us feel better. One advantage of Facebook is that it is a totally reliable best friend. Even at 3 a.m., when not even our bestest best friend wants to be disturbed, we can turn to Facebook, feel connected with all those other lives and come out less lonely and less bored, though, of course, we may also end up more depressed or jealous because of the revelations about all those very active other people who don't seem lonely and bored. But this can also happen after face-to-face chats with actual best friends. Following from the previous point, there are people who see themselves as irredeemably unattractive and shunned by those who, in public, don't want to be associated with them. Fieldwork suggested this was not uncommon, especially for school-age children. Such people often find Facebook a lot more forgiving and benign. You can't say that the photos on someone else's Facebook site were posted specifically for you to see, but neither can you say they weren't. Once there, they are part of your social life.

Journalism is already rife with extreme stories of Facebook's negative impacts. It may be held responsible for people becoming jealous and murdering their lover, or for paedophilic grooming. To a lesser extent, there are also positive stories about how Facebook has stopped someone from committing suicide and helps those who are depressed. With 500 million users, we can be pretty sure that most stories and anecdotes about what Facebook might be capable of doing are true, however extreme. But one reason this volume barely refers to journalism and anecdote, preferring more systematic research, is that such instances may be so exceptional as to be largely inconsequential except for the people directly involved in those cases. It is, however, not necessary to suggest that Facebook as a meta-best friend necessarily cures depression or prevents suicide. We can still recognize that it is plausible that, for a certain proportion of people, it does act to complement offline friendships to become significant as a friend in its own right.

Facebook is somewhere we can talk as much as we like, with or without responses from others. It is a site that genuinely addresses the perennial problem of boredom, especially teenage boredom, without necessarily imposing on the time of others. It has its limits; it doesn't get drunk when we do. It doesn't always comment back when we want it to. You can only 'sort of' have sex with it. But at a meta-level, it may serve. Some of the most poignant examples we found included the case of a person who posted constantly about a premature baby, and another of someone who posted about a parent afflicted with terminal illness. It was observed that these individuals did not seem too concerned if the responses they received were not always from people they knew well. Facebook was the public sharing of suffering, the feeling that Facebook was a 'witness' to suffering that might be cathartic in its own right. The fact that Facebook is made up of actual people may give it unprecedented power and plausibility to act in this meta-person-like manner. The downside to this relationship was very evident in the portrait of Joseph and Nneka and the BlackBerry. We may use the phrase 'addicted to Facebook' a little too easily and loosely. But for Joseph, Nneka's addiction was as lethal to their relationship as if she had been addicted to heroin. Clearly, we cannot dismiss the possibility that Facebook may indeed become a fetish.

Facebook as transforming our relationship to privacy

If there is one thing that shocks those who either rarely use or do not use Facebook, it is the awareness of how little regard people may have for Facebook's potential to destroy privacy. What perturbs them most is not that there is a failure to understand these consequences but that nonetheless there is the deliberate and intentional use of Facebook to transform the private into the public. Why on earth would a husband utter tender words of endearment to his wife on Facebook? Isn't that something for the privacy of their bedroom? Why should people admit to hugely embarrassing incidents and even post photos of those incidents where a huge number of other people can see them? One of the earliest papers on the topic was called 'Facebook's "Privacy Trainwreck"'.[6] It has dominated discussion about the consequences of Facebook, including several associated 'moral panics'.[7] It is also the issue

---

[6]   boyd, d. (2006), 'Facebook's "Privacy Trainwreck": Exposure, Invasion, and Drama', *Apophenia Blog*. September 8, www.danah.org/papers/FacebookAndPrivacy. html.

[7]   Debatin, B., Lovejoy, J., Horn, A.-K. and Hughes, B. (2009), 'Facebook and Online

around which Facebook has most often had to retreat in the face of user concerns and accusations that it has tended to make transparency, as opposed to privacy, its default setting.[8] But it is also clear that the shock is as much a result of the way users seem comfortable with far more transparency than had been anticipated. Academics are increasingly curbed by state and institutional authorities concerned with the legal issues of data protection yet, simultaneously, they study a world in which the prophylactics of privacy are being steadily removed and the most private parts are being waved in public. In response, academics are coming up with concepts, such as 'participatory surveillance',[9] which recognize that users of Facebook seem to see positive as well as negative consequences to this loss of privacy.

Once again, we need to address such issues, not with prurient interest, but with a more cautious and sensitive evaluation of our findings. One of the most striking portraits in this collection is surely that of Ajani. She is not an invention of fiction. She exists as an intensely private person, someone really quite obsessive about her inner privacy. And yet at the same time she is one of the most prolific Facebook posters. Ajani has no qualms about blogging, or appearing in the media or any other number of public spaces. She is a consummate performer who has a keen interest in all manner of arts intended to experiment and play with the very idea of the performative. What becomes clear from her portrait is that, far from there being a contradiction between these two facets of her personality, she uses the public posting on Facebook as a means to help create and preserve her vital privacy. The portrait ends with a vision of the avatar, the unknown silent and hidden self that manipulates another highly public active self. Ajani is surely extreme, but she may thereby help clarify something that is relatively common.

The mistake is to imagine people only in terms of the particular

---

Privacy: Attitudes, Behaviors, and Unintended Consequence', *Journal of Computer-Mediated Communication* 15(1): 83–108; Marwick, A. (2008), 'To Catch a Predator? The MySpace Moral Panic', *First Monday* 13: 6; Raynes-Goldie, K. (2010), 'Aliases, Creeping, and Wall Cleaning: Understanding Privacy in the Age of Facebook', *First Monday* 15: 1–4; Rosen, L. (2006), 'Adolescents in MySpace: Identity Formation, Friendship and Sexual Predators', at www.csudh.edu/psych/lrosen.htm (accessed 19 July 2010).

8   Kirkpatrick (2010), p. 201.
9   Albrechtslund, A. (2008), 'Online Social Networking as Participatory Surveillance', *First Monday* 13: 3 March.

media with which we are concerned. Facebook never exists in isolation; it is never the totality of the lives of the people we meet. It is not surprising that it is at least as often the complement to offline lives as the expression of offline lives. Those shy East Indian girls who become extravert on Facebook may remain shy East Indian girls when they are not on Facebook. Or Facebook may be facilitating a cultural transformation that will lead to the eventual extinction of this stereotype of the shy East Indian girl.

There is however no reason to deny the obvious: that Facebook is extremely public compared to any precedent, and yet is already commonly the medium for expressing the private and intimate. Different people have very different ideas about how far they would or should make their private lives public: 'I am uncomfortable with the photos thing, where my sister will have tons of photos on Facebook. You would know all her business just through her profile pictures, the different boyfriends she has had, as you scroll backwards through the photos. So that's what I think is weird.' Things can also just leak or spiral out of control from the private to the public:

> 'My sister's friend had her whole breakup documented by her Facebook status. She and her ex-boyfriend were communicating to each other through their statuses. I think it started, like, she put up a song lyric that represented how she felt.[10] So he put up one that represented how he felt. And they went back and forth to the point where it became totally obvious and all subtlety has disappeared. And it was name calling, and it was interesting.'

Critics in Trinidad suggested that such couples might be able to work out their issues in private but putting this into the public domain makes that less likely. In one case, it was noted that constantly posting about the process of reconciliation the couple was undergoing was probably not the best idea. As Gershon notes, there are a wide variety of responses to the act of making a change within a relationship 'Facebook official'.[11]

The normal distinction between public and private does not work for Facebook. There is no longer a contrast between the

---

[10] This use of pop song lyrics to hint at feelings seems to be very common amongst the US students documented in Gershon (2010), pp. 125–30.

[11] Gershon (2010), pp. 65–78.

private and an entirely unbounded anonymous mass that might constitute the kind of public sphere that reads celebrity magazines or watches *Big Brother*. The 'public' represented by Facebook is better understood as an aggregate of private spheres. It consists of all the people one knows privately, but in one place and open to each other. Still, there are important and specific consequences of addressing this larger body of aggregate private connections through text and photos on Facebook rather than in conversation with particular individuals. The bacchanal and discomfort that derives from Facebook are often a consequence of the way transient feelings and actions, once inscribed in text, come to have longer-term effects than intended. There were many instances in this fieldwork of someone losing their temper, getting angry or drunk, or otherwise being in a state that would normally be a passing phase. However, during that time they posted something on Facebook that they would subsequently come to regret: a nasty remark about their then partner, or a revelation about themselves. Once in the public domain, this could not be ignored. This might include children expressing strong feelings of anguish and anger about their parents. Although examples of this did not appear during this research in Trinidad, it was an important component during an earlier research trip carried out with Mirca Madianou in the Philippines. There we encountered cases of children posting feelings of anger and resentment that seemed to imply abuse. This public airing could have a beneficial effect in revealing actual abuse, but it is such a crude and undirected outpouring of emotions that it was probably something that many would regret in the longer term. Once such a suggestion is out there, it can no longer be put into a bottle called 'private and past'. It is hard for it not to be remembered, even when retracted.

Another issue that comes up in the portrait of the businessman Burton, but also that of others, is the difference it makes when one's work colleagues, and more specifically one's boss, becomes a Facebook friend. There were many stories about problems that arose (recall the admonition not to post a photo of yourself on the beach when you have taken a day's sick leave) or even people losing their jobs as a result of incautious revelations. The most extreme example of inadvertent exposure is the case of the singer Josanne.

A more specific privacy issue is the threat to confidentiality when networks come together on Facebook that were previously distinct. In our earlier research on the Philippines, the most important example was the juxtaposition of kinship and friendship. Trinidad may be unusual in that Trinis seem more concerned to be more careful about what they post in relation to a work colleague than to a relative. They were largely relaxed about the juxtaposition of friends and kin. In the Philippines and elsewhere, the quintessential moment of clash tended to be when one's mother asked to be one's friend. The most heated discussion on my own Facebook page was in response to my posing the question of how people would respond to such a request. It came to the fore in our Philippine research because this is a study of long-distance relationships between mothers who live mainly as domestic workers in the UK and their children left behind in the Philippines. In the most extreme case, a son was traumatized by seeing the mother whom he had idolized at a distance appear on Friendster, where her photos made her look, in his words, 'like a prostitute'. Another child traumatized the new family of her father (who hadn't previously known of her existence) merely by getting in touch. More common, though, is the embarrassment of a family whose quarrels may be exposed to public view on Facebook and the discomfiture of children whose everyday activities are being examined in fine detail by their parents.[12]

Facebook as the transformation of self and self-consciousness

This is a work of anthropology rather than psychology,[13] but it is worth at least speculating upon the role of Facebook in facilitating the fantasy worlds of individuals. Imagine a novel in which two work colleagues barely exchange more than a few sentences, an occasional comment on what the other is wearing, but little more. Yet in the mind of one, each word actually spoken, each glance is

---

[12] For details, see Madianou, M. and Miller, D. (forthcoming), *Migration and New Media: Transnational Families and Polymedia.*

[13] There are many books and papers that try and claim general psychological consequences of using Facebook and the internet. Some tend to platitudes and 'counselling', e.g. Osuagwu, N. (2009), *Facebook Addiction.* New York: Ice Cream Melts Publishing; or Rise, J. (2009), *The Church of Facebook.* New York: David C. Cook. For more serious popular psychology, see Carr, N. (2010), *The Shallows: What the Internet Is Doing to Our Brains.* Colorado Springs: W. W. Norton; or Shirky, C. (2010), *Cognitive Surplus.* London: Penguin Press.

dissected in minute detail. The man thereby convinces himself that he is now completely in love and in thrall to this work colleague and would surely leave his wife for her if only he didn't have children. He knows exactly which Greek island will be the site of their passionate tryst. A little molehill of conversation becomes the mountain that moves Tristan and Isolde. My evidence for the impact of Facebook in this regard is very limited but it seems likely that the increased ability of people to observe passively and 'follow' another person gives even more licence to their internal fantasy world where they can imagine whatever they may choose to happen between them. It is therefore possible that one of the most significant impacts of Facebook will be on an internal world of fantasy and imagination, where many people spend much of their time.

One of the first discussions regarding the impact of the internet that looked more deeply into its possible consequences was the book, *The Second Self,* by Sherry Turkle.[14] Much of her discussion concerned the implications of anonymity and the way people could appear quite different from their offline selves when online. Although she doesn't make explicit use of his work, her discussion leads back to Erving Goffman,[15] the author of the most rewarding of all social science writings about the self. Yet Facebook points us in the opposite direction to this concern with anonymity, indicating rather an end to anonymity. This alone should give pause for thought for anyone who thinks such digital technologies lay down a consistent path in any given direction. In either case, such debates release us from any simple or colloquial assumption that there is evidence of a truer or less true self, or that these correspond to the distinction between online and offline selves. What Goffman and Turkle reveal is that all versions of the self are to some degree performative and based on certain frames of expectation. We play a variety of roles in life with different degrees of attachment and distance.

Vishala reveals that the Trinidadian concept of truth with regard to who a person really is differs significantly from what you would

---

[14] Turkle, S. (1984), *The Second Self*. Cambridge, MA: MIT Press.
[15] Goffman. E. (1956), *The Presentation of Self in Everyday Life*. Edinburgh: University of Edinburgh Social Sciences Research Centre; Goffman, E. (1974) *Frame Analysis*. Cambridge, MA: Harvard University Press.

be likely to encounter in England. In a recent edited collection,[16] several papers investigate the way different populations conceive of the individual. The concept of a self and self-consciousness is often bound up with a deeper idea of truth, the existential question of how far a person feels they are being true to themselves. This is exemplified in the final portrait of Nicole who only found herself to be pretty through viewing the 400 photos her boyfriend posted of her on Facebook. Some people feel that the person they create on Facebook is a seamless expression of how they are in other contexts. Vishala, however, believes the online person is a truer reflection than the person we meet. Others would strongly assert the opposite is true. Even more complex is Ajani, since neither the incredibly public Ajani you meet on Facebook nor the even more private Ajani you never meet at all constitutes Ajani. Any truth of who she is exists in the extreme nature of this contrast and the relation between them.

To determine whether, or to what degree, Facebook itself makes a difference to the nature of the self or self-consciousness is extremely difficult. For example, one could argue that the sheer number of postings of photographs of a person online must create a new self-consciousness about one's appearance. As one person commented,

> 'I think for teenagers Facebook is just dangerous, and seeing every-body's photos, it makes you so superficial. It's like constantly looking in a mirror and seeing yourself reflected. But through other people's eyes. So you have everybody's opinions coming down on you, because everyone will comment on your photos. "And, oh I love your top" or this and that, and you never know, it's just con-stant. So I don't think it's healthy for teenagers at all or anybody who has insecurities.'

There were many versions of this idea that Facebook makes us more concerned with appearances and thus more superficial but often such arguments work by contrasting the present with a mythical, more authentic past. I was conducting fieldwork in Trinidad long before the invention of the internet, and at times I would spend several hours with young women who were deciding

---

[16] Miller, D. (ed.) (2009), *Anthropology and the Individual*. Oxford: Berg.

what to wear before going out for an evening. They would try on seven different outfits to get the right image. It's hard to imagine they could be any more self-conscious about their public appearance now than they were then. At that time, I argued that in an egalitarian society, such as Trinidad, the concept of the self is less dependent upon some interior being or institutionalized position or role. The self is a more transient creation, largely formed by other people's response to your appearance which alone tells you who you are. So if the truth of who you are exists largely in other people's response to your appearance, it may not be that unreasonable to be obsessed about one's public image.

To take this a stage further, Marilyn Strathern[17] argues with respect to Melanesian societies that making things visible is itself constitutive of relationships. For example, when there is a new baby, this is the visual evidence for the relationship that created that baby and gives rise to the social establishment of that relationship. On Facebook, the category 'relationship status' is much more than a reflection of the status of a relationship. Facebook can become the medium of visibility which helps to create or to break relationships, partly because it brings to the fore knowledge that could have remained in the back of your mind (e.g. your partner's other relationships).

This idea that making a relationship visible also creates that relationship can extend to the self. Facebook is a virtual place where you discover who you are by seeing a visible objectification of yourself. Central to Trinidadian cosmology, as found in Carnival, is the belief that a mask or outward appearance is not a disguise. As something you have crafted or chosen and not merely been born with, the mask is a better indication of the actual person than your unmasked face. This is why Vishala states that the true person is the person you meet on Facebook not the person you meet face to face. It follows that the truth about yourself is revealed to yourself by what you post on Facebook. On Facebook, you find out who you are.

The next stage is to account for the more general compulsion to post things about the self in this public domain. The question raised by the issue of privacy was why people put such private and intimate exchanges online. In the final essay on Melanesia,

[17] Strathern, M. (1986), *The Gender of the Gift*. Berkeley: University of California Press.

reference will be made to Jean Paul Sartre's concept of 'witnessing'. There are powerful religious undercurrents to the idea that everything we do is seen, or should be seen, by another, perhaps divine, force. A common trope in the various forms of Christianity found in Trinidad is the idea of an all-witnessing God from whom nothing is or should be hidden. There is a secular equivalent in Freud's concept of the superego, the introjected image of one's own parents who see everything and again become the foundation for our moral evaluations. In philosophy, this becomes central to the work of Levinas[18] and the proposition that we are constituted as moral agents only in relation to this third observing other, which corresponds to the divine. It is the belief that there is a witness out there that is often the drive behind moral action.

These reflections imply a kind of necessity people may feel with regard to ensuring there is a higher and wider scrutiny of their personal exchanges and self-presentations, that is, people may want an assurance that there is some higher or moral evaluation, and use Facebook to ensure that this exists, in which case what Facebook provides is not only some particular friends who may comment, nor even a meta-best friend. We have reached the point where Facebook may be regarded as providing a crucial medium of visibility and public witnessing. It gives us a moral encompassment within which we have a sense not only of who we are but of who we ought to be. Facebook is normative not just in the sense of a consensual netiquette, but also as a force for witnessing the moral order of the self – not for all people, and not necessarily. But without some kind of explanation of this ilk it is hard to account for what often appears as a compulsion to place things under a generic public gaze rather than to post them to any particular person. Such an argument would render Facebook anything but superficial. It may perhaps, for some, be equivalent to the presence of the divine as witness in their lives.

---

[18] Levinas, E. (1985), *Ethics and Infinity*, trans. Richard Cohen. Pittsburgh, PA: Duquesne University Press. See also Borgerson, J. (2010), 'Witnessing and Organization: Existential Phenomenological Reflections on Intersubjectivity', *Philosophy Today* 54(1): 78–87 for a specific discussion of the impact of witnessing on relationships and engagement more generally.

Facebook and the community

Facebook has reversed two centuries of flight from community

The last essay ended with a speculative thesis with regard to the impact of Facebook on our inner being, for which there exists little evidence. By contrast, we can now turn to the best-documented and the most significant impact that Facebook can be seen to have had in the world. Over the last century and more, almost all writings about modern life have emphasized the diminishing presence of tightly-knit social communities. There is no discipline more affected by this contention than anthropology. One reason students are drawn to the study of anthropology is the feeling that they are no longer living in a community and are driven to understand what has thereby been lost. The classic texts of the discipline from Malinowski or Boas satisfy this interest. They are further confirmed by a sociological tradition rooted in Durkheim, Tönnies and Simmel, a sociology whose leitmotif is this same decline of community and the subsequent drift towards the isolation and anonymity of urban crowds. Common within such critiques is an association between this loss of community and the rise of capitalism and industrialization. The resurrection of community is the green heart of environmentalism.

Books such as Putnam's *Bowling Alone* or Sennett's *The Fall of Public Man*[19] add substance to this general trend in contemporary and historical studies. This study of Facebook may be considered in some respects a sequel to my earlier book, *The Comfort of Things*.[20] That book, like the current volume, presented a series of portraits but made some very different points. The final chapter of *The Comfort of Things* examines the degree to which people in London live in the relative isolation of households. Typically, they expect only minimal contact with neighbours or neighbourhoods. They may have social networks around the workplace or a church, but increasingly they do not. Up to now this flight from close-knit community has seemed inexorable, and it is this which makes Facebook quite extraordinary. It flies in the face of most

[19] Putnam, R. (2001), *Bowling Alone*. New York: Simon and Schuster; Sennett, R. (1977), *The Fall of Public Man*. New York: Knopf.
[20] Miller, D. (2008), *The Comfort of Things*. Cambridge: Polity.

generalizations made by social scientists to explain this historical trajectory away from close-knit community. The precise definition of community is subject to considerable debate,[21] but participants in this research seemed comfortable using the word 'community' to compare their experience of Facebook and their offline lives. In this volume, the term has referred simply to this colloquial usage as encountered in Trinidad. But whatever exactly we mean by the word 'community', Facebook seems to have revived and expanded it.

What almost all users say about their pattern of friending on Facebook is that they are loath to include people they have not met in person. Friending usually begins by replicating a core group of offline friends but it quickly expands to include pretty much anyone that a person did at some time or other know personally, even if they have subsequently lost touch with them. The classic act of Facebook friending is to find and friend an individual with whom you once went to school, or a cousin who migrated abroad and with whom you lost touch. Facebook seems like the end of what previously was the natural attrition of social networks. It brings all those once disregarded back into the frame of current regard. Equally important is the facility of Facebook to bring back diaspora populations and ameliorate the effect of their residence in different countries.

Once a friend is on Facebook, it does not mean at all that they become people with whom you directly exchange comments or messages. That category remains a relatively small group of close friends. There is a danger that we might dismiss Facebook, once we see evidence that most people remain in constant contact with the same small group of people. But while they may not be in constant dyadic communication, individuals will commonly observe the postings of this wider sphere. Trinidadians constantly view the photos that a much wider range of others put online than those they talk to. This seems to convince them that they once again know these people. They feel they are now aware of what these more remote contacts are up to, and have become sufficiently concerned that they now want to keep up with a narrative of their

---

[21] Posthill provides many good reasons for not using the word 'community' as an academic term, but I see an advantage in the familiarity of this as a colloquial term in a book such as this which is seeking a wide audience. See Postill, J. (2008), 'Localising the Internet beyond Communities and Networks', *New Media and Society* 10(3): 413–31.

lives. But then most offline communities always were a kind of soap opera, comprising other people's narratives.

Rather than arguing the point abstractly, we can take advantage of the fact that this fieldwork included people, such as Alana, who were born and brought up in conditions generally regarded as a real community: small hamlets or villages where everyone knows each other, are largely descended from the same kin groups, and where there is considerable collective activity. If people like Alana seem to agree that Facebook does indeed represent something they recognize as community, there seems little reason to refute their claims. When her school meets online after midnight, Facebook is not just an aggregate of personal networks, it is a group activity. Critical to this observation is the question of whether people who interact online do so at the expense of offline interaction. A paper by the sociologists Hampton and Wellman,[22] which compared two communities in Canada, suggests that the group who were heavily networked online tended also to extend their social interaction offline in contrast to those who lacked these online facilities. When Facebook was first invented as a facility for students, it was assumed that it would be used to help people organize themselves to go drinking or to parties or even lectures and to share their subsequent experiences. This is what more or less happened, with Facebook facilitating rather than substituting for offline interaction.

So, although the fear was often expressed, there was no evidence in Trinidad that people spent less time together as a result of Facebook. Rather, Facebook is assumed to be a facility people used to coordinate and organize offline events, from occasional family reunions to daily discussion of homework. As noted in the previous section, it is more that Facebook can assist where people find offline sociality difficult. In the earlier portraits, several references were made to both the high level of violence, especially murder, and the very heavy traffic as two reasons why Trinidadians felt constrained from face-to-face socializing. Clearly, there are some people who are unwilling to go out at night for fear, and others who flinch from being delayed in their cars for hours. They would reason, quite plausibly that, while

---

[22] Hampton, K. and Wellman, B. (2003), 'Neighboring in Netville', *City and Community* 2(4): 277–311.

an interaction with someone on Facebook is not a substitute for seeing them face to face, it is preferable to seeing them in a state of fear and anxiety about how they are going to get home safely and quickly.

Particularly important are the observations about Facebook made by Alana. She suggested that people who have intense offline sociality in small communities may take refuge in the less intense and mediated communication represented by Facebook. Conversely, those whose offline social lives are lacking will flock to Facebook to gain something of what they have lost, even if they don't thereby regain all the sensual contact of meeting people in the flesh. Alana's comments with regard to community reiterate those made with regard to the individual. Facebook works best when used to compensate for the deficiencies or stresses of other forms of communication. This may be regarded as one of the principal conclusions of this study.

Facebook reacquaints us with the downside of community

The term community is problematic, not just in terms of definition but because it has accrued romantic, often bucolic, significance. The less we give time to it in practice, the more we seem to fetishize community as some kind of paradise lost. Community in modern politics appears as an unalloyed good which provides the individual with support, concern and physical help. It is viewed as a bulwark against loneliness and depression. Facebook is hugely helpful in pushing us back to a more balanced and realistic understanding of the meaning and experience of close-knit community. It really does seem to possess the characteristic of most traditional face-to-face communities – a good many of which are negative. There are many reasons for the previous decline in community. It is not simply that it is no longer an option. Many people of their own volition have systematically opted for more urban and isolated lives. This may seem incomprehensible to those for whom community represents some ideal state lost in the mists of history. It was not until I lived for a year in a village in India, while conducting research for a PhD, that the cruelty, abuse and oppression, especially of women, which is potentially characteristic of village life became apparent. This was the other side to its solidarity, friendship and feelings of common identity. There are many good reasons why people are desperate to escape such close-knit communities.

By contrast, the focus upon the term bacchanal as the self-conceptualization of Trinidadian society points us directly to these problems of community. Bacchanal presumes a situation where everyone is constantly aware of each other's business. No one can hope to begin a relationship, get a tear in their clothes, or perform less well than expected in an exam without the entire world knowing about it and commenting upon it. In London, people talk sentimentally about the loss of family and kinship, and yet these same people often resent even the small amount of time they are nowadays expected to devote to family and family rituals. They are far too busy for such things. Alana, as well as others interviewed and encountered who do not appear here as portraits, seemed to regard Facebook as a milder version of offline community. What they meant was not that it is less good, but less bad. Facebook creates bacchanal and, while it could be blamed for the destruction of Marvin's marriage, it is less likely to cause physical conflict than traditional quarrels within a village and other kinds of long-term dispute and reciprocal revenge that comes with proximity over generations.

This emphasis on the dark side of community is only presented to balance our understanding, not to deny its worth. We have also seen that individuals gain comfort and support when they receive comments on their Facebook wall from people other than their close friends. At times of grief or depression, this evidence of a wider community of concern may be of considerable importance. Facebook is also directly employed to create solidarity and practical support, for example coordinating the Trinidadian response to the catastrophic earthquake in Haiti. Facebook enabled the mobilization of aid from ordinary people which might not otherwise have been possible.

To conclude, like other forms of community, Facebook has contradictory consequences. A final anecdote makes this point. A young person was diagnosed with cancer but he didn't feel ready to discuss this more generally. However, within a day or two, 'Trinidad being as it is', the news spread via Facebook. Soon he was receiving messages such as 'We are praying for you' and 'Cherish your friends and family that you have now', without anyone actually saying he had cancer. Initially, these messages made him feel as though his death was a foregone conclusion; he would have much rather no one had known. Yet later, all sorts of events and fund-raisers were organized on his behalf through Facebook.

Facebook as a site of normativity and netiquette

Central to the word 'culture' is the idea of values enshrined as normative action. In any given society, people's actions are judged according to the degree to which they seem normal, where the term 'normal' carries clear moral overtones. It is a judgement as to how people should behave. The most common expression Facebook users employ to refer to this principle of normativity is netiquette. Despite the fact that most of these participants have only used Facebook for a couple of years, or even just a couple of months, there is an expectation that they should already be aware of the various genres and codes of usage and, if they fail to abide by these, they should be subject to moral pressure and sanctions.

The very structure of Facebook tends to create normativity. This is found in the language of posting, comment, relationship status, liking, and similar terms. But in addition there are many norms and genres that are not determined by this infrastructure, for example, the various styles of postings, or the expectations of their frequency. Every time we compare Trinidadian usage with non-Trinidadian, we imply culture as normativity. Different groups of users may have different norms and may be quite explicit about them. For example, a teenager talking about the problem of 'de-friending':

'You can't do that, yeah, that's very inappropriate. That's the equivalent of saying that you are not part of my life, and that's extreme. To break that up would have affected all of my friends' lives as well. Not just the three of us who are fighting. It would have affected everybody.'

Yet in another milieu, de-friending is no big deal.[23]

---

[23] Much of Gershon (2010) is devoted to the lack of standardization in netiquette and the misunderstanding and confusions that arise precisely because people wrongly assume that others share their expectations of netiquette, especially with regard to this topic of relationship break-up, and with respect to which medium people choose to use for that break-up.

There can be direct sanctions against misbehaviour. For example, there were several stories about parents intervening to prevent their children misusing Facebook:

'About a year ago a woman, when I went to a parent–teacher's meeting in school, came and told me my son had posted some awful comments about her son on Facebook, and if I was aware of that. And I said no. And she said "well you should speak to him about it". And I spoke to him and he agreed that he did say that and he did not like that person. I said "You must be very aware of how this Facebook thing works." And I never got another complaint.'

But this form of explicit control is far less common than the rise of a more consensual netiquette conforming to emerging genres without anyone having to enforce them.

The use of Facebook often reflects pre-existing modes of normative control. The earliest established extensive social networking site was probably that of Cyworld in South Korea, a country often regarded as one of the most conformist societies in the world. Soon after its inception, there were reports of an intensification of social conformity through social networking. For example, a person who allowed their dog to foul the street was photographed on a mobile phone. This was then posted and quickly identified online, allowing almost the entire country to unite in condemnation of what was seen as anti-social behaviour.[24] Trinidad is a land of comparative licence. It will take some time to determine whether Facebook independently increases or decreases the pressures of conformity. In all likelihood, we will find instances of both.

Facebook and politics

Kirkpatrick's book, *The Facebook Effect*, begins with an example of Facebook activism, the establishment in Columbia in January 2008 of a group against FARC (Revolutionary Armed Forces of Colombia), more specifically opposing the practice within FARC of kidnapping innocent citizens for ransom and how the mere act of setting up a Facebook profile to protest led, just over a month later, to ten million people taking to the streets in an anti-FARC

---

[24] Miran Shin (pers. comm.).

demonstration. There has been much note taken of the impact of Facebook and Twitter on the anti-government protests in Iran. In teaching, I use the example of usage in response to the typhoon destruction in the Philippines. The catastrophic earthquake in Haiti occurred during the period of this research and it was very clear that Facebook had become a genuinely important medium for galvanizing the response of Trinidadians to a tragedy about which many felt very deeply.

All of this is welcome and genuine, but at the same time we should be cautious about the idea that we have finally reached some brave new public sphere representing a kind of mass, authentic politics which is what politics should always have been. Many of the same claims tend to be made in turn for any new media. For example, when mobile phones first emerged, the 'EDSA' popular overthrow of the Philippines president was credited to the use of texting to coordinate political protest, but more sober analysis suggests the impact was exaggerated[25] and today the mobile phone is no longer seen as quite so revolutionary in its political consequence, partly because the hype has moved on to social networking sites. Surely the most impressive examples of this kind of spontaneous political action culminating in the overthrow of government came with the collapse of communism in Eastern Europe. One may recall in particular the suddenness with which the apparently immovable regime of Ceauşescu in Romania was crushed in a mass uprising. None of this owed much to these new technologies.

At a lower level, there has been much enthusiasm for the more constant potential for activism facilitated by Facebook, and the example that came up several times in these portraits was the protest movement against the proposed aluminium smelter in Trinidad. Facebook certainly was used to publicize such activism internationally and to coordinate activist events locally. Similarly, Dr Karamath found that a life devoted to a series of human rights issues was effectively rescued by Facebook which became the medium that allowed him to be just as effective in this coordination as he had ever been. But again we should be cautious. Most of the Trinidadians in this project showed no interest in political action and no evidence that this was a feature of their Facebook

---

[25] Pertierra et al. (2002), *Txt-ing Selves: Cellphones and Philippine Modernity*. Manila: De La Salle University Press.

lives. Indeed, many made explicit their desire to avoid all form of political discussion as something divisive to the personal relationships which were their primary interest in Facebook. So the fact that activists clearly use Facebook is not evidence that Facebook turns more people into activists. There is at least as much hype about the internet making us more shallow than deep or more passive than active.

The other problem with this discussion of politics is the assumed benign nature of Facebook activism. Currently (July 2010), the newspapers are full of discussion of a confrontation between the UK prime minister, David Cameron, and Facebook.[26] This followed the death of Raoul Moat who shot himself in front of the police after shooting his ex-girlfriend, her current partner and a policeman. The politicians were incensed that a callous murderer now had a Facebook site, called 'R.I.P. Raoul Moat You Legend', which very quickly attracted 38,000 fans. Once again, there is nothing new about conspiracy theories against government or the use of such events to galvanize various forms of alienation and opposition. In the event, Facebook refused to have the site taken down. Nor should public action that is spontaneous and massive be seen as necessarily significant. A quintessential example of such an event was the extraordinary response to the death of Diana, Princess of Wales, yet the expected long-term memorialization never happened, and the scale of response proved of almost no significance, other than as a cathartic reaction to the event itself. So the evidence is that Facebook will become just one more medium for facilitating political action rather than a tool for the revolutionary transformation of politics. It is a sign of this more mundane presence that political candidates in Maryland will now have their usage of social networking sites regulated alongside other media.[27]

Complementary to this more direct usage in politics and activism is the suggestion that the internet more generally represents a revolutionary new form of political economy, a thesis most forcefully expressed in the three-volume work published by the sociologist Castells.[28] The problem with this and other writings

---

[26] For opposed views, compare *Daily Mirror*, 18 July 2010, 'Sick Moat a Legend? No, but PC He Shot Is' with *The Guardian*, 15 July 2010, 'Raoul Moat Page Reaction Shows PM Doesn't Get Social Media'.

[27] *Baltimore Sun*, 20 June 2010.

[28] Castells, M. (2000), *The Information Age: Economy, Society and Culture*, updated edn,

that use terms such as actor network is the tendency to fetishize the network in and of itself, and to envisage that the modern (or to use that most banal of academic terms, the postmodern) world exists principally in a more direct relationship between individuals on the one hand and a global network on the other. Nothing in this volume supports such a contention. There is no evidence for a global network, and no evidence for isolated individualism. The entire volume is focused upon social relationships that reduce to neither of these two extremes. People in Trinidad are clearly less individualistic as a result of Facebook.

Within the writings about Facebook itself, there is also a tendency to misunderstand or misuse the idea of Facebook as global. Yes, Facebook is global in the sense that Facebook is used pretty much everywhere today but that is true of telephones and whisky. It does not follow that it is becoming some kind of aggregate entity like a global consciousness or brain. When a user goes onto Facebook, they are communicating potentially with a few hundred friends – actually most often with about fifteen – but certainly not with the world. Although Facebook may help ideas and fashions spread virally and quickly, this was happening just as widely prior to Facebook with regard to news about a celebrity or opinion about a politician's gaffe. Facebook in Trinidad is not Facebook in London. In short, Facebook is important but it is not transcendent. Its primary effects are on close social relationships.

For all these reasons, the emphasis here has not been on the hype of the new but actually on the more conservative aspect of Facebook, that it is really far more interesting and extraordinary to dwell on the manner in which Facebook seems to reverse trends towards individualism and the decline of close social relationships. Although Facebook is a new form of communication, the content of this communication, such as gossip, dating and banter, seems to hark back to older forms and is not necessarily best understood by the term 'network'. More valuable has been a series of studies associated with Barry Wellman and his colleagues[29] that demon-

Blackwell, 3 vols. For a summary, see Castells, M. (2000), 'Materials for an Exploratory Theory of the Network Society', *British Journal of Sociology* 51(1): 5–24.
29 Kennedy, L., Smith, A., Wells, A., and Wellman, B. (2008), *Networked Families*. Pew Internet and American Life Project; Wang, H. and Wellman, B. (2010), 'Social Connectivity in America: Changes in Adult Friendship Network Size from 2002 to 2007', *American Behavioral Scientist* 53(8): 1148–69.

strated through research how, even prior to Facebook, the use of the internet tended to reinforce rather than substitute for wider social relationships, including face-to-face relationships.

Further consequences of Facebook

Facebook changes our relationship to time

It is tempting to see Facebook as merely consolidating what some have seen as the prior tendency of the internet to concertina time into a relentless fixation with the present. This can form part of an argument that Facebook represents a new mode of superficiality, or 'shallows'.[30] But this volume suggests much more complex developments. Facebook's first impact has tended to be the resurrection of connections with people from earlier parts of participants' lives, such as old schoolfriends or migrated relatives. This revitalization of the past makes one less focused on the people with whom one happens to be in immediate contact. If Facebook thereby reconnects with the longer time depth of an individual's prior life, then this would seem to be the exact opposite of any dismissal of Facebook as an orientation to the present. It is possible that this association with the present is a legacy of Facebook's initial association with students. It is likely to be viewed quite differently as it becomes associated with wider usage such as that of Dr Karamath.

One of the most surprising findings, expressed in the portrait of Nicole, is that Facebook has, in a very short time, already accumulated quite a profound history of its own, one that is meaningful as history to many of its users. This is the history of its development, first from a few elite universities to universities of all kinds, then spilling out to teenagers generally, and finally drifting upwards towards the more elderly. These shifts, along with changes in the way its infrastructure has been altered by the Facebook company, makes Nicole, 'the history woman', quite defensive about her role as a pioneer and quite nostalgic about the 'old days' of its first iteration. Similarly, after an initial concentration on good news and things of the moment, Facebook is becoming an important

---

[30] Carr, N. (2010), *The Shallows: What the Internet Is Doing to Our Brains*. New York: Norton.

site for people responding to death, loss and memorialization. As it develops its own history, it seems also to be turning its attention towards the past.

What Facebook does effectively complete is a stripping away of the inefficiencies of delay in communications. It transmits, sometimes several times a day, the current state of many people. We no longer depend on the mediation of others to obtain such information. Previously, we would never have gained this kind of everyday trivial knowledge of people we didn't meet on a daily basis. Facebook makes the present richer and more attuned to the co-occurrence of other people's lives. It would be mere conservatism to assume that prior delays and inefficiencies in communication were necessarily more natural or healthier than this instantaneous updating of social information. This may also apply to more formal news. It might be better if people actually watched the news media. But for those who don't, key events, such as the Haiti earthquake, can make their appearance quite quickly through online comment. Of course, this may also be true of less significant news. It was Trini Facebook discussion of the Kanye West–Taylor Swift MTV debacle that first made this evident to me.

A more plausible accusation against Facebook is the idea that it is a 'time suck', that people spend quite remarkable amounts of their lives on Facebook. Using this term as the title for one of the portraits might imply that what most people do with time on Facebook may be regarded as incredibly tedious. But again, it is easy to be glibly dismissive. If we actually consider how this time might otherwise be spent, it is hard to be other than grudgingly positive. At least in Trinidad, it seems to be mainly a switch from other forms of entertainment, such as watching television and gaming. Although TV watching is more sociable in many countries than is typical in the UK or US, and gaming is increasingly multi-player, these still seem less intrinsically socialized than Facebook.

A rather more profound consequence may follow from the identification of Facebook time as narrative time. In three volumes called *Time and Narrative*,[31] the philosopher Paul Ricoeur delved deeply into the central role played by narrative in the constitution of our humanity and in the sharing of experience, especially suffer-

---

[31] Ricoeur, P. (1984–8), *Time and Narrative*, 3 vols. Chicago: University of Chicago Press.

ing. Although he was concerned with the writings of Aristotle and St Augustine, perhaps the best exemplification of his point is the global attraction of soap opera. Soap opera appeals because the characters appear in real-time narrative. Programmes such as *Big Brother* broke the link between soap opera and fiction by substituting real-life narrative. It seems possible that at least to a degree, *Big Brother* then paved the way for Facebook. Facebook confirms Ricoeur's argument that we relate best to other people when we encounter them within established genres of narrative. Facebook is the culmination of this trajectory since finally we have real people intermittently updated in real time.

Equally complex is the anthropological perspective of cultural relativism as applied to the experience of time itself. For an anthropologist, time is experienced differently in different places, and even at different times. Trinidad time is not equally spread throughout the year. It has a clear climax in Carnival and slows down for Lent. People transform themselves in accordance with this rhythm. For Carnival, ordinary women turn into the 'Glamazons' who take over the streets. There is a crescendo of activity that allows people to escape from mundane time and act in ways they would shun otherwise. This more Rabelaisian reversal may be threatened by Facebook. Trinidadians now worry that they will be recognized, photographed and exposed. They can no longer afford to engage in this kind of liberation from conventional roles and time. Carnival is a festival dedicated to the moment, and depends on an escape from the longer-term consequences of actions at other times. So once again we can conclude that Facebook seems to make an orientation to the present more difficult rather than easier.

Facebook changes our relationship to space

The death of distance seems to be an even more obvious consequence of Facebook than the assumed death of time. Once again, we need to pause and consider before assuming that we fully understand the consequences of such a phrase, with its implication that distance no longer matters. After all, in the first instance Facebook consolidated the traditional parochialism of the family-based household. It is a common complaint that young people now seem glued to the computer in their bedrooms as they spend hours online. Horst[32] has noted that they may even create an aesthetic for their online sites, for example in MySpace, which produces continuity with the aesthetics of the bedroom itself. It is also possible to use Facebook to expand the house as a site of sociality. This is what Ajani achieves by making her home the equivalent of the French Salon, a centre for arts and creative activity for the town she lives in. As with many new technologies, the first impact is often to intensify conservatism rather than to establish some radical break because we use the technology to accomplish tasks we previously felt unable to perform. So if there is an initial death of distance, it is likely to be an attempt to counter the dispersal of families, to bring the family closer to how it used to be, rather than to make it radically different. When siblings migrate to other countries, Facebook allows them to retain an intense level of family and household interaction. While other new forms of communication such as email helped maintain dyadic sibling relationships, Facebook comes closer to the sense of the family as a whole group in constant interaction with each other.

The death of distance is equally implicated in the new efficiencies of transnational communication. On Facebook, it really doesn't matter where that person is offline; your interaction can be just as intimate or personal whether they live in the next street or the next continent. Again, the most obvious illustration is Dr Karamath who expands his global connectivity precisely because he is now effectively housebound. More subtle is the dissolution of diaspora that is evident when one looks more closely at the Doubles site. This is the portrait that includes the greatest degree of diaspora presence, quite likely precisely because its content is the most parochial and specific to Trinidad. It is when people are living in effective exile somewhere in Toronto or Miami that they seem most moved to engage in a heated debate about which particular street corner in Trinidad is the best place to buy a Doubles. The death of distance is also effective when the distance itself is relatively short, as in the case of Nicole as a young mother, stuck at home with children, who can become much more aware of what her friends are doing without her. They may be only a few streets

---

[32] Horst, H. (2009), 'Aesthetics of the Self: Digital Mediations', in D. Miller (ed.), *Anthropology and the Individual*. Oxford: Berg.

away but from her perspective, unable to leave her house, the distance is as insuperable as if they were continents apart.

Facebook changes the relationship between work and leisure

It is not just time and space that are being reconfigured by Facebook. One of the most dramatic consequences of new media has been the reversal of what had seemed an inevitable and entrenched separation of work and leisure. For decades, commercial institutions have policed the boundaries between work and personal life, almost as though work itself would collapse if workers were allowed to acknowledge that they had a life other than at work. This was true until very recently. And yet today it is like the Berlin wall – once it has fallen, one cannot imagine it being reinstated. There seems to be no way to stop most people carrying on with their personal lives while in the workplace. The Trojan horse that led to the collapse of this wall from the inside is the personal computer. The computer has become vital to almost any and every kind of work but it remains a technology that is very difficult to keep focused entirely on the job in hand.

A high proportion of the Facebook activity observed, and even more of that reported during fieldwork, took place at work. The very first portrait of Marvin and his marriage breakup was observed in its entirety as part of Marvin's working day. Many of the participants in Trinidad report that Facebook is effectively on in the background for much of the time they are formally at work. One of the reasons this is so hard to prevent is that work communication takes place between people who, by virtue of working together, are also in a social relationship. In academia, it is very difficult to differentiate between communication that operates between colleagues and students about work and about matters pertaining to friendship. Indeed, a communication about a work matter that does not include some framing that makes it more personal and friendly is becoming almost unacceptable. As a result, companies are casting about, trying to measure how much productivity in work has been lost as a result of the rise of social networking.[33] Facebook doesn't just intrude into work; it swarms all over it.

---

[33] *The Economist*, 28 January 2010.

In this trend, Facebook is by no means alone. Rather, it builds upon a whole plethora of new communication technologies whose use for personal purposes, while at work, has been extensively studied by Stefana Broadbent.[34] These developments may indeed be at the expense of a narrow definition of work efficiency. But for parents worried about their children and needing to deal with household tasks, it seems to be regarded as a hugely progressive and emancipatory form of welfare. It certainly makes work more pleasant. For many people, especially in management and the professions, this trend would be more than countered by the tendency of the internet and email to allow people to continue working in their leisure time. The constant siren song of emails arriving on the screen summons many people back to work during what otherwise should be their leisure hours and has surely led to an overall increase in their working time. But the evidence from Trinidad, outside of these managerial and professional classes, would be the reverse. Office workers and mechanics are much more prone to bring their private life into work than their work into their private life. Several people also remarked that Facebook was enabling them to turn work colleagues into friends. For example, previously people tended to lose touch with such colleagues if they moved jobs, but it was reported that Facebook enabled them to remain in contact with ex-colleagues. In fact, they sometimes got to know them better outside of the work environment and were able to incorporate them within more sustained friendship relations.

Why Facebook is not just corporate

One of the most popular words used by those who wish to dismiss Facebook as a proper subject for anthropology, is 'corporate'. To call Facebook corporate is to render it incapable of being anything other than an extension of the power and intention of the commercial interests that brought it into being and maintain it, so all one would be studying is the ability of a company to impose structures upon populations. The term 'corporate' seems self-evidently correct. Facebook is a company; the main imperative for its founders and investors and many of those involved outside perhaps of

---

[34] Broadbent, S. and Bauwens, V. (2008), 'Understanding Convergence', *Interactions* 15: 23–7.

Mark Zuckerberg himself has probably been the desire to become rich, though there was a remarkable amount of bacchanal consequent upon their pursuit of that goal.[35] Its employees are tasked with creating income streams that profit from its success. It does not follow, however, that because Facebook is a company, whatever anyone does with the website it produces is somehow intrinsically 'capitalist', 'neo-liberal' or indeed 'corporate'.

The twelve portraits that comprise this volume suggest nothing of the kind. The consequences of Facebook for people's lives are not one iota less authentic because Facebook is created by others. None of us are the authors of our own conditions of life. We are all historically created. The final essay concerns Gawa, an island in Melanesia that is pretty much exactly the kind of place you would have expected an anthropologist to study. Gawa may be described in terms of culture but that is not because it is devised by those who practise that culture. They are brought up with cultural expectations that descend from their ancestors. An individual Gawan is not necessarily expressing intention, will or agency in their actions. Actually, far more than on Facebook, Gawans are subject to sanctions, rules, controls and orders that they did not themselves devise. Gawan culture does not come from a corporation but it does come from history. An individual is born into a pre-existing set of rules. As another anthropologist, Bourdieu,[36] has pointed out, there is a strategy in how you apply these rules. But, in the main, Gawan people do as they are brought up to do. The little villages that are used as symbols of authentic and deeply rooted society in anthropology often arose from brutal movements in political economy, such as the consolidation of landholdings by aristocrats. Tribes often result from conquest, or flight from warfare, or from what today would be regarded as xenophobic cults. So the idea that the non-commercial creation of social worlds is necessarily more benign is largely the product of our ignorance of history.

One reason for setting this study of Facebook in Trinidad is to demonstrate how Facebook, as so many modern phenomena, simultaneously creates new forms of local heterogeneity as well as

---

[35] Mezrich, B. (2010), *The Accidental Billionaires*. London: Arrow Books.
[36] Bourdieu, P. (1977), *Outline of a Theory of Practice*. Cambridge: Cambridge University Press.

a global homogeneity. Only after the study of *Fasbook* in Trinidad did it become safe to speculate about Facebook. Yet there is no reason to think that the company behind Facebook has the faintest idea that *Fasbook* even exists. The idea that Facebook is necessarily neo-liberal is particularly misleading. I disagree with Gershon in this respect.[37] The term 'neo-liberal' implies that Facebook is an example of relentless individualism at the behest of capitalist necessity in which individuals become in effect micro, business-like entities. By contrast, Facebook, as a form of social networking, is one of the most powerful challenges in quite some time to that individualism. The previous thesis discussed how business has tried, for decades, to prevent workers from using devices such as Facebook that keep them in touch with their wider social world when they should be working. While other internet technologies balance this trend by facilitating the extension of work into leisure time, this seems far less true of Facebook, especially in the case of low-paid labour, in which case Facebook seems to represent a comprehensive victory by the workers of the world who have united against capitalism.

The portraits in this volume are of individuals but they are used to demonstrate the effects of social working. They seem to confirm that Facebook in its actual usage is an instrument for increasing social interaction. Most users of Facebook, including myself, tend to resent any active intervention by those who built it and control it. We bridle at changes in the way privacy settings or status updates may operate. Yet this is partly because users often become quickly conservative about something that, to a surprising degree, they tend to feel they actually 'own'.

We are not entirely wrong in this. *The Economist* magazine, in a survey of social networking (28 January 2010), reveals that a technical innovation in Facebook, such as MultiFeed which works in the background, has been successful but another, called Beacon, which pushed a more commercial application, was quickly resented by users and had to be dropped. Less famously than the iPhone, Facebook has also spread creativity in usage through approving 'apps' that they do not themselves create. *FarmVille*, *Mafia Wars* and the other games Trinis play are developed by a

---

[37] Gershon, I. (forthcoming), 'Un-Friend My Heart: Facebook, Promiscuity and Heartbreak in a Neoliberal Age', *Anthropology Quarterly*.

separate company, Zynga. So businesses, such as Facebook, are learning that they tend to be more successful through facilitating rather than through intervening. If Facebook tries to transform itself in ways that may bring it greater profits but are unwelcome to its users, or even if another network emerges that provides better functionality or is seen as 'cooler', then however extraordinary the speed with which Facebook has grown, its demise may be still more rapid.

A previous study showed why we need to recognize local heterogeneity not just in the effects of business but within capitalism itself.[38] Already Facebook is becoming an important vehicle for a wide variety of commercial pursuits. Several participants noted that it is much easier to browse the products of their favourite clothing shop on Facebook than to have to go to another website, let alone having to brave the traffic to reach the shop itself. The most effective example, within the portraits of Facebook as a commercial utility, was its use by Burton's nephew for his music business, a trend previously well established within MySpace but now emerging as a property of Facebook. But in Trinidad the urge to consolidate online experience around the one site makes it the obvious place to develop economic activities of all kinds. This book started with Marvin's attempts to move the marketing of a cocoa plantation onto Facebook.

The concept of the neo-liberal tends to creep back when analysis turns to the way individuals promote themselves on Facebook. It may be argued that acts of self-representation on Facebook are a kind of one-person branding, a form of self-promotion that emulates the techniques and rationale of branding. But it is worth reflecting on a rather different example of this process, in a paper by Bean,[39] on the history of Mahatma Gandhi as represented through his clothing. Bean traces the way Gandhi started by asserting himself through the power-dressing of a modern lawyer in a suit and tie. He then tried out various modes of sartorial expression, including what later became the Nehru style associated with the Congress party. Finally, he settles into the garb of the classic ascetic, which is his best-known visual image. The history

[38] Miller, D. (1997), *Capitalism: An Ethnographic Approach*. Oxford: Berg.
[39] Bean, S. (1989), 'Gandhi and Khadi: The Fabric of Indian Independence', in A. Weiner and S. Schneier (eds), *Cloth and Human Experience*. Washington: Smithsonian Press.

of branding is not indebted to the life of Gandhi but it could easily have been. It is undoubtedly the case that Facebook is the site for relentless self-promotion and a never-ending concern for crafting personal image. But this is an expression of an individual's anxiety over how they appear within the social domain, not mere individualism. As such, it has always been of paramount human concern from the Code of Hammurabi onwards. As various portraits reveal, the idioms employed, such as sexy and funny, derive from Trinidadian, rather than commercial, precedents. So the fact that Facebook is a company and generated by commercial interests should not extend to a glib dismissal of its consequences as corporate.

Facebook within polymedia

The term 'polymedia' is a neologism coined by Mirca Madianou and myself as an acknowledgement of a radical transformation in human communication that we would argue for most people in the world has only really happened in the last couple of years. The need for this neologism arose from our study of Filipina mothers in the UK and their reliance upon media for almost all aspects of parenting of their children left behind in the Philippines.[40] Until the last couple of years, a hugely significant factor had been the constraints and costs of media. By contrast within the last two years, such people are finding they have access to relatively inexpensive but also much more diverse forms of media. These can include texting, email, IM, webcam, voice-phone, Skype, blogging, as well as social networking. In that work, we are more concerned with the impact upon parenting seen from the perspectives of both mothers and of children. In this volume, the important point is that Facebook has come into being at pretty much the same time that Skype and webcam have developed, as well as smartphones such as the BlackBerry and the iPhone.

The context of polymedia reinforces a point made merely by examining Facebook from the perspective of anthropology. The argument has been that a book about Facebook has to be mainly about the wider context of people's lives rather than about the

---

[40] Madianou, M. and Miller, D. (forthcoming), *Migration and New Media: Transnational Families and Polymedia*. London: Routledge and Kegan Paul.

technology or the interface. So the portraits are as much about religion and sex, friendship and betrayal, business and leisure as about how many photos people tag or how often they post. Only with this more holistic approach can one appreciate that a person may go public on Facebook in order to be private elsewhere, or that Facebook is more a balance to community than community per se. These arguments have now become equally true for the narrower field of communication media, that is to say, the meaning and significance of Facebook has become the decision to use that site as opposed to a series of alternative media, and not just what Facebook constitutes as an independent entity.

In a situation of polymedia, one technology is preferred to another because it seems a better medium for being emotional or for hiding emotion, for showing one's face or for foregrounding one's voice, for having arguments or avoiding them, and above all for choosing between dyadic communication involving only two people or conversing within a much wider public sphere. There were many examples within the portraits where people considered carefully what Facebook was essentially good for before deciding to use this as opposed to some other communicative vehicle. Vishala discusses this in quite some detail as it pertains to her sense of truth (see chapter 4).

The reason we invented the term 'polymedia' was because alternative and existing terminologies were inadequate or misleading. 'Multi-media' refers to the simultaneous use of media, not alternative uses of media. There exist terms such as 'multi-platform' or 'multi-channel' but these raise issues as to what kind of entity Facebook itself is. This is something of concern not just to users but clearly to the company itself. In Kirkpatrick's account,[41] Mark Zuckerberg is trying to distance Facebook from Google by arguing that the latter is more orientated towards the computer, while he sees Facebook as potentially something more like a communication utility able to flow through many platforms and even retreat into the background. So terms such as multi-platform and multi-channel are likely to remain quite confusing. A point emphasized by Gershon,[42] given the emphasis within her volume, is that users take good note of the choices of media that others make and hold

[41] Kirkpatrick (2010), pp. 324–7.
[42] Gershon (2010).

them more responsible precisely because the selection of media is now seen as more of an individual choice than a constraint of price or availability. Our evidence from the Filipino study entirely supports Gershon in holding that the main consequence of poly-media is that it socializes media communication more generally in the sense that people now have to make such decisions and then take responsibility for their selection of one medium rather than another.

Facebook as the internet

The last thesis was largely derived from other research and other literature. For the final thesis, we can extend the point through a perspective more explicitly expressed by Trinidadians themselves. One of the clearest distinctions between discussions of Facebook in Trinidad as against those encountered in the UK is that Trinis are far more explicit about their desire that Facebook should effectively replace the internet itself. They argue that previously the internet was an unwieldy mess of different applications that one was required to open and close and move between in order to carry out a variety of tasks. What Trinidadians want from Facebook is a consolidation of all such activities within a single site. They want an IM facility for private chatting and an email-like facility for private messaging. They want to be able to surf internally for news and for window-shopping for clothes. Facebook should be the place for entertainment and games while simultaneously the centre of their social lives. They want better integration of webcams and organizational tools. The expression used locally is that Facebook should become a 'one-stop shop'.

This extends a point made earlier about corporations. Time and time again, users welcomed the likes of Microsoft, Apple and Google, especially when they initially appear as underdogs, challenging some previous incumbent power. The products of such companies allowed users to do things more effectively and more stylishly than before and to communicate without having incompatible formats. Once these companies became large, domi-nant and apparently hegemonic, love turned to resentment and even hate, regardless of how much money Bill Gates puts into philanthropy. A recent article suggested Facebook has become extremely unpopular in its turn.[43] But when it comes to Facebook in Trinidad, it is very apparent that the desire for dominance and centralization is coming at least as much from users as from the company. It is the Trinis themselves who want Facebook to replace all other applications on the internet. They consider this to form part of a self-evident drive towards efficiency and ease in internet use. By the same token, those Trinidadians who can afford it have seized upon the BlackBerry for the most seamless interactivity between their mobile phone and social networking. Again and again, Trinis pushed communications and other activities back onto Facebook. The teacher in Alana's class wanted to use a group blog for collaborative work, but her students insisted on doing this through Facebook instead, so that they could consolidate home-work within their socializing and gossiping, between midnight and 3 a.m. This does not mean people have the slightest affection for, or even interest in, Facebook as a company. If someone else offers this seamless internet, they will switch with alacrity.

The drive to consolidation is matched by the increasing differentiation and splintering of Facebook into separate genres and groups. It is quite hard to read the portrait called *Time Suck* since most of it consists of a teenage language that is understood mainly by other teenagers. It is not supposed to be of any interest to anyone else. The consolidation of the internet does not mean the consolidation of its users. boyd[44] notes the way Facebook tends to retrench the specificity of teenagers as a separate cultural sphere within contemporary US culture. What is striking about the twelve portraits is that, even within Trinidad, they seem to represent multiple worlds, each with their own Facebook, each with their own consequences.

What is more difficult to ascertain at this stage is whether the use of Facebook, and the internet more generally, changes, as well as consolidates, particular patterns of cultural expression. As a final example, it is possible that Facebook alters the balance between the visual and verbal in personal communication. Certainly in Trinidad there is increasing focus on photographs as against text. But this is extremely hard to interpret. It is entirely possible that

[43] Bosker, B. (2010) 'Facebook's User Satisfaction Bombs: Site Rates Slightly above IRS', *Huffington Post*, 20 July.

[44] boyd, d. (2010) 'Friendship', in M. Ito et al., *Hanging Out, Messing Around, and Geeking Out*. Cambridge, MA: MIT Press.

it merely reflects a deficiency in previous media, rather than any push by the technology of Facebook itself towards the visual. In other words, given the choice, Trinidadians would always have privileged the visual over the verbal. It's just that when technology was dominated by IM and email, this was extremely difficult to accomplish. It was the technology that was the constraint. But now Facebook enables what we might regard as the missing presence of the visual, in much the same way that webcams add the visual to verbal Skype in personal communication. This is why it is difficult to claim that any of these media are somehow more natural or closer to some proper mode of communicating. All we can do is to pay attention to these often rapid transformations and try to think through any significant consequences.

These issues may pertain to the future of Facebook itself, or they may foreshadow new instruments which will eventually come to replace it. For example, Foursquare seems to have been favoured in the kind of arenas that already have a reputation for featuring the next big thing, such as the SXSW festival in Austin, Texas. What Foursquare adds to social networking is the broadcasting of real-time spatial location. Such advances seem to highlight the problematic issues of public exposure and security even more strongly than Facebook since, for example, it allows potential thieves to know that you are not at home. It also suggests further movement towards the smartphone, rather than computer-based, integration and convergence. Time will tell. Given the shift from a concern that the internet was problematic because of the way it promoted anonymity to the current concern with the difficulty of retaining anonymity on Facebook, we should be wary of any assumption that these technological developments are necessarily a consistent movement in any one direction. What is clear is that new developments will be as swift as they are unpredictable. But the key consequence of Facebook – the expansion and transformation of social relations, which has been the subject of this book – is likely to remain. And the task of trying to understand its consequences for the five hundred million people who already use it has only just begun.

C

The Fame of Facebook

In another publication,[1] I describe the ultimate ambition of anthropology as that of extremism. Firstly, there is an extreme devotion to research, for instance spending at least a year observing a population before one feels one has the authority to talk about it. Extreme also is anthropology's ambition to balance the parochialism of time spent with only one very particular population with a desire to theorize about humanity as a whole. Finally, extremism is represented in the commitment to always try and forge connections between this empirical grounding and this theoretical abstraction. Retaining this commitment to extremism is an ever more important task in a world in which the abstractions of generalization and the specifics of populations seem to grow further and further apart. This book exemplifies such an approach by starting with the minutiae of individual Trinidadians but ending with an attempt to create a theory of Facebook.[2]

The discipline of anthropology has many branches but the trunk consists of the comparative ethnography of small-scale societies. Anthropologists live for extended periods of time learning the

[1]   Miller, D. (2010), *Stuff*. Cambridge: Polity, pp. 6–10.
[2]   This is the most explicitly anthropological and theoretical section of the book. I am hoping that some people, having followed the story so far, might have a go at this final 'puzzle' represented by an attempt to create a theory of Facebook. But I recognize that this will only appeal to some readers, so don't feel obliged to keep going if this is not the sort of thing you enjoy or feel the need of. I am content if you have found that which you have encountered so far rewarding.

language and trying to empathetically understand the customs of specific groups of people. For British students learning anthropology, it was Bronislaw Malinowski who most clearly initiated these rites of ethnographic study. And it was through one example, in particular, that Malinowski revealed how ethnography leads us to key questions about the nature of culture. In his book *Argonauts of the Western Pacific*,[3] Malinowski showed that the people of the Trobriand Islands, off the coast of New Guinea where he lived for several years, were associated with a much larger circle called the Kula ring that linked many such island groups. Around this ring circulate valuables, shell necklaces in a clockwise direction and shell armbands in the other, valuables which give honour and fame to those through whose hands they passed. The exchanges take place between neighbouring groups who then pass them on. The Kula as a whole is not under the control of any of its own participants; it exists only as the aggregate of these smaller dyadic exchanges between neighbouring island groups. So as culture it transcends its own constituent parts or the intentions of those who participate in it.

Of the various subsequent studies of the Kula ring, my personal favourite has always been *The Fame of Gawa* by the Chicago-based anthropologist Nancy Munn,[4] a book which seemed to me the culmination of Malinowski's project. The island of Gawa is, like the Trobriand Islands, part of the Kula ring. At the time of her study, the population was only 532. Munn managed not only to study Gawa, and by extension Kula, but also thereby to create theories of value and culture. Social scientists are not natural scientists, but I now want to suggest that if we imagine *The Fame of Gawa* were a theorem, then Facebook would be its proof.

To theorize about culture, we can start by imagining its absence. We might have been rather like the animals we watch in a nature programme. They wake up, spend the day obtaining and consuming food, mate, protect their young till they are old enough to survive for themselves and then die. When it comes to the primates, we see the development of obligations to kin and even some rudiments of culture and custom. Nevertheless, these are

[3] Malinowski, B. (1922), *Argonauts of the Western Pacific*. London: Routledge and Kegan Paul.
[4] Munn, N. (1986), *The Fame of Gawa*. Cambridge: Cambridge University Press.

very small worlds. By contrast, human societies, such as the people of Gawa, create vast arrays of custom and expectation, rituals based on spirits of good and evil, arts and artefacts, etiquettes of behaviour, all of which make for a vastly more elaborate world. This wealth of culture rests in turn upon fundamental values by which people are expected to live and by which they judge each other. In turn, these values create goals in life which make that life rich and complex. Not only that but, thanks to the Kula ring, the cultural universe of Gawa in turn gives rise to the excitement and challenge of Argonauts within a still more expansive universe, those who negotiate transactions with other islands, making for even wider possibilities and accomplishments beyond the shores of Gawa itself.

The book is called *The Fame of Gawa* because it rests upon a series of sanctions and exhortations designed to create, maintain and increase these values. If there is not a great world out there in which we can do deeds and become known for them, there is no possibility of fame, and much less to live our lives for. Culture provides the platform which allows every person to become a player. For the people of Gawa, culture is understood as a series of increasingly expanding exchanges. If we simply grow our food and consume the same food that we grow, then that food has no capacity to create this cultural world of Fame. We would live in a much smaller world, more like that of animals. People in Gawa are therefore forbidden to consume the crops that they themselves grow. Instead, that food is exchanged with their extended family members. This leads to wider exchanges of labour, such as wood carving or other obligations, through which more complex things can be produced such as canoes or marriages. Next, these intra-island exchanges feed into the Kula exchanges between islands, where the products of Gawa can be exchanged with and become known in more distant inter-island worlds. The objects from those other islands which have been obtained in exchange for the products of Gawa are then reintroduced to Gawa through a series of increasingly local exchanges within Gawa, until finally they return as the food which it is appropriate for people to eat. But there has been a huge value added between producing food and consuming it. All this activity finally comes back as *The Fame of Gawa*, the reputation that Gawa people have gained through these far-flung interactions and, most especially, through the exchange of Kula

valuables which themselves can become quite famous. Kula valuables and the people who exchange them become the 'celebrities'
of the Kula ring. To use modern parlance, culture is then what
ensures that the people of Gawa 'get a life'.

In theoretical terms, Munn reasons that this activity represents
an expansion of what she calls intersubjective spacetime: the
scale of the world within which people can live and gain Fame.
Fame refers to reputation gained over a greater time and space.
There are positive transformations that expand this spacetime
and negative transformations that shrink it. The first chapters of
The Fame of Gawa are mainly concerned with the establishment
of positive transformations: the complex systems of exchanges
based on principles of reciprocity and mutual obligation and
expectations that grow spacetime, first exchanges within Gawa,
and then through Kula with other islands. The final chapters are
more concerned with witchcraft, an aspect of these same activities
which can destroy and shrink our social relationships and the field
within which we can gain Fame. So culture itself can grow or it
can shrink.

Curiously, when we turn to the lives of people who live in
large cities such as London, then we see modern life as almost
the inverse of these arguments. Although there has been a huge
growth in the external and material world, this has been matched
by a reduction in our social world, based on the increasing self-
sufficiency of households who can obtain resources more directly
from markets and the state. Our social spacetime seems to be
shrinking. By contrast, every single discussion of Facebook in
Trinidad includes the observation that it is an expansion of communication between an individual and others. To be on Facebook
is to initiate a process of ever-widening circles, starting with lost
relatives and schoolfriends. Even if we do not have very active
communication with them, we are able to constantly update our
knowledge about who they are and what they do. In theoretical
terms, Facebook is clearly a positive transformation in the expansion of intersubjective spacetime. Thanks to Facebook, most of us
live within a considerably wider social world than a few years ago.

If Facebook can be regarded as a kind of social 'big bang'
leading to an expanding social universe, then an analogy seems
warranted with Munn's arguments about culture. For this analogy
to be useful we would have to see in Facebook something equiva-

lent to both the positive expansion and negative shrinking of spacetime. To start with expansion, in Gawa the contrast is drawn between merely eating the food you grow yourself or sending it out into ever-expanding networks of exchange. Similarly, in Trinidad, a person might use some experience or reflection in mere dyadic exchanges with someone close to them, by reporting them in a personal conversation with one other person. I tell you about something that happened to me, and that's as far as it goes. But instead, with Facebook, they can harvest those same observations from the garden of experiences and post them onto a site where not just one other person will be able to consume them, but hundreds. Even if no direct messages are sent to and from individuals, they are made aware of aspects of others' lives through textual and visual postings. As spacetime, it enables this information to carry across continents and diasporas, allowing news and information to travel vast distances with extraordinary effect. Similarly, there is an unprecedented simultaneity, but also a digital inscription that lasts. As such, Facebook is as precisely a positive transformation and expansion of spacetime as a social medium.

To call a book *The Fame of Gawa* is to imply that eventually Fame accrues not just to the individual but also to the island of Gawa itself. Thanks to the network represented by Kula, Gawa can become known well beyond its own boundaries. Trinis are, in general, just as keen as the people of Gawa that their individual reputations be matched by enhanced respect for the island of Trinidad itself. In the earlier work on the internet carried out with Don Slater,[5] we showed that individual Trinidadians would often set up whole websites designed to export knowledge about, and generate interest in, Trinidad and Tobago. Often they hid the fact that these were merely the creations of an individual in order to try and represent Trinidad itself. Thanks to Facebook, the achievements of Trinidadians abroad, the degrees they pass, the children they have, are re-internalized within the local networks of Trinidad, ready for discussion and assessment. By the same token, Facebook internationalizes events in Trinidad, initially to the diaspora and then, if of sufficient interest, to others. As seen in the Doubles site, it can also create an expanded spacetime that

[5] Miller, D. and Slater, D. (2000), *The Internet: An Ethnographic Approach*. Oxford: Berg.

seamlessly integrates internal and external contributors. It is clear from the content that much of the Doubles posting comes from the wider diaspora of people who miss the food itself but still want to insist that they know the best street corner in Trinidad to buy it.

As an example, several of the portraits in this book mention the anti-smelter movement. The key figures in this movement are well aware that a street demonstration only reported locally will have limited effect. Increasingly, they use the way Facebook links intra-island and inter-island networks to ensure that such political protest is covered by international and not just national media. They argue that it is only when their actions are acknowledged first at this international level that it is subsequently deemed significant within Trinidad itself. Similarly, there is a consensual desire to export interest in particular aspects of Trinidadian culture, such as steelband or Carnival.

If Munn's work stretches back to Malinowski, both are indebted to one of the founding texts of anthropology itself. The significance of *The Gift*[6] by Mauss is that it stands as an exemplary theory of society. Mauss argued that we often think of the gift as a voluntary giving by one person to another but in practice, and in most societies, gifts are grounded in a principle of reciprocity. If I give you something, that puts you in my debt, and you have an obligation to give me something back. This will in turn put me in your debt. So the gift is rarely voluntary. It is a relationship bonded by sequential obligation. This is one of the most common ways relationships are created and sustained. Such reciprocity is almost as critical to Trinidadian Facebook as to Gawan cultural practice. The degree to which people post comments is often roughly equivalent to the degree to which they are commented upon. Many Facebook gifts, produced by the company, have quite explicit references to more immediate reciprocity. For example, one person may send a cartoon gift to a friend but with a note that it only 'counts' if they send one back within two days. The most obvious case of reciprocity is Arvind's use of *FarmVille* with its infrastructure based on the ideal of neighbours who help each other, and without whom one cannot progress in the game. As Mauss argued, reciprocity can also lead to hierarchy, especially when a gift cannot be returned. A famous person receives more

---

[6]   Mauss, M. (1990 [1922]), *The Gift*. London: Routledge.

comments than they make and tends to attract followers who hope for fame by constantly commenting on people better known than themselves. A well-known Trinidadian DJ complained that people you 'friend' on Facebook should know that doesn't entitle them to think of themselves as your actual friends. Such lack of reciprocity creates a hierarchical relationship.

Because these reciprocal exchanges are carried out publicly on Facebook, rather than privately, they are subject to viewing by hundreds of other people. Munn develops a theory partly derived from the concept of witness as employed by the philosopher Jean-Paul Sartre. Although writing prior to the advent of the internet, she speaks of a virtual presence:

> In Gawan images of kula fame, the virtual third party is the distant other who hears about, rather than directly observes the transaction. . . . As iconic and reflexive code, fame is the *virtual form of influence*. Without fame a man's influence would, as it were, go nowhere: successful acts would in effect remain locked within themselves in given times and places of their occurrence or be limited to immediate transactors. (Munn 1986: 116–17; my italics)

It is not so far-fetched to suggest that Facebook represents a realization of this ideal of a virtual component in the construction of Fame. Most of what people do on Facebook gathers either no response or merely a handful of comments. But Facebook works because there is a virtual audience, usually of hundreds, that stands for this much larger witnessing by the 'anybody' and the 'everybody', the imagined community through which it is possible for one's Fame to be broadcast.

In *The Fame of Gawa*, Munn uses the term *qualisign* to express the way particular qualities are signified. She explores the way qualities of heaviness associated with the land become transformed into images of mobility that relate to the sea and to Kula. For example, the static properties of a tree must be symbolically converted to the swift movement over the water of the canoe that is carved from the tree. Similarly, the postings of Trinis are not random in content but correspond to particular cultural idioms which express key qualities central to Trini culture. These form patterns of usage that are easily recognizable after a while. For example, the use of text in status updates tends to revolve around a few typical modes. Firstly, there is a genre of news posting which is simply the way one individual alerts others to information they might not have come across. This can be political and international news and commentary, but also news about local parties or fetes, or even something that is happening at school. By contrast, a second mode of posting consists of constant, but trivial, updates on the minutiae of someone's life, such as going out to Kentucky Fried Chicken or washing the car. Each individual posting is essentially inconsequential but the overall effect is the gift of virtual co-presence in real time – ambient intimacy. So if someone is feeling lonely and bored, they can go onto Facebook and feel they are sharing the mundane routines of another person's life, with an illusion of the kind of intimacy one might associate with a long-term marriage. A third genre is the gifting of sayings and ruminations. A more sophisticated participant, such as Ajani, often posts lines from mystical poetry, while the less educated Vishala posts sayings such as 'Be bold in what you stand for, but careful in what you fall for . . . hmmmmm.' A fourth genre of posting is that of jokes and various kinds of humour. Each genre tends to create its own expected frequency of posting so that, after a while, you expect that one person will post every few days while another person posts every few hours. It can be quite disconcerting when they don't.

Within these patterns can be found particular cultural genres of content. Probably the most important in Trinidad consists of a balance between two qualities, that of appearing 'sexy' and 'funny'. It is almost unimaginable for a Trinidadian not to have at least some component of their Facebook presence devoted to the art of looking sexy. This is the appropriate term. It's not just trying to be good looking, because there is clearly both an erotic and seductive intention. This is most especially true of profile pictures. These are the pictures that you see whenever you go online and come across a posting by that individual. There is no age limit to the possibility of looking seductive. It is as expected of a sixty-year old much as of a twenty-year old. Men are a little coyer than women but there is plenty of muscle and tone. Usually these are used intermittently with other types of profile picture.

But a person who only ever tried to look sexy would be the subject of derision. Almost all Trini sites also include something that is almost the direct opposite of this sexy image. The imperative to be funny usually requires photos taken when one looks most ugly, least well dressed, most unguarded and generally stupid or daft: one's mouth crammed with pizza when someone made you laugh, a moment when you just fell, or when you were pulling a ridiculous face. These portraits of self-ridicule are usually complemented by more artificial forms of humour, such as replacing one's profile picture with a cartoon figure, a joke, or some other fun piece of Facebook paraphernalia. On balance, men tend to have a higher proportion of funny to sexy images, but most people regard both as essential. One man in his thirties only has comic pictures of himself, often transposing his face onto other figures such as John Travolta, the Mona Lisa or a prison mugshot but, in addition, adding a silly moustache to his face. It may be that he knows he is so clearly good looking and fit that he simply doesn't need to construct images of his attractiveness except in this mediated form.

This balance is perhaps even more important with textual comments. To be positively appraised in Trinidad demands that whatever one's pretensions to cleverness and success, this must be balanced with humour. To fail in this would leave you open to ridicule. A good deal of posting consists of jokes and innuendoes. For the more accomplished, these are self-composed. They are often quite rapid responses to someone else's photo or posting. They represent the quick banter that is central to most social life. But for many, especially younger users such as schoolchildren, it is more like shopping. There are a huge number of jokes that pass through Facebook, texts and jokes about teachers or about Facebook itself, and an equal number of funny groups or things to be a fan of, as featured in Aaron's portrait. The individual then makes a selection from these and posts them on his or her own site so that they are appraised for the quality of this selection as against the deluge of alternative postings. The effect is almost an 'I wish I had said that first' club, so central to visual posting are people in social situations where they are seen by others to be both sexy and funny. Just making a claim to a quality will not do: equally important is the process by which it is seen that other people attest to that quality. So although the *qualisigns* of Trinidadian Facebook are quite different from those *qualisigns* that Munn discusses for Gawa, the idea that culture operates through the signing of core and key qualities is as true for the former as for the latter.

So having seen the positive expansion of spacetime as fame, and now the specific qualities by which people are appraised, the last chapters of *The Fame of Gawa* are devoted to the negative transformations of spacetime. This implies that any cultural form that creates expansion has to have within itself the opposite quality which would destroy and shrink spacetime. Bacchanal corresponds to the Gawan concept of witchcraft because it derives from gossip and the exchange of news, which is part and parcel of what makes Facebook work. But equally it is that aspect which destroys its ability to positively expand spacetime. The very first portrait is one in which viewing has turned into stalking, and stalking into jealousy, and jealousy has destroyed this marriage. At the end of 2010, everyone had to hand a quintessential example of Facebook's relationship to bacchanal. This was the release onto the internet of Josanne's private sex tape. It was almost as though this sequence of events had been crafted to make this point since Josanne was not just anyone but had become one of the key celebrity figures of the island. As noted in the chapter on Josanne, this was by no means an isolated case. There were many other stories circulating about inadvertent or sometimes deliberate exposure of sexual material, ranging from schoolgirls to people's own relatives.

Mostly bacchanal relates to much less significant exposures, such as when a photographer has recorded something and tagged the photograph or, as is common with teenagers, the mere hint that one person's boyfriend was observed with another girl. These can cause an explosion of recrimination publicly aired on Facebook itself. When such bacchanal occurs, it often has the effect of either demolishing specific relationships or making people in general frightened of the consequences of exposure through their online community. Bacchanal thereby directly contributes to the negative transformative possibilities of Facebook as spacetime. It shrinks social worlds. During the period of fieldwork, it became particularly difficult for Josanne to engage in any kind of wider social life, though there were signs of early rehabilitation. Trinidad is a relatively liberal society in relation to sex, and there was a general appreciation that she was a very decent and respected person who had been betrayed by the release of a private tape. But for her and for any bacchanal that follows from one teenager's revelation about another, the immediate impact will most likely be a negative transformation of spacetime and a shrinking of their social domain.

The other significant impact of bacchanal is that, just as witchcraft in *The Fame of Gawa,* it also operates as an important sanction which secures normative and moral usage of Facebook. In Gawa, witchcraft provides a sanction against those who would rather not bother to take part in these complex exchanges. Those we could term the 'couch yams' of Gawa who just can't be bothered to help build a canoe or participate in a ritual come to fear witchcraft. In Trinidad, defining culture itself as bacchanal creates a fierce and continual debate about netiquette: how to determine what is proper and improper behaviour in the use of Facebook. Typical are conversations about the immaturity of teenagers who fail to see the consequences of their desire to look sexier than the girl next door, or how much they will regret losing their temper when they vent their spleen against a parent or best friend on Facebook. Equally, many negative comments appear about people who photograph private quarrels or tag too many photos or otherwise behave inappropriately. The existence of this negative potential, the bacchanal inherent in Facebook that could destroy community, is one of the main factors that help people build consensus as to how they should behave on Facebook, at least if they want to stave off such destructive acts of witchcraft.

The Fame of Gawa is, then, far more than a descriptive ethnography of one place: it is also a theory of culture. Culture exists in the human capacity to expand worlds towards distant horizons and more complex outcomes of life, and in the negative potentials of the very same mechanism that creates that expansive potential. It was suggested earlier that if Munn's book was a theorem, then Facebook would be its proof; that the true significance of her arguments only really becomes evident when they are applied, not only to Gawa, but to an entirely different context; that her theory can work not just for a few hundred people on an island in Melanesia but helps us comprehend the vast network that is Facebook. By the same token, this act of theorization makes another point which is central to the decision to study Facebook from an anthropological perspective because it follows from this essay that if Kula exemplifies what anthropologists mean by the word culture, then so does Facebook.

Conclusion

To date, there is one rather poor[1] and one very good[2] description of the rise of Facebook and the role of Mark Zuckerberg. On the basis of Kirkpatrick's plausible and informed account, it seems that the vision and decisions of a single individual have been of considerable importance in understanding the specifics of Facebook's transformations and trajectory. It seems that Mark Zuckerberg has always had a remarkably ambitious belief and vision that Facebook could become as basic as a household utility[3] because it would facilitate a movement that was in any case inevitable towards transparency and the sharing of ever more personal information. This vision, rather than the search for profitability per se, has led to the company being consistently ahead of its user base in pushing towards this greater openness. However, at the same time there has had to be a growing appreciation that the company needs to beat a swift retreat whenever the evidence is that the user base is unwilling to go as far as the company.

What this book has tried to argue is that, if we want to understand Facebook and its consequences, it is at least as important to appreciate Nicole, the history woman, and the range of other users represented in these portraits as it is to understand Mark

---

[1] Mezrich (2010).
[2] Kirkpatrick (2010).
[3] Op. cit., p. 201.

Zuckerberg. In fact, Facebook is not so entirely different from rivals such as Friendster and the social networking sites that preceded it. Probably the most important factor in its more recent overwhelming success is not the vision of Zuckerberg but the desire by nearly everyone on our planet to be on the same network as everyone else. The portrait of Nicole is not especially different from the company's understanding of early users, as is evident in Kirkpatrick's account. Nicole shows a strong sense of loyalty, emotional attachment and even of ownership, with the corollary of deep conservatism and resistance to both change and expansion within Facebook.

More challenging perhaps is the conclusion one would draw from the range of portraits. That the key to Facebook's success is not really the dialectic of openness and privacy that so commands the attention of journalism, critics and indeed the company itself. Nor is it that Facebook represents some brave new world of global networking. My conclusion is that the secret of Facebook's success, along with that of similar social networks, lies not in change but in conservatism. Above all, Facebook really is quite literally a social network. Its importance lies in its perceived and actual ability to reconstruct relationships, especially within families and with absent friends, that had been gradually fading away due to the attrition of other aspects of modern life, such as increasing mobility. Facebook helps in some measure to reverse this decline in sociality and repair what is viewed as the damage inflicted on people by this loss of close relationships. So the single most important attribute of Facebook is not what is new about it, but the degree to which it seems to help us return to the kind of involvement in social networks that we believe we have lost.

The final essay juxtaposed the study of Facebook with a classic anthropological study of Island Melanesia. It suggested that even in a world where technology is mainly what people do with trees rather than with computers, culture itself gives rise to a series of tensions and contradictions whereby people wish to expand their horizons without losing the benefits of close kinship and relationships. If there are contradictions inherent in Facebook, they are not so different or incommensurable from our appreciation of contradictions in any other cultural context that is amenable to anthropological study. One of the considerable benefits of Facebook is that it contributes to our study of social networking as an intrinsic condition of social life, irrespective of the technologies employed.

My focus has been on this reconstruction of our orientation to kinship and close social relationships with the technology compensating for increasing distance and absence. The evidence in this book suggests that the main impact of Facebook is on aspects of those relationships such as dating, feelings of isolation and boredom, gossip, maintaining long-distance relationships, sharing of news and other rather similar unremarkable activities. For those reasons, this book has little in common with the main raft of popular work about Facebook and generally eschews the idea that there is some profound or peculiar link either in Facebook, or the internet more generally, with some psychological or cognitive function, or with what may be regarded as a rather romantic and one-dimensional notion of traditional community.

As Facebook becomes global, cultural difference will become more, not less, important. As Kirkpatrick notes, 'Facebook has exploded across Asia in the last year or so, but for different reasons in each country.'[4] Indeed, within this volume, although various usages have been generalized as Trinidadian, the twelve portraits show highly eclectic and different interactions between particular Trini individuals.

The importance of this conservative imperative to Facebook's success is quite possibly not something the company is particularly aware of. But this simply may not matter very much. It is, however, hugely significant to the users of Facebook, since for most people it is their immediate family and closest social relationships that dominate their lives and it is these close relationships that typically are the main determinant of happiness or unhappiness. If anthropology is resolutely focused upon kinship and close relationships, then this is not just some disciplinary obstinacy but properly reflects an empathetic appreciation that what matters most to people should also matter to us.

---

[4] Kirkpatrick (2010), p. 283.